BILL GATES

WITH NATHAN MYHRVOLD
AND PETER RINEARSON

THE
ROAD
AHEAD

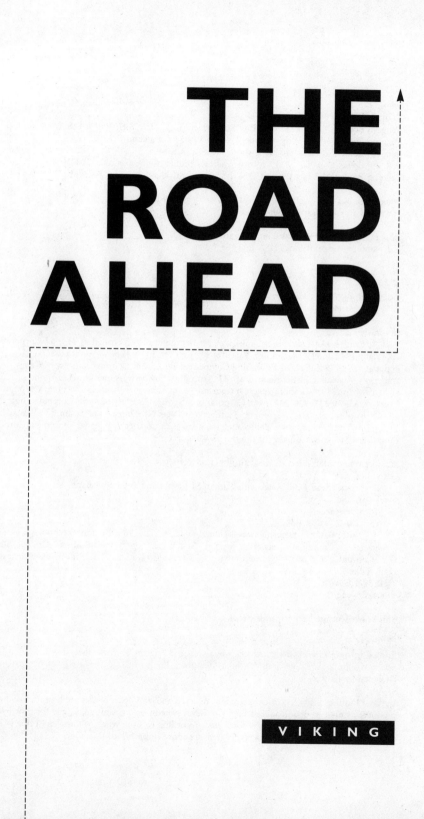

VIKING

VIKING
Published by the Penguin Group
Penguin Books USA Inc., 375 Hudson Street, New York, New York 10014, U.S.A.
Penguin Books Ltd, 27 Wrights Lane, London W8 5TZ, England
Penguin Books Australia Ltd, Ringwood, Victoria, Australia
Penguin Books Canada Ltd, 10 Alcorn Avenue, Toronto, Ontario, Canada M4V 3B2
Penguin Books (N.Z.) Ltd, 182–190 Wairau Road, Auckland 10, New Zealand

Penguin Books Ltd, Registered Offices:
Harmondsworth, Middlesex, England

First published in 1995 by Viking Penguin,
a division of Penguin Books USA Inc.

10 9 8 7 6 5 4 3 2 1

Illustration credits:
Page 3: Courtesy of Lakeside School; Page 13: Reproduced by permission of Intel Corporation, copyright 1972 Intel Corporation; Page 16: Reproduced from *Popular Electronics,* January 1975, copyright © 1975 Ziff-Davis Publishing Company; Page 25: Illustrations courtesy of Carey, Keller, Anderson; Page 28: UPI/Bettmann; Page 32: Reproduced by permission of Intel Corporation, copyright 1994 Intel Corporation; Page 49: Courtesy of International Business Machines Corporation; Pages 52, 53, 74, 117, 220: Microsoft Corporation; Page 55: Courtesy of Apple Computer, Inc.; Page 70: Copyright 1995 Davis Freeman, Seattle, WA; Page 71: Courtesy of Scientific-Atlanta, Inc./ Illustration courtesy of Carey, Keller, Anderson; Page 73: Courtesy of Digital Equipment Corporation; Pages 217, 219: Courtesy of Intergraph Corporation

LIBRARY OF CONGRESS CATALOGING IN PUBLICATION DATA
Gates, Bill, date.
    The road ahead / Bill Gates with Nathan Myhrvold and Peter Rinearson.
        p.   cm.
    Includes index.
    ISBN 0-670-77289-5
    1. Information superhighway—United States. 2. Information technology—United
States. 3. Computer networks—United States. 4. Telecommunication—United States.
5. Computer industry—United States. I. Myhrvold, Nathan. II. Rinearson, Peter, date.
III. Title.
HE7572.U6G38   1995
004.6'7—dc20   95-43803

This book is printed on acid-free paper.
(∞)

Printed in the United States of America by Quebecor Printing/Fairfield Inc.
Set in Minion by Creative Graphics, Inc., Allentown, PA
Designed by Katy Riegel

To my parents

CONTENTS

ACKNOWLEDGMENTS

Bringing a major software project to market can require the combined talents of hundreds of people. Not quite that many helped me with this book, but I certainly couldn't have done it alone. If I've inadvertently left someone out below, I'm really sorry, and thank you too.

For everything from conception to marketing, and lots of stops along the way, thanks to Jonathan Lazarus and his team: Kelli Jerome, Mary Engstrom, Wendy Langen, and Debbie Walker. Without Jonathan's guidance and persistence this book never would have happened.

For their helpful suggestions throughout the project, special thanks to Tren Griffin, Roger McNamee, Melissa Waggener, and Ann Winblad.

For their incisive review comments, thanks to Stephen Arnold, Steve Ballmer, Harvey Berger, Paul Carroll, Mike Delman, Kimberly Ellwanger, Brian Fleming, Bill Gates, Sr., Melinda Gates, Bernie Gifford, Bob Gomulkiewicz, Meg Greenfield, Collins Hemingway, Jack Hitt, Rita Jacobs, Erik Lacitis, Mich Matthews, Scott Miller, Craig Mundie, Rick Rashid, Jon Shirley, Mike Timpane, Wendy Wolf, Min Yee, and Mark Zbikowski.

For help with research, transcription, and resource material, my gratitude to Kerry Carnahan, Ina Chang, Peggy Gunnoe, Christine Shannon, Sean Sheridan, and Amy Dunn Stephenson. I'm also grateful to Elton Welke and his able staff at Microsoft Press, including Chris Banks, Judith Bloch, Jim Brown, Sally Brunsman, Mary DeJong, Jim Fuchs, Dail Magee, Jr., Erin O'Connor, JoAnne Woodcock, and Mark Young.

I'm also grateful to those at my English-language publisher, Viking Penguin, for their help and patience. In particular, I'd like to thank Peter Mayer, Marvin Brown, Barbara Grossman, Pamela Dorman, Cindy Achar, Kate Griggs, Theodora Rosenbaum, Susan Hans O'Connor, and Michael Hardart.

Thanks, too, for editorial help, go to Nancy Nicholas and Nan Graham.

My special gratitude to my collaborators, Peter Rinearson and Nathan Myhrvold.

FOREWORD

The past twenty years have been an incredible adventure for me. It started on a day when, as a college sophomore, I stood in Harvard Square with my friend Paul Allen and pored over the description of a kit computer in *Popular Electronics* magazine. As we read excitedly about the first truly personal computer, Paul and I didn't know exactly how it would be used, but we were sure it would change us and the world of computing. We were right. The personal-computer revolution happened and it has affected millions of lives. It has led us to places we had barely imagined.

We are all beginning another great journey. We aren't sure where this one will lead us either, but again I am certain this revolution will touch even more lives and take us all farther. The major changes coming will be in the way people communicate with each other. The benefits and problems arising from this upcoming communications revolution will be much greater than those brought about by the PC revolution.

There is never a reliable map for unexplored territory, but we can learn important lessons from the creation and evolution of the $120-billion personal-computer industry. The PC—its evolving hardware, business applications, on-line systems, Internet connections, electronic mail, multimedia titles, authoring tools, and games—is the foundation for the next revolution.

During the PC industry's infancy, the mass media paid little attention to what was going on in the brand-new business. Those of us who were enthralled by computers and the possibilities they promised were unnoticed outside our own circles and definitely not considered trendy.

But this next journey, to the so-called information highway, is the topic of endless newspaper and magazine articles, television and radio broadcasts, conferences, and rampant speculation. There has been an unbelievable amount of interest in this subject during the last few years, both inside and outside the computer industry. The interest is not confined only to developed countries, and it goes well beyond even the very large numbers of personal-computer users.

Thousands of informed and uninformed people are now speculating publicly about the information highway. The amount of misunderstanding about the technology and its possible pitfalls surprises me. Some people think the highway—also called the network—is simply today's Internet or the delivery of 500 simultaneous channels of television. Others hope or fear it will create computers as smart as human beings. Those developments will come, but they are not the highway.

The revolution in communications is just beginning. It will take place over several decades, and will be driven by new "applications"—new tools, often meeting currently unforeseen needs. During the next few years, major decisions will have to be made by governments, companies, and individuals. These decisions will have an impact on the way the highway will roll out and how much benefit those deciding will realize. It is crucial that a broad set of people—not just technologists or those who happen to be in the computer industry—participate in the debate about how this technology should be shaped. If that can be done, the highway will serve the purposes users want. Then it will gain broad acceptance and become a reality.

I'm writing this book now as part of my contribution to the debate and, although it's a tall order, I hope it can serve as a travel guide for the forthcoming journey. I do this with some trepidation. We've all smiled at predictions from the past that look silly today. You can flip through old *Popular Science* magazines and read about conveniences to come, such as the family helicopter and nuclear power "too cheap to meter." History is full of now ironic examples—the Oxford professor who in 1878 dismissed the electric light as a gimmick; the commissioner of U.S. patents who in 1899 asked that his office be abolished because "everything that can be invented has been invented." This is meant to be a serious book, although ten years from now it may not appear that way. What I've said that turned out to be right will be considered obvious and what was wrong will be humorous.

I believe the course of the creation of the highway will mirror, in many ways, the history of the personal-computer industry. I'm including a bit of my history—yes, I too talk about the house—and that of computing in general, to help explain some concepts and lessons from the past. Anyone expecting an autobiography or a treatise on what it's like to have been as lucky as I have been will be disappointed. Perhaps when I've retired I will get around to writing that book. This book looks primarily to the future.

Anyone hoping for a technological treatise will be disappointed, too. Everyone will be touched by the information highway, and everyone ought to be able to understand its implications. That's why my goal from the very beginning was to write a book that as many people as possible could understand.

The process of thinking about and writing *The Road Ahead* took longer than I expected. Indeed, estimating the time it would take proved to be as difficult as projecting the development schedule of a major software project. Even with able help from Peter Rinearson and Nathan Myhrvold, this book was a major undertaking. The only part that was easy was the cover photo by Annie Leibovitz, which we finished well ahead of schedule. I enjoy writing speeches and had thought writing a book would be like writing them. I innocently imagined writing a chapter would be the equivalent of writing a speech. The fallacy in my thinking was similar to the one software developers often run into—a program ten times as long is about one hundred times more complicated to write. I should have known better. To complete the book, I

------------------------->

had to take time off and isolate myself in my summer cabin with my PC.

And here it is. I hope it stimulates understanding, debate, and creative ideas about how we can take advantage of all that's sure to be happening in the decade ahead.

THE
ROAD
AHEAD

A REVOLUTION BEGINS

I wrote my first software program when I was thirteen years old. It was for playing tic-tac-toe. The computer I was using was huge and cumbersome and slow and absolutely compelling.

Letting a bunch of teenagers loose on a computer was the idea of the Mothers' Club at Lakeside, the private school I attended. The mothers decided that the proceeds from a rummage sale should be used to install a terminal and buy computer time for students. Letting students use a computer in the late 1960s was a pretty amazing choice at the time in Seattle—and one I'll always be grateful for.

This computer terminal didn't have a screen. To play, we typed in our moves on a typewriter-style keyboard and then sat around until the results came chug-chugging out of a loud printing device on paper. Then we'd rush over to take a look and see who'd won or decide our next move. A game of tic-tac-toe, which would take thirty seconds with a pencil and paper, might consume most of a lunch period. But who cared? There was just something neat about the machine.

I realized later part of the appeal was that here was an enormous, expensive, grown-up machine and we, the kids, could control it. We were too young to drive or to do any of the other fun-seeming adult activities, but we could give this big machine orders and it would always obey. Computers are great because when you're working with them you get immediate results that let you know if your program works. It's feedback you don't get from many other things. That was the beginning of my fascination with software. The feedback from simple programs is particularly unambiguous. And to this day it still thrills me to know that if I can get the program right it will always work perfectly, every time, just the way I told it to.

As my friends and I gained confidence, we began to mess around with the computer, speeding things up when we could or making the games more difficult. A friend at Lakeside developed a program in BASIC that simulated the play of Monopoly. BASIC (**B**eginner's **A**ll-purpose **S**ymbolic **I**nstruction **C**ode) is, as its name suggests, a relatively easy-to-learn programming language we used to develop increasingly complex programs. He figured out how to make the computer play hundreds of games really fast. We fed it instructions to test out various methods of play. We wanted to discover what strategies won most. And—chug-a-chug, chug-a-chug—the computer told us.

Like all kids, we not only fooled around with our toys, we changed them. If you've ever watched a child with a cardboard carton and a box of crayons create a spaceship with cool control panels, or listened to their improvised rules, such as "Red cars can jump all others," then you know that this impulse to make a toy do more is at the heart of innovative childhood play. It is also the essence of creativity.

Of course, in those days we were just goofing around, or so we thought. But the toy we had—well, it turned out to be some toy. A few of us at Lakeside refused to quit playing with it. In the minds of a lot of people at school we became linked with the computer, and it with us. I was asked by a teacher to help teach computer programming, and that seemed to be OK with everyone. But when I got the lead in the school play, *Black Comedy*, some students were heard muttering, "Why did they pick the computer guy?" That's still the way I sometimes get identified.

It seems there was a whole generation of us, all over the world, who

1968: Bill Gates (standing) and Paul Allen working at the computer terminal at Lakeside School.

dragged that favorite toy with us into adulthood. In doing so, we caused a kind of revolution—peaceful, mainly—and now the computer has taken up residence in our offices and homes. Computers shrank in size and grew in power, as they dropped dramatically in price. And it all happened fairly quickly. Not as quickly as I once thought, but still pretty fast. Inexpensive computer chips now show up in engines, watches, antilock brakes, facsimile machines, elevators, gasoline pumps, cameras, thermostats, treadmills, vending machines, burglar alarms, and even talking greeting cards. School kids today are doing amazing things with personal computers that are no larger than textbooks but outperform the largest computers of a generation ago.

Now that computing is astoundingly inexpensive and computers inhabit every part of our lives, we stand at the brink of another revolution. This one will involve unprecedentedly inexpensive communication; all the computers will join together to communicate with us and for us. Interconnected globally, they will form a network, which is being called the information highway. A direct precursor is the present Internet, which is a group of computers joined and exchanging information using current technology.

The reach and use of the new network, its promise and perils, is the subject of this book.

Every aspect of what's about to happen seems exciting. When I was nineteen I caught a look at the future, based my career on what I saw, and I turned out to have been right. But the Bill Gates of nineteen was in a very different position from the one I'm in now. In those days, not only did I have all the self-assurance of a smart teenager, but also nobody was watching me, and if I failed—so what? Today I'm much more in the position of the computer giants of the seventies, but I hope I've learned some lessons from them.

At one time I thought I might want to major in economics in college. I eventually changed my mind, but in a way my whole experience with the computer industry has been a series of economics lessons. I saw firsthand the effects of positive spirals and inflexible business models. I watched the way industry standards evolved. I witnessed the importance of compatibility in technology, of feedback, and of constant innovation. And I think we may be about to witness the realization of Adam Smith's ideal market, at last.

But I'm not using those lessons just for theorizing about this future—I'm betting on it. Back when I was a teenager, I envisioned the impact that low-cost computers could have. "A computer on every desk and in every home" became Microsoft's corporate mission, and we have worked to help make that possible. Now those computers are being connected to one another, and we're building software—the instructions that tell the computer hardware what to do—that will help individuals get the benefits of this connected communication power. It is impossible to predict exactly what it will be like to use the network. We'll communicate with it through a variety of devices, including some that look like television sets, some like today's PCs; some will look like telephones, and some will be the size and something like the shape of a wallet. And at the heart of each will be a powerful computer, invisibly connected to millions of others.

There will be a day, not far distant, when you will be able to conduct business, study, explore the world and its cultures, call up any great entertainment, make friends, attend neighborhood markets, and show pictures to distant relatives—without leaving your desk or armchair. You won't leave your network connection behind at the office or in the classroom. It will be more than an object you carry or an appliance you purchase. It will be your passport into a new, mediated way of life.

Firsthand experiences and pleasures are personal and unmediated. No one, in the name of progress, will take away from you the experience of lying on a beach, walking in the woods, sitting in a comedy club, or shopping at a flea market. But firsthand experiences aren't always rewarding. For example, waiting in line is a firsthand experience, but we have been trying to invent ways to avoid it ever since we first queued up.

Much of human progress has come about because someone invented a better and more powerful tool. Physical tools speed up work and rescue people from hard labor. The plow and the wheel, the crane and the bulldozer, amplify the physical abilities of those using them.

Informational tools are symbolic mediators that amplify the intellect rather than the muscle of their users. You're having a mediated experience as you read this book: We're not actually in the same room, but you are still able to find out what's on my mind. A great deal of work now involves decision making and knowledge, so information tools have become, and will continue increasingly to be, the focus of inventors. Just as any text could be represented with an arrangement of letters, these tools allow information of all types to be represented in digital form, in a pattern of electrical pulses that is easy for computers to deal with. The world today has more than 100 million computers whose purpose is to manipulate information. They are helping us now by making it much easier to store and transmit information that is already in digital form, but in the near future they will allow us access to almost any information in the world.

In the United States, the connecting of all these computers has been compared to another massive project: the gridding of the country with interstate highways, which began during the Eisenhower era. This is why the new network was dubbed the "information superhighway." The term was popularized by then-senator Al Gore, whose father sponsored the 1956 Federal Aid Highway Act.

The highway metaphor isn't quite right though. The phrase suggests landscape and geography, a distance between points, and embodies the implication that you have to travel to get from one place to another. In fact, one of the most remarkable aspects of this new communications technology is that it will eliminate distance. It won't matter if someone you're contacting is in the next room or on another continent, because this highly mediated network will be unconstrained by miles and kilometers.

The term "highway" also suggests that everyone is driving and following the same route. This network is more like a lot of country lanes where everyone can look at or do whatever his individual interests suggest. Another implication is that perhaps it should be built by the government, which I think would be a major mistake in most countries. But the real problem is that the metaphor emphasizes the infrastructure of the endeavor rather than its applications. At Microsoft we talk about "Information At Your Fingertips," which spotlights a benefit rather than the network itself. A different metaphor that I think comes closer to describing a lot of the activities that will take place is that of the ultimate market. Markets from trading floors to malls are fundamental to human society, and I believe this new one will eventually be the world's central department store. It will be where we social animals will sell, trade, invest, haggle, pick stuff up, argue, meet new people, and hang out. When you hear the phrase "information highway," rather than seeing a road, imagine a marketplace or an exchange. Think of the hustle and bustle of the New York Stock Exchange or a farmers' market or of a bookstore full of people looking for fascinating stories and information. All manner of human activity takes place, from billion-dollar deals to flirtations. Many transactions will involve money, tendered in digital form rather than currency. Digital information of all kinds, not just as money, will be the new medium of exchange in this market.

The global information market will be huge and will combine all the various ways human goods, services, and ideas are exchanged. On a practical level, this will give you broader choices about most things, including how you earn and invest, what you buy and how much you pay for it, who your friends are and how you spend your time with them, and where and how securely you and your family live. Your workplace and your idea of what it means to be "educated" will be transformed, perhaps almost beyond recognition. Your sense of identity, of who you are and where you belong, may open up considerably. In short, just about everything will be done differently. I can hardly wait for this tomorrow, and I'm doing what I can to help make it happen.

You aren't sure you believe this? Or want to believe it? Perhaps you'll decline to participate. People commonly make this vow when some new technology threatens to change what they're familiar and comfortable with. At first, the bicycle was a silly contraption; the automobile, a noisy intruder; the pocket calculator, a threat to the study of mathematics; and the radio, the end of literacy.

But then something happens. Over time, these machines find a place in our everyday lives because they not only offer convenience and save labor, they can also inspire us to new creative heights. We warm to them. They assume a trusted place beside our other tools. A new generation grows up with them, changing and humanizing them. In short, playing with them.

The telephone was a major advance in two-way communication. But at first, even it was denounced as nothing more than a nuisance. People were made uncomfortable and awkward by this mechanical invader in their homes. Eventually, though, men and women realized they were not just getting a new machine, they were learning a new kind of communication. A chat on the telephone wasn't as long or as formal as a face-to-face conversation. There was an unfamiliar and, for many, an off-putting efficiency to it. Before the phone, any good talk entailed a visit and probably a meal, and one could expect to spend a full afternoon or evening. Once most businesses and households had telephones, users created ways to take advantage of the unique characteristics of this means of communicating. As it flourished, its own special expressions, tricks, etiquette, and culture developed. Alexander Graham Bell certainly wouldn't have anticipated the silly executive game of "Have My Secretary Get Him Onto the Line Before Me." As I write, a newer form of communication—electronic mail, or e-mail—is undergoing the same sort of process: establishing its own rules and habits.

"Little by little, the machine will become a part of humanity," the French aviator and author Antoine de Saint-Exupéry wrote in his 1939 memoir, *Wind, Sand, and Stars.* He was writing about the way people tend to react to new technology and using the slow embrace of the railroad in the nineteenth century as an example. He described the way the smoke-belching, demonically loud engines of the primitive locomotives were decried at first as iron monsters. Then as more tracks were laid, towns built train stations. Goods and services flowed. Interesting new jobs became available. A culture grew up around this novel form of transportation, and disdain became acceptance, even approval. What had once been the iron monster became the mighty bearer of life's best products. Again, the change in our perception was reflected in the language we used. We began calling it "the iron horse." "What is it today for the villager except a humble friend who calls every evening at six?" Saint-Exupéry asked.

The only other single shift that has had as great an effect on the history of communication took place in about 1450, when Johann Gutenberg, a goldsmith from Mainz, Germany, invented movable type and introduced the first printing press to Europe (China and Korea already had presses). That event changed Western culture forever. It took Gutenberg two years to compose the type for his first Bible, but once that was done, he could print multiple copies. Before Gutenberg, all books were copied by hand. Monks, who usually did the copying, seldom managed more than one text a year. Gutenberg's press was a high-speed laser printer by comparison.

The printing press did more than just give the West a faster way to reproduce a book. Until that time, despite the passing generations, life had been communal and nearly unchanging. Most people knew only about what they had seen themselves or been told. Few strayed far from their villages, in part because without reliable maps it was often nearly impossible to find the way home. As James Burke, a favorite author of mine, put it: "In this world all experience was personal: horizons were small, the community was inward-looking. What existed in the outside world was a matter of hearsay."

The printed word changed all that. It was the first mass medium—the first time that knowledge, opinions, and experiences could be passed on in a portable, durable, and available form. As the written word extended the population's reach far beyond a village, people began to care about what was happening elsewhere. Printing shops quickly sprang up in commercial cities and became centers of intellectual exchange. Literacy became an important skill that revolutionized education and altered social structures.

Before Gutenberg, there were only about 30,000 books on the entire continent of Europe, nearly all Bibles or biblical commentary. By 1500, there were more than 9 million, on all sorts of topics. Handbills and other printed matter affected politics, religion, science, and literature. For the first time, those outside the canonical elite had access to written information.

The information highway will transform our culture as dramatically as Gutenberg's press did the Middle Ages.

Personal computers have already altered work habits, but they haven't really changed our lives much yet. When tomorrow's powerful information machines are connected on the highway, people, machines, entertainment, and information services will all be accessible. You will be able to stay in touch with anyone, anywhere, who wants to stay in touch with you; to browse through any of thousands of libraries, day or night. Your misplaced or stolen camera will send you a message telling you exactly where it is, even if it's in a different city. You'll be able to answer your apartment intercom from your office, or answer any mail from your home. Information that today is difficult to retrieve will be easy to find:

Is your bus running on time?

Are there any accidents right now on the route you usually take to the office?

Does anyone want to trade his or her Thursday theater tickets for your Wednesday tickets?

What is your child's school-attendance record?

What's a good recipe for halibut?

Which store, anywhere, can deliver by tomorrow morning for the lowest price a wristwatch that takes your pulse?

What would someone pay for my old Mustang convertible?

How is the hole in a needle manufactured?

Are your shirts ready yet at the laundry?

What's the cheapest way to subscribe to *The Wall Street Journal*?

What are the symptoms of a heart attack?

Was there any interesting testimony at the county courthouse today?

Do fish see in color?

What does the Champs-Élysées look like right now?

Where were you at 9:02 P.M. last Thursday?

Let's say you're thinking about trying a new restaurant and want to see its menu, wine list, and specials of the day. Maybe you're wondering what your favorite food reviewer said about it. You may also want to know what sanitation score the health department gave the place. If you're leery of the restaurant's neighborhood, perhaps you'll want to see a safety rating based on police reports. Still interested in going? You'll want reservations, a map, and driving instructions based on current traffic conditions. Take the instructions in printed form or have them read to you—and updated—as you drive.

All of this information will be readily accessible and completely personal, because you'll be able to explore whatever parts of it interest you in whatever ways and for however long you want. You'll watch a program when it's convenient for you, instead of when a broadcaster chooses to air it. You'll shop, order food, contact fellow hobbyists, or publish information for others to use when and as you want to. Your nightly newscast will start at a time you determine and last exactly as long as you want it to. It will cover subjects selected by you or by a service that knows your interests. You'll be able to ask for reports from Tokyo or Boston or Seattle, request more detail on a news item, or inquire whether your favorite columnist has commented on an event. And if you prefer, your news will be delivered to you on paper.

Change of this magnitude makes people nervous. Every day, all over the world, people are asking about the implications of the network, often with terrible apprehension. What will happen to our jobs? Will people withdraw from the physical world and live vicariously through their computers? Will the gulf between the haves and have-nots widen irreparably? Will a computer be able to help the disenfranchised in East St. Louis or the starving in Ethiopia? There are some major challenges that will come with the network and the changes it will bring. In chapter 12,

I talk at length about the many legitimate concerns I hear expressed again and again.

I've thought about the difficulties and find that, on balance, I'm confident and optimistic. Partly this is just the way I am, and partly it's because I'm enthusiastic about what my generation, which came of age the same time the computer did, will be able to do. We'll be giving people tools to use to reach out in new ways. I'm someone who believes that because progress will come no matter what, we need to make the best of it. I'm still thrilled by the feeling that I'm squinting into the future and catching that first revealing hint of revolutionary possibilities. I feel incredibly lucky that I am getting the chance to play a part in the beginning of an epochal change for a second time.

I first experienced this particular euphoria as a teenager when I understood how inexpensive and powerful computers would become. The computer we played tic-tac-toe on in 1968 and most computers at that time were mainframes: temperamental monsters that resided in climate-controlled cocoons. After we had used up the money the Mothers' Club had provided, my school friend Paul Allen, with whom I later started Microsoft, and I spent a lot of time trying to get access to computers. They performed modestly by today's standards, but seemed awesome to us because they were big and complicated and cost as much as millions of dollars each. They were connected by phone lines to clackety Teletype terminals so they could be shared by people at different locations. We rarely got close to the actual mainframes. Computer time was very expensive. When I was in high school, it cost about $40 an hour to access a time-shared computer using a Teletype—for that $40 an hour you got a slice of the computer's precious attention. This seems odd today, when some people have more than one PC and think nothing of leaving them idle for most of the day. Actually, it was possible even then to own your own computer. If you could afford $18,000, Digital Equipment Corporation (DEC) made the PDP-8. Although it was called a "mini-computer," it was large by today's standards. It occupied a rack about two feet square and six feet high and weighed 250 pounds. We had one at our high school for a while, and I fooled around with it a lot. The PDP-8 was very limited compared to the mainframes we could reach by phone; in fact, it had less raw computing power than some wristwatches do today. But it was programmable the same way the big, expensive ones were: by giving it software instructions. Despite its limitations, the PDP-8 inspired us to indulge in the dream that one day millions of individuals could possess their own computers. With each passing year, I became more certain that computers and computing were destined to be cheap and ubiquitous. I'm sure that one of the reasons I was so determined to help develop the personal computer is that I wanted one for myself.

At that time software, like computer hardware, was expensive. It had to be written specifically for each kind of computer. And each time computer hardware changed, which it did regularly, the software for it pretty much had to be rewritten. Computer manufacturers provided some standard software program building blocks (for example, libraries of mathematical functions) with their machines, but most software was written specifically to solve some business's individual problems. Some software was shared, and a few companies were selling general-purpose software, but there was very little packaged software that you could buy off the shelf.

My parents paid my tuition at Lakeside and gave me money for books, but I had to take care of my own computer-time bills. This is what drove me to the commercial side of the software business. A bunch of us, including Paul Allen, got entry-level software programming jobs. For high school students the pay was extraordinary—about $5,000 each summer, part in cash and the rest in computer time. We also worked out deals with a few companies whereby we could use computers for free if we'd locate problems in their software. One of the programs I wrote was the one that scheduled students in classes. I surreptitiously added a few instructions and found myself nearly the only guy in a class full of girls. As I said before, it was hard to tear myself away from a machine at which I could so unambiguously demonstrate success. I was hooked.

Paul knew a lot more than I did about computer hardware, the machines themselves. One summer day in 1972, when I was sixteen and Paul was nineteen, he showed me a ten-paragraph article buried on page 143 of *Electronics* magazine. It was announcing that a young firm named Intel had released a microprocessor chip called the 8008.

A microprocessor is a simple chip that contains the entire brain of a whole computer. Paul and I realized this first microprocessor was very limited, but he was sure that the chips would get more powerful and computers on a chip would improve very rapidly.

At the time, the computer industry had no idea of building a real computer around a microprocessor. The *Electronics* article, for example, described the 8008 as suitable for "any arithmetic, control, or decision-making system, such as a smart terminal." The writers didn't see that a microprocessor could grow up to be a general-purpose computer. Microprocessors were slow and limited in the amount of information they could handle. None of the languages programmers were familiar with was available for the 8008, which made it nearly impossible to write complex programs for it. Every application had to be programmed with the few dozen simple instructions the chip could understand. The 8008 was condemned to life as a beast of burden, carrying out uncomplicated and unchanging tasks over and over. It was quite popular in elevators and calculators.

To put it another way, a simple microprocessor in an embedded application, such as an elevator's controls, is a single instrument, a drum or a horn, in the hands of an amateur: good for basic rhythm or un-

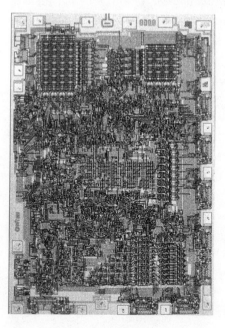

1972: Intel's 8008 microprocessor

complicated tunes. A powerful microprocessor with programming languages, however, is like an accomplished orchestra. With the right software, or sheet music, it can play anything.

Paul and I wondered what we could program the 8008 to do. He called up Intel to request a manual. We were a little surprised when they actually sent him one. We both dug into it. I had worked out a version of BASIC, which ran on the limited DEC PDP-8, and was excited at the thought of doing the same for the little Intel chip. But as I studied the 8008's manual, I realized it was futile to try. The 8008 just wasn't sophisticated enough, didn't have enough transistors.

We did, however, figure out a way to use the little chip to power a machine that could analyze the information counted by traffic monitors on city streets. Many municipalities that measured traffic flow did so by stringing a rubber hose over a selected street. When a car crossed the hose, it punched a paper tape inside a metal box at the end of the hose. We saw that we could use the 8008 to process these tapes, to print out graphs and other statistics. We baptized our first company "Traf-O-Data." At the time it sounded like poetry.

I wrote much of the software for the Traf-O-Data machine on cross-state bus trips from Seattle to Pullman, Washington, where Paul was attending college. Our prototype worked well, and we envisioned selling lots of our new machines across the country. We used it to process traffic-volume tapes for a few customers, but no one actually wanted to buy the machine, at least not from a couple of teenagers.

Despite our disappointment, we still believed our future, even if it was not to be in hardware, might have something to do with microprocessors. After I started at Harvard College in 1973, Paul somehow managed to coax his clunky old Chrysler New Yorker cross-country from Washington State and took a job in Boston, programming mini-computers at Honeywell. He drove over to Cambridge a lot so we could continue our long talks about future schemes.

In the spring of 1974, *Electronics* magazine announced Intel's new 8080 chip—ten times the power of the 8008 inside the Traf-O-Data machine. The 8080 was not much larger than the 8008, but it contained 2,700 more transistors. All at once we were looking at the heart of a real computer, and the price was under $200. We attacked the manual. "DEC can't sell any more PDP-8s now," I told Paul. It seemed obvious to us that if a tiny chip could get so much more powerful, the end of big unwieldy machines was coming.

Computer manufacturers, however, didn't see the microprocessor as a threat. They just couldn't imagine a puny chip taking on a "real" computer. Not even the scientists at Intel saw its full potential. To them, the 8080 represented nothing more than an improvement in chip technology. In the short term, the computer establishment was right. The 8080 was just another slight advance. But Paul and I looked past the limits of that new chip and saw a different kind of computer that would be perfect for us, and for everyone—personal, affordable, and adaptable. It was absolutely clear to us that because the new chips were so cheap, they soon would be everywhere.

Computer hardware, which had once been scarce, would soon be readily available, and access to computers would no longer be charged for at a high hourly rate. It seemed to us people would find all kinds of new uses for computing if it was cheap. Then, software would be the key to delivering the full potential of these machines. Paul and I speculated that Japanese companies and IBM would likely produce most of the hardware. We believed we could come up with new and innovative software. And why not? The microprocessor would change the structure of the industry. Maybe there was a place for the two of us.

This kind of talk is what college is all about. You have all kinds of new experiences, and dream crazy dreams. We were young and assumed we had all the time in the world. I enrolled for another year at Harvard and kept thinking about how we could get a software company going. One plan was pretty simple. We sent letters from my dorm room to all the big computer companies, offering to write them a version of BASIC for the new Intel chip. We got no takers. By December, we were pretty discouraged. I was planning to fly home to Seattle for the holidays, and Paul was staying in Boston. On an achingly cold Massachusetts morning a few days before I left, Paul and I were hanging out at the Harvard Square newsstand, and Paul picked up the January issue of *Popular Electronics*. This is the moment I described at the beginning of the Foreword. This gave reality to our dreams about the future.

On the magazine's cover was a photograph of a very small computer,

-------------------------------▶

January 1975 issue of
Popular Electronics

not much larger than a toaster oven. It had a name only slightly more dignified than Traf-O-Data: the Altair 8800 ("Altair" was a destination in a *Star Trek* episode). It was being sold for $397 as a kit. When it was assembled, it had no keyboard or display. It had sixteen address switches to direct commands and sixteen lights. You could get the little lights on the front panel to blink, but that was about all. Part of the problem was that the Altair 8800 lacked software. It couldn't be programmed, which made it more a novelty than a tool.

What the Altair did have was an Intel 8080 microprocessor chip as its brain. When we saw that, panic set in. "Oh no! It's happening without us! People are going to go write real software for this chip." I was sure it would happen sooner rather than later, and I wanted to be involved from the beginning. The chance to get in on the first stages of the PC revolution seemed the opportunity of a lifetime, and I seized it.

Twenty years later I feel the same way about what's going on now. Then I was afraid others would have the same vision we did; today I know thousands do. The legacy of the earlier revolution is that 50 million PCs are sold each year worldwide, and that fortunes have been completely reordered in the computer industry. There have been plenty of winners and losers. This time lots of companies are rushing to get in early while change is taking place and there are endless opportunities.

When we look back at the last twenty years it is obvious that a number of large companies were so set in their ways that they did not adapt properly and lost out as a result. Twenty years from now we'll look back and see the same pattern. I know that as I write this there's at least one young person out there who will create a major new company, convinced that his or her insight into the communications revolution is the right one. Thousands of innovative companies will be founded to exploit the coming changes.

In 1975, when Paul and I naively decided to start a company, we were acting like characters in all those Judy Garland and Mickey Rooney movies who crowed, "We'll put on a show in the barn!" There was no time to waste. Our first project was to create BASIC for the little computer.

We had to squeeze a lot of capability into the computer's small memory. The typical Altair had about 4,000 characters of memory. Today most personal computers have 4 or 8 million characters of memory. Our task was further complicated because we didn't actually own an Altair, and had never even seen one. That didn't really matter because what we were really interested in was the new Intel 8080 microprocessor chip, and we'd never seen that, either. Undaunted, Paul studied a manual for the chip, then wrote a program that made a big computer at Harvard mimic the little Altair. This was like having a whole orchestra available and using it to play a simple duet, but it worked.

Writing good software requires a lot of concentration, and writing BASIC for the Altair was exhausting. Sometimes I rock back and forth or pace when I'm thinking, because it helps me focus on a single idea and exclude distractions. I did a lot of rocking and pacing in my dorm room the winter of 1975. Paul and I didn't sleep much and lost track of night and day. When I did fall asleep, it was often at my desk or on the floor. Some days I didn't eat or see anyone. But after five weeks, our BASIC was written—and the world's first microcomputer software company was born. In time we named it "Microsoft."

----------------------------➤

We knew getting a company started would mean sacrifice. But we also realized we had to do it then or forever lose the opportunity to make it in microcomputer software. In the spring of 1975, Paul quit his programming job and I decided to go on leave from Harvard.

I talked it over with my parents, both of whom were pretty savvy about business. They saw how much I wanted to try starting a software company and they were supportive. My plan was to take time off, start the company, and then go back later and finish college. I never really made a conscious decision to forgo a degree. Technically, I'm just on a really long leave. Unlike some students, I loved college. I thought it was fun to sit around and talk with so many smart people my own age. However, I felt the window of opportunity to start a software company might not open again. So I dove into the world of business when I was nineteen years old.

From the start, Paul and I funded everything ourselves. Each of us had saved some money. Paul had been well paid at Honeywell, and some of the money I had came from late-night poker games in the dorm. Fortunately, our company didn't require massive funding.

People often ask me to explain Microsoft's success. They want to know the secret of getting from a two-man, shoestring operation to a company with 17,000 employees and more than $6 billion a year in sales. Of course, there is no simple answer, and luck played a role, but I think the most important element was our original vision.

We glimpsed what lay beyond that Intel 8080 chip, and then acted on it. We asked, "What if computing were nearly free?" We believed there would be computers everywhere because of cheap computing power and great new software that would take advantage of it. We set up shop betting on the former and producing the latter when no one else was. Our initial insight made everything else a bit easier. We were in the right place at the right time. We got there first and our early success gave us the chance to hire many smart people. We built a worldwide sales force and used the revenue it generated to fund new products. From the beginning we set off down a road that was headed in the right direction.

Now there is a new horizon, and the relevant question is, "What if communicating were almost free?" The idea of interconnecting all homes and offices to a high-speed network has ignited this nation's imagination as nothing has since the space program. And not just this nation's—imaginations around the world have caught fire. Thousands of companies are committed to the same vision, so individual focus, understanding of the intermediate steps, and execution will determine their relative successes.

I spend a good deal of time thinking about business because I enjoy my work so much. Today, a lot of my thoughts are about the highway. Twenty years ago, when I was thinking about the future of microchip personal computers, I couldn't be certain where they were leading me either. I kept to my course, however, and had confidence we were moving in the right direction to be where we wanted to be when everything became clear. There's a lot more at stake now, but I feel that same way again. It's nerve-wracking, but exhilarating too.

All sorts of individuals and companies are betting their futures on building the elements that will make the information highway a reality. At Microsoft, we're working hard to figure out how to evolve from where we are today to the point where we can unleash the full potential of the new advances in technology. These are exciting times, not only for the companies involved but for everyone who will realize the benefits of this revolution.

2

THE BEGINNING OF
THE INFORMATION AGE

The first time I heard the term "Information Age" I was tantalized. I knew about the Iron Age and the Bronze Age, periods of history named for the new materials men used to make their tools and weapons. Those were specific eras. Then I read academics predicting that countries will be fighting over the control of information, not natural resources. This sounded intriguing too, but what did they mean by information?

The claim that information would define the future reminded me of the famous party scene in the 1967 movie *The Graduate*. A businessman buttonholes Benjamin, the college graduate played by Dustin Hoffman, and offers him a single word of unsolicited career advice: "Plastics." I wondered whether, if the scene had been written a few decades later, the businessman's advice would have been: "One word, Benjamin. 'Information.'"

I imagined nonsensical conversations around a future office watercooler: "How much information do you have?" "Switzerland is a great country because of all the information they have there!" "I hear the Information Price Index is going up!"

It sounds nonsensical because information isn't as tangible or measurable as the materials that defined previous ages, but information has become increasingly important to us. The information revolution is just beginning. The cost of communications will drop as precipitously as the cost of computing already has. When it gets low enough and is combined with other advances in technology, "information highway" will no longer be just a phrase for eager executives and excited politicians. It will be as real and as far-reaching as "electricity." To understand why information is going to be so central, it's important to know how technology is changing the ways we handle information.

The majority of this chapter is devoted to such an explanation. The material that follows is to give less-informed readers without a background in computer principles and history sufficient information to enjoy the rest of the material in the book. If you understand how digital computers work, you probably already know the material cold, so feel free to skip to chapter 3.

The most fundamental difference we'll see in future information is that almost all of it will be digital. Whole printed libraries are already being scanned and stored as electronic data on disks and CD-ROMs. Newspapers and magazines are now often completely composed in electronic form and printed on paper as a convenience for distribution. The electronic information is stored permanently—or for as long as anyone wants it—in computer databases: giant banks of journalistic data accessible through on-line services. Photographs, films, and videos are all being converted into digital information. Every year, better methods are being devised to quantify information and distill it into quadrillions of atomistic packets of data. Once digital information is stored, anyone with access and a personal computer can instantaneously recall, compare, and refashion it. What characterizes this period in history is the completely new ways in which information can be changed and manipulated, and the increasing speeds at which we can handle it. The computer's abilities to provide low-cost, high-speed processing and transmission of digital data will transform the conventional communication devices in homes and offices.

The idea of using an instrument to manipulate numbers isn't new. The abacus had been in use in Asia for nearly 5,000 years by 1642, when the nineteen-year-old French scientist Blaise Pascal invented a mechanical calculator. It was a counting device. Three decades later, the German mathematician Gottfried von Leibniz improved on Pascal's design. His "Stepped Reckoner" could multiply, divide, and calculate square roots. Reliable mechanical calculators, powered by rotating dials and gears, descendants of the Stepped Reckoner, were the mainstay of business until their electronic counterparts replaced them. When I was a boy, a cash register was essentially a mechanical calculator linked to a cash drawer.

More than a century and a half ago, a visionary British mathematician glimpsed the possibility of the computer and that glimpse made him famous even in his day. Charles Babbage was a professor of mathematics at Cambridge University who conceived the possibility of a mechanical device that would be able to perform a string of related calculations. As early as the 1830s, he was drawn to the idea that information could be manipulated by a machine if the information could be converted into numbers first. The steam-powered machine Babbage envisioned would use pegs, toothed wheels, cylinders, and other mechanical parts, the apparatus of the then-new Industrial Age. Babbage believed his "Analytical Engine" would be used to take the drudgery and inaccuracy out of calculating.

He lacked the terms we now use to refer to the parts of his machine. He called the central processor, or working guts of his machine, the "mill." He referred to his machine's memory as the "store." Babbage imagined information being transformed the way cotton was—drawn from a store (warehouse) and milled into something new.

His Analytical Engine would be mechanical, but he foresaw how it would be able to follow changing sets of instructions and thus serve different functions. This is the essence of software. It is a comprehensive set of rules a machine can be given to "instruct" it how to perform particular tasks. Babbage realized that to create these instructions he would need an entirely new kind of language, and he devised one using numbers, letters, arrows, and other symbols. The language was designed to let Babbage "program" the Analytical Engine with a long series of conditional instructions, which would allow the machine to modify its actions in response to changing situations. He was the first to see that a single machine could serve a number of different purposes.

For the next century mathematicians worked with the ideas Babbage had outlined and finally, by the mid-1940s, an electronic computer was built based on the principles of his Analytical Engine. It is hard to sort out the paternity of the modern computer, because much of the thinking and work was done in the United States and Britain during World War II under the cloak of wartime secrecy. Three major contributors were Alan Turing, Claude Shannon, and John von Neumann.

In the mid-1930s, Alan Turing, like Babbage a superlative Cambridge-trained British mathematician, proposed what is known today as a Turing machine. It was his version of a completely general-purpose calculating machine that could be instructed to work with almost any kind of information.

In the late 1930s, when Claude Shannon was still a student, he demonstrated that a machine executing logical instructions could manipulate information. His insight, the subject of his master's thesis, was about how computer circuits—closed for true and open for false—could perform logical operations, using the number 1 to represent "true" and 0 to represent "false."

This is a binary system. It's a code. Binary is the alphabet of electronic computers, the basis of the language into which all information is translated, stored, and used within a computer. It's simple, but so vital to the understanding of the way computers work that it's worth pausing here to explain it more fully.

Imagine you have a room that you want illuminated with as much as 250 watts of electric lighting and you want the lighting to be adjustable, from 0 watt of illumination (total darkness) to the full wattage. One way to accomplish this is with a rotating dimmer switch hooked to a 250-watt bulb. To achieve complete darkness, turn the knob fully counterclockwise to Off for 0 watt of light. For maximum brightness, turn the knob fully clockwise for the entire 250 watts. For some illumination level in between, turn the knob to an intermediate position.

This system is easy to use but has limitations. If the knob is at an intermediate setting—if lighting is lowered for an intimate dinner, for example—you can only guess what the lighting level is. You don't really know how many watts are in use, or how to describe the setting precisely. Your information is approximate, which makes it hard to store or reproduce.

What if you want to reproduce exactly the same level of lighting next week? You could make a mark on the switch plate so that you know how far to turn it, but this is hardly exact, and what happens when you want to reproduce a different setting? What if a friend wants to reproduce the same level of lighting? You can say, "Turn the knob about a fifth of the way clockwise," or "Turn the knob until the arrow is at about two o'clock," but your friend's reproduction will only approximate your setting. What if your friend then passes the information on to another friend, who in turn passes it on again? Each time the information is handed on, the chances of its remaining accurate decrease.

That is an example of information stored in "analog" form. The dimmer's knob provides an analogy to the bulb's lighting level. If it's turned halfway, presumably you have about half the total wattage. When you measure or describe how far the knob is turned, you're actually storing information about the analogy (the knob) rather than about the lighting level. Analog information can be gathered, stored, and reproduced, but it tends to be imprecise—and runs the risk of becoming less precise each time it is transferred.

Now let's look at an entirely different way of describing how to light the room, a digital rather than analog method of storing and transmitting information. Any kind of information can be converted into numbers using only 0s and 1s. These are called binary numbers—numbers composed entirely of 0s and 1s. Each 0 or 1 is called a bit. Once the information has been converted, it can be fed to and stored in computers as long strings of bits. Those numbers are all that's meant by "digital information."

Instead of a single 250-watt bulb, let's say you have eight bulbs, each with a wattage double the one preceding it, from 1 to 128. Each of these bulbs is hooked to its own switch, with the lowest-watt bulb on the right. Such an arrangement can be diagrammed like this:

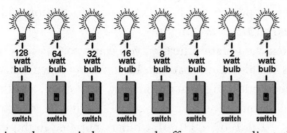

By turning these switches on and off, you can adjust the lighting level in 1-watt increments from 0 watt (all switches off) to 255 watts (all switches on). This gives you 256 possibilities. If you want 1 watt of light, you turn on only the rightmost switch, which turns on the 1-watt bulb. If you want 2 watts of light, you turn on only the 2-watt bulb. If you want 3 watts of light, you turn on both the 1-watt and 2-watt bulbs, because 1 plus 2 equals the desired 3 watts. If you want 4 watts of light, you turn on the 4-watt bulb. If you want 5 watts, you turn on just the 4-watt and 1-watt bulbs. If you want 250 watts of light, you turn on all but the 4-watt and 1-watt bulbs.

If you have decided the ideal illumination level for dining is 137 watts of light, you turn on the 128-, 8-, and 1-watt bulbs, like this:

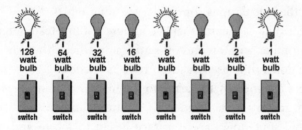

This system makes it easy to record an exact lighting level for later use or to communicate it to others who have the same light-switch setup. Because the way we record binary information is universal—low number to the right, high number to the left, always doubling—you don't have to write down the values of the bulbs. You simply record the pattern of switches: on, off, off, off, on, off, off, on. With that information a friend can faithfully reproduce the 137 watts of light in your room. In fact, as long as everyone involved double-checks the accuracy of what he does, the message can be passed through a million hands and at the end every person will have the same information and be able to achieve exactly 137 watts of light.

To shorten the notation further, you can record each "off" as 0 and each "on" as 1. This means that instead of writing down "on, off, off, off, on, off, off, on," meaning turn on the first, the fourth, and the eighth of the eight bulbs, and leave the others off, you write the same information as 1, 0, 0, 0, 1, 0, 0, 1, or 10001001, a binary number. In this case it's 137. You call your friend and say: "I've got the perfect lighting level! It's 10001001. Try it." Your friend gets it exactly right, by flipping a switch on for each 1 and off for each 0.

This may seem like a complicated way to describe the brightness of a light source, but it is an example of the theory behind binary expression, the basis of all modern computers.

Binary expression made it possible to take advantage of electric circuits to build calculators. This happened during World War II when a group of mathematicians led by J. Presper Eckert and John Mauchly at the University of Pennsylvania's Moore School of Electrical Engineering began developing an electronic computational machine, the Electronic Numerical Integrator And Calculator, called ENIAC. Its purpose was to speed up the calculations for artillery-aiming tables. ENIAC was more like an electronic calculator than a computer, but instead of representing a binary number with on and off settings on wheels the way a mechanical calculator did, it used vacuum tube "switches."

Soldiers assigned by the army to the huge machine wheeled around squeaking grocery carts filled with vacuum tubes. When one burned out, ENIAC shut down and the race began to locate and replace the burned-out tube. One explanation, perhaps somewhat apocryphal, for why the tubes had to be replaced so often was that their heat and light attracted moths, which would fly into the huge machine and cause short circuits. If this is true, it gives new meaning to the term "bugs" for the little glitches that can plague computer hardware or software.

When all the tubes were working, a staff of engineers could set up ENIAC to solve a problem by laboriously plugging in 6,000 cables by hand. To make it perform another function, the staff had to reconfigure the cabling—every time. John von Neumann, a brilliant Hungarian-born American, who is known for many things, including the development of game theory and his contributions to nuclear weaponry, is credited with the leading role in figuring out a way around this problem. He created the paradigm that all digital computers still follow. The "von Neumann architecture," as it is known today, is based on principles he articulated in 1945—including the principle that a computer could avoid cabling changes by storing instructions in its memory. As soon as this idea was put into practice, the modern computer was born.

Today the brains of most computers are descendants of the micro-processor Paul Allen and I were so knocked out by in the seventies, and personal computers often are rated according to how many bits of infor-mation (one switch in the lighting example) their microprocessor can process at a time, or how many bytes (a cluster of eight bits) of memory or disk-based storage they have. ENIAC weighed 30 tons and filled a large room. Inside, the computational pulses raced among 1,500 electro-mechanical relays and flowed through 17,000 vacuum tubes. Switching it on consumed 150,000 watts of energy. But ENIAC stored only the equivalent of about 80 characters of information.

By the early 1960s, transistors had supplanted vacuum tubes in con-sumer electronics. This was more than a decade after the discovery at Bell Labs that a tiny sliver of silicon could do the same job as a vacuum tube. Like vacuum tubes, transistors act as electrical switches, but they require significantly less power to operate and as a result generate much less heat and require less space. Multiple transistor circuits could be combined onto a single chip, creating an integrated circuit. The com-puter chips we use today are integrated circuits containing the equiva-lent of millions of transistors packed onto less than a square inch of silicon.

In a 1977 *Scientific American* article, Bob Noyce, one of the founders of Intel, compared the $300 microprocessor to ENIAC, the moth-infested mastodon from the dawn of the computer age. The wee micro-processor was not only more powerful, but as Noyce noted, "It is twenty times faster, has a larger memory, is thousands of times more reliable, consumes the power of a lightbulb rather than that of a locomotive, oc-cupies 1/30,000 the volume and costs 1/10,000 as much. It is available by mail order or at your local hobby shop."

Of course, the 1977 microprocessor seems like a toy now. And, in

1946: A view inside a part of the ENIAC computer

fact, many inexpensive toys contain computer chips that are more powerful than the 1970s chips that started the microcomputer revolution. But all of today's computers, whatever their size or power, manipulate information stored as binary numbers.

Binary numbers are used to store text in a personal computer, music on a compact disc, and money in a bank's network of cash machines. Before information can go into a computer it has to be converted into binary. Machines, digital devices, convert the information back into its original, useful form. You can imagine each device throwing switches, controlling the flow of electrons. But the switches involved, which are usually made of silicon, are extremely small and can be thrown by applying electrical charges extraordinarily quickly—to produce text on the screen of a personal computer, music from a CD player, and the instructions to a cash machine to dispense currency.

The light-switch example demonstrated how any number can be represented in binary. Here's how text can be expressed in binary. By convention, the number 65 represents a capital A, the number 66 represents a capital B, and so forth. On a computer each of these numbers is expressed in binary code: the capital letter A, 65, becomes 01000001.

The capital B, 66, becomes 01000010. A space break is represented by the number 32, or 00100000. So the sentence "Socrates is a man" becomes this 136-digit string of 1s and 0s:

01010011 01101111 01100011 01110010 01100001 01110100
01100101 01110011 00100000 01101001 01110011 00100000
01100001 00100000 01101101 01100001 01101110

It's easy to follow how a line of text can become a set of binary numbers. To understand how other kinds of information are digitized, let's consider another example of analog information. A vinyl record is an analog representation of sound vibrations. It stores audio information in microscopic squiggles that line the record's long, spiral groove. If the music has a loud passage, the squiggles are cut more deeply into the groove, and if there is a high note the squiggles are packed more tightly together. The groove's squiggles are analogs of the original vibrations—sound waves captured by a microphone. When a turntable's needle travels down the groove, it vibrates in resonation with the tiny squiggles. This vibration, still an analog representation of the original sound, is amplified and sent to loudspeakers as music.

Like any analog device for storing information, a record has drawbacks. Dust, fingerprints, or scratches on the record's surface can cause the needle to vibrate inappropriately and create clicks or other noises. If the record is not turning at exactly the right speed, the pitch of the music won't be accurate. Each time a record is played, the needle wears away some of the subtleties of the squiggles in the groove and the reproduction of the music deteriorates. If you record a song from a vinyl record onto a cassette tape, any of the record's imperfections will be permanently transferred to the tape, and new imperfections will be added because conventional tape machines are themselves analog devices. The information loses quality with each generation of rerecording or retransmission.

On a compact disc, music is stored as a series of binary numbers, each bit (or switch) of which is represented by a microscopic pit on the surface of the disc. Today's CDs have more than 5 billion pits. The reflected laser light inside the CD player—a digital device—reads each of the pits to determine if it is switched to the 0 or the 1 position, and then reassembles that information back into the original music by generating specified electrical signals that are converted by the speakers into sound waves. Each time the disc is played, the sounds are exactly the same.

It's convenient to be able to convert everything into digital representations, but the number of bits can build up quite quickly. Too many bits of information can overflow the computer's memory or take a long time to transmit between computers. This is why a computer's capacity to compress digital data, store or transmit it, then expand it back into its original form is so useful and will become more so.

Quickly, here's how the computer accomplishes these feats. It goes back to Claude Shannon, the mathematician who in the 1930s recognized how to express information in binary form. During World War II, he began developing a mathematical description of information and founded a field that later became known as information theory. Shannon defined information as the reduction of uncertainty. By this definition, if you already know it is Saturday and someone tells you it is Saturday, you haven't been given any information. On the other hand, if you're not sure of the day and someone tells you it is Saturday, you've been given information, because your uncertainty has been reduced.

Shannon's information theory eventually led to other breakthroughs. One was effective data-compression, vital to both computing and communications. On the face of it what he said is obvious: Those parts of data that don't provide unique information are redundant and can be eliminated. Headline writers leave out nonessential words, as do people paying by the word to send a telegraph message or place a classified advertisement. One example Shannon gave was the letter *u*, redundant in English whenever it follows the letter *q*. You know a *u* will follow each *q*, so the *u* needn't actually be included in the message.

Shannon's principles have been applied to the compression of both sound and pictures. There is a great deal of redundant information in the thirty frames that make up a second of video. The information can be compressed from about 27 million to about 1 million bits for transmission and still make sense and be pleasant to watch.

However, there are limits to compression and in the near future we'll be moving ever-increasing numbers of bits from place to place. The bits will travel through copper wires, through the air, and through the structure of the information highway, most of which will be fiber-optic cable (or just "fiber" for short). Fiber is cable made of glass or plastic so smooth and pure that if you looked through a wall of it 70 miles thick, you'd be able to see a candle burning on the other side. Binary signals, in the form of modulated light, carry for long distances through these optic fibers. A signal doesn't move any faster through fiber-optic cable than it does in copper wire; both go at the speed of light. The enormous advantage fiber-optic cable has over wire is the bandwidth it can carry. Bandwidth is a measure of the number of bits that can be moved through a circuit in a second. This really is like a highway. An eight-lane interstate has more room for vehicles than a narrow dirt road. The greater the bandwidth, the more lanes available—thus, that many more cars, or bits of information, can pass in a second. Cables with limited bandwidth, used for text or voice transmissions, are called narrow-band circuit. Cables with more capacity, which carry images and limited animation, are "midband capable." Those with a high bandwidth, which can carry multiple video and audio signals, are said to have broadband capacity.

The information highway will use compression, but there will still have to be a great deal of bandwidth. One of the main reasons we don't already have a working highway is that there isn't sufficient bandwidth in today's communications networks for all the new applications. And there won't be until fiber-optic cable is brought into enough neighborhoods.

Fiber-optic cable is an example of technology that goes beyond what Babbage or even Eckert and Mauchly could have predicted. So is the speed at which the performance and capacity of chips have improved.

In 1965, Gordon Moore, who later cofounded Intel with Bob Noyce, predicted that the capacity of a computer chip would double every year. He said this on the basis of having examined the price/performance ratio of computer chips over the previous three years and projecting it forward. In truth, Moore didn't believe that this rate of improvement would last long. But ten years later, his forecast proved true, and he then predicted the capacity would double every two years. To this day his predictions have held up, and the average—a doubling every eighteen months—is referred to among engineers as Moore's Law.

No experience in our everyday life prepares us for the implications of a number that doubles a great number of times—exponential improvements. One way to understand it is with a fable.

King Shirham of India was so pleased when one of his ministers invented the game of chess that he asked the man to name any reward.

"Your Majesty," said the minister, "I ask that you give me one grain of wheat for the first square of the chessboard, two grains for the second square, four grains for the third, and so on, doubling the number of grains each time until all sixty-four squares are accounted for." The king was moved by the modesty of the request and called for a bag of wheat.

The king asked that the promised grains be counted out onto the chessboard. On the first square of the first row was placed one small grain. On the second square were two specks of wheat. On the third square there were 4, then 8, 16, 32, 64, 128. By square eight at the end of the first row, King Shirham's supply master had counted out a total of 255 grains.

The king probably registered no concern. Maybe a little more wheat was on the board than he had expected, but nothing surprising had hap-

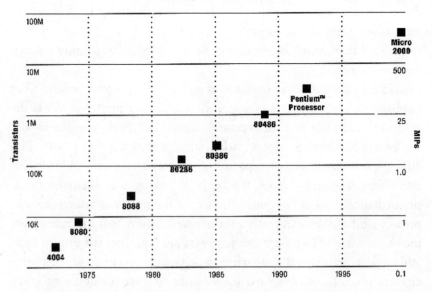

Intel Microprocessor Evolution

Intel microprocessors have doubled in transistor count approximately every eighteen months, in accordance with Moore's Law.

pened. Assuming it would take one second to count each grain, the counting so far had taken only about four minutes. If one row was done in four minutes, try to guess how long it would take to count out the wheat for all sixty-four squares of the board. Four hours? Four days? Four years?

By the time the second row was complete, the supply master had worked for about eighteen hours just counting out 65,535 grains. By the end of the third of the eight rows, it took 194 days to count the 16.8 million grains for the twenty-fourth square. And there were still forty empty squares to go.

It is safe to say that the king broke his promise to the minister. The final square would have gotten 18,446,744,073,709,551,615 grains of wheat on the board, and required 584 billion years of counting. Current estimates of the age of the earth are around 4.5 billion years. According to most versions of the legend, King Shirham realized at some point in the counting that he had been tricked and had his clever minister beheaded.

Exponential growth, even when explained, seems like a trick.

Moore's Law is likely to hold for another twenty years. If it does, a computation that now takes a day will be more than 10,000 times faster, and thus take fewer than ten seconds.

Laboratories are already operating "ballistic" transistors that have switching times on the order of a femtosecond. That is 1/1,000,000,000,000,000 of a second, which is about 10 million times faster than the transistors in today's microprocessors. The trick is to reduce the size of the chip circuitry and the current flow so that moving electrons don't bump into anything, including each other. The next stage is the "single-electron transistor," in which a single bit of information is represented by a lone electron. This will be the ultimate in low-power computing, at least according to our current understanding of physics. In order to make use of the incredible speed advantages at the molecular level, computers will have to be very small, even microscopic. We already understand the science that would allow us to build these superfast computers. What we need is an engineering breakthrough, and these are often quick in coming.

By the time we have the speed, storing all those bits won't be a problem. In the spring of 1983, IBM released its PC/XT, the company's first personal computer with an interior hard disk. The disk served as a built-in storage device and held 10 megabytes, or "megs," of information, about 10 million characters or 80 million bits. Existing customers who wanted to add these 10 megs to their original computers could, for a price. IBM offered a $3,000 kit, complete with separate power supply, to expand the computer's storage. That's $300 per megabyte. Today, thanks to the exponential growth described by Moore's Law, personal-computer hard drives that can hold 1.2 gigabytes—1.2 billion characters of information—are priced at $250. That's 21 cents per megabyte! And we look toward an exotic improvement called a holographic memory, which can hold terabytes of characters in less than a cubic inch of volume. With such capability, a holographic memory the size of your fist could hold the contents of the Library of Congress.

As communications technology goes digital, it becomes subject to the same exponential improvements that have made today's $2,000 laptop computer more powerful than a $10 million IBM mainframe computer of twenty years ago.

At some point not far in the future, a single wire running into each home will be able to deliver all of a household's digital data. The wire will either be fiber, which is what long-distance telephone calls are carried on now, or coaxial cable, which currently brings us cable television signals. If the bits are interpreted as voice calls, the phone will ring. If there are video images, they will show up on the television set. If they are on-line news services, they will arrive as written text and pictures on a computer screen.

That single wire bringing the network will certainly carry much more than phone calls, movies, news. But we can no more imagine what the information highway will carry in twenty-five years than a Stone Age man using a crude knife could have envisioned Ghiberti's Baptistery doors in Florence. Only when the highway arrives will all its possibilities be understood. However, the last twenty years of experience with digital breakthroughs allow us to understand some of the key principles and possibilities for the future.

3

LESSONS FROM THE COMPUTER INDUSTRY

Success is a lousy teacher. It seduces smart people into thinking they can't lose. And it's an unreliable guide to the future. What seems the perfect business plan or latest technology today may soon be as out-of-date as the eight-track tape player, the vacuum-tube television, or the mainframe computer. I've watched it happen. Careful observation of many companies over a long period of time can teach you principles that will help with strategies for the years ahead.

Companies investing in the highway will try to avoid repeating the mistakes made in the computer industry over the past twenty years. I think most of these mistakes can be understood by looking at a few critical factors. Among them are negative and positive spirals, the necessity of initiating rather than following trends, the importance of software as opposed to hardware, and the role of compatibility and the positive feedback it can generate.

You can't count on conventional wisdom. That only makes sense in conventional markets. For the last three decades the market for computer hardware and software has definitely been unconventional. Large established companies that one day had hundreds of millions of dollars in sales and lots of satisfied customers had disappeared in a short time. New companies, such as Apple, Compaq, Lotus, Oracle, Sun, and Microsoft, appeared to go from nothing to a billion dollars of revenue in a flash. These successes were driven, in part, by what I call the "positive spiral."

When you have a hot product, investors pay attention to you and are willing to put their money into your company. Smart kids think, Hey, everybody's talking about this company. I'd like to work there. When one smart person comes to a company, soon another does, because talented people like to work with each other. This creates a sense of excitement. Potential partners and customers pay more attention, and the spiral continues, making the next success easier.

Conversely, there is a negative spiral companies can get caught in. A company in a positive spiral has an air of destiny, while one in a negative spiral feels doomed. If a company starts to lose market share or delivers one bad product, the talk becomes "Why do you work there?" "Why would you invest in that company?" "I don't think you should buy from them." The press and analysts smell blood and begin telling inside stories about who's quarreling and who's responsible for mismanagement. Customers begin to question whether, in the future, they should continue to buy the company's products. Within a sick company everything is questioned, including things that are being done well. Even a fine strategy can get dismissed with the argument "You are just defending the old way," and that can cause more mistakes. Then down the company spirals. Leaders such as Lee Iacocca who have been able to reverse a negative spiral deserve a lot of credit.

Throughout my youth the hot computer firm was Digital Equipment Corporation, known as DEC. For twenty years its positive spiral seemed unstoppable. Ken Olsen, the company's founder, was a legendary hardware designer and a hero of mine, a distant god. In 1960 he had created the minicomputer industry by offering the first "small" computers. The earliest was the PDP-1, the ancestor of my high school's PDP-8. A buyer, instead of paying the millions asked by IBM for its "Big Iron," could get one of Olsen's PDP-1s for $120,000. It wasn't nearly as powerful as the big machines, but it could be used for a wide variety of applications. DEC grew to a $6.7 billion company in eight years by offering a wide range of computers in different sizes.

Two decades later, Olsen's vision faltered. He couldn't see the future of small desktop computers. Eventually he was forced out of DEC, and part of his legend now is that he is the man famous for repeatedly, and publicly, dismissing the personal computer as a passing fad. I am sobered by stories like Olsen's. He was brilliant at seeing new ways of doing things, and then—after years of being an innovator—he missed a big bend in the road.

Another visionary who faltered was An Wang, the Chinese immigrant who built Wang Laboratories into the dominant supplier of electronic calculators in the 1960s. In the 1970s he ignored the advice of everyone around him and left the calculator market just before the arrival of low-cost competition that would have ruined him. It was a brilliant move. Wang reinvented his company to be the leading supplier of word-processing machines. During the 1970s, in offices around the world, Wang word-processing terminals began to replace typewriters. The machines contained a microprocessor but weren't true personal computers, because they were designed to do only one thing—handle text.

Wang was a visionary engineer. The kind of insight that had led him to abandon calculators could have led to success in personal-computer software in the 1980s, but he failed to spot the next industry turn. Even though he developed great software, it was tied proprietarily to his word processors. His software was doomed once general-purpose personal computers appeared that could run a variety of word-processing software applications such as WordStar, WordPerfect, and MultiMate (which imitated Wang software). If Wang had recognized the importance of compatible software applications, there might not be a Microsoft today. I might be a mathematician or an attorney somewhere, and my adolescent foray into personal computing might be little more than a distant personal memory.

IBM was another major company that missed technological changes at the start of the PC revolution. The company's leader had been a hard-driving former cash-register salesman, Thomas J. Watson. Technically, Watson wasn't the founder of IBM, but it was thanks to his aggressive management style that by the early 1930s IBM dominated the market for accounting machines.

IBM began working on computers in the middle 1950s. It was one of many companies in the business vying for leadership in the field. Until 1964 each computer model, even from the same manufacturer, had had a unique design and required its own operating system and application software. An operating system (sometimes called a disk-operating system, or just DOS) is the fundamental software that coordinates a computer system's components, tells them how to work together, and performs other functions. Without an operating system, a computer is useless. The operating system is a platform on which all the software programs for applications—such as accounting or payroll or word-processing or electronic-mail programs—are built.

Computers at different price levels had different designs. Some models were dedicated to scientific study, others to commerce. As I discovered when I wrote the BASIC for various personal computers, significant work was required to move software from one computer model to another. This was true even if the software was written in a standard language such as COBOL or FORTRAN. Under the direction of young Tom, as Watson's son and successor was known, the company gambled $5 billion on the novel notion of scalable architecture—all the computers in the System/360 family, no matter what size, would respond to the same set of instructions. Models built with different technology, from the slowest to the fastest, from small machines that could fit into a normal office to water-cooled giants that sat in climate-controlled glass rooms, could run the same operating system. Customers could move their applications and peripherals, accessories such as disks, tape drives, and printers, freely from one model to the next. Scalable architecture completely reshaped the industry.

System/360 was a runaway success and made IBM the powerhouse in mainframe computers for the next thirty years. Customers made large investments in the 360, confident that their commitment to software and training would not be wasted. If they needed to move to a larger computer, they could get an IBM that ran the same system, and shared the same architecture. In 1977, DEC introduced its own scalable-architecture platform, the VAX. The VAX family of computers ultimately ranged from desktop systems to mainframe-size machine clusters and did for DEC what System/360 did for IBM. DEC became overwhelmingly the leader in the minicomputer market.

The scalable architecture of the IBM System/360 and its successor, the System/370, drove many of IBM's competitors out of business and scared away potential newcomers. In 1970, a new competing company was founded by Eugene Amdahl, who had been a senior engineer at IBM. Amdahl had a novel business plan. His company, also called Amdahl, would build computers fully compatible with the IBM 360 software. Amdahl delivered hardware that not only ran the same operating systems and applications as IBM, but, because it took advantage of new technology, also outperformed IBM's comparably priced systems. Soon Control Data, Hitachi, and Itel all also offered mainframes that were "plug-compatible" to IBM. By the mid-1970s, the importance of 360 compatibility was becoming obvious. The only mainframe companies doing well were those whose hardware could run IBM's operating systems.

Before the 360, computer designs were intentionally incompatible with those from other companies because the manufacturer's goal was to make it discouragingly difficult and expensive for customers heavily invested in one company's computer to switch to a different brand. Once a customer committed to a machine, he or she was stuck with offerings from the computer's manufacturer because changing the software could be done but was too difficult. Amdahl and the others ended that. Market-driven compatibility is an important lesson for the future personal-computer industry. It should also be remembered by those creating the highway. Customers choose systems that give them a choice of hardware suppliers and the widest variety of software applications.

While this was going on, I was busy enjoying school and experimenting with computers. I arrived at Harvard in the fall of 1973. In college there is a lot of posturing, and appearing to slack off was considered a great way to establish your coolness. Therefore, during my freshman year I instituted a deliberate policy of skipping most classes and then studying feverishly at the end of the term. It became a game—a not uncommon one—to see how high a grade I could pull while investing the least time possible. I filled in my leisure hours with a good deal of poker, which had its own attraction for me. In poker, a player collects different shards of information—who's betting boldly, what cards are showing, what's this guy's pattern of betting and bluffing—and then crunches all that information together to devise a plan for his own hand. I got pretty good at this kind of information processing.

The experience of poker strategizing—and the money—were helpful when I got into business, but the other game I was playing, the postponing one, didn't serve me well at all. But I didn't know that then. In fact, I was encouraged that my dilatory practices were shared by a new friend, Steve Ballmer, a math major whom I met freshman year, when we lived in the same student dorm, Currier House. Steve and I led very different lives, but we were both trying to pare down to the minimum the course time needed to get top grades. Steve is a man of endless energy, effortlessly social. His activities took a lot of his time. By his sophomore year he was a manager of the football team, the advertising manager for the *Harvard Crimson*, the school newspaper, and president of a literary magazine. He also belonged to a social club, the Harvard equivalent of a fraternity.

He and I would pay very little attention to our classes and then furiously inhale the key books just before an exam. Once we took a tough graduate-level economics course together—Economics 2010. The professor allowed you to bet your whole grade on the final if you chose. So Steve and I focused on other areas all semester, and did absolutely nothing for the course until the week before the last exam. Then we studied like mad and ended up getting A's.

After Paul Allen and I started Microsoft, however, I found out that that sort of procrastination hadn't been the best preparation for running a company. Among Microsoft's first customers were companies in Japan so methodical that the minute we got behind schedule they would fly someone over to baby-sit us. They knew their man couldn't really help, but he stayed in our office eighteen hours a day just to show us how much they cared. These guys were serious! They would ask, "Why did the schedule change? We need a reason. And we're going to change the thing that caused it to happen." I can still feel how painful being late on some of those projects got to be. We improved and mended our ways. We're still late with projects sometimes but a lot less often than we would have been if we hadn't had those scary baby-sitters.

Microsoft started out in Albuquerque, New Mexico, in 1975 because that's where MITS was located. MITS was the tiny company whose Altair 8800 personal-computer kit had been on the cover of *Popular Electronics*. We worked with it because it had been the first company to sell an inexpensive personal computer to the general public. By 1977, Apple, Commodore, and Radio Shack had also entered the business. We provided BASIC for most of the early personal computers. This was the crucial software ingredient at that time, because users wrote their own applications in BASIC rather than buying packaged applications.

In the early days, selling BASIC was one of my many jobs. For the first three years, most of the other professionals at Microsoft focused solely on technical work, and I did most of the sales, finance, and marketing, as well as writing code. I was barely out of my teens, and selling intimidated me. Microsoft's strategy was to get computer companies such as Radio Shack to buy licenses to include our software with the personal computers they sold (the Radio Shack TRS-80, for example) and pay us a royalty. One reason we took that approach was software piracy.

In the early years of selling Altair BASIC, our sales had been far lower than the widespread usage of our software suggested they should be. I wrote a widely disseminated "Open Letter to Hobbyists," asking the early users of personal computers to stop stealing our software so that we could make money that would let us build more software. "Nothing would please me more than being able to hire ten programmers and deluge the hobby market with good software," I wrote. But my argument didn't convince many hobbyists to pay for our work; they seemed to like it and used it, but preferred to "borrow" it from each other.

Fortunately, today most users understand that software is protected by copyright. Software piracy is still a major issue in trade relations because some countries still don't have—or don't enforce—copyright laws. The United States insists that other governments do more to enforce copyright laws for books, movies, CDs, and software. We will have to be extremely careful to make sure the upcoming highway doesn't become a pirate's paradise.

Although we were very successful selling to U.S. hardware companies, by 1979 almost half of our business was coming from Japan, thanks to an amazing guy named Kazuhiko (Kay) Nishi. Kay telephoned me in 1978 and introduced himself in English. He had read about Microsoft and thought he should be doing business with us. As it happened, Kay and I had a lot in common. We were the same age, and he too was a college student on leave because of his passion for personal computers.

We met some months later at a convention in Anaheim, California, and he flew back with me to Albuquerque, where we signed a page-and-a-half contract that gave him exclusive distribution rights for Microsoft BASIC in East Asia. There were no attorneys involved, just Kay and me, kindred spirits. We did more than $150 million of business under that contract—more than ten times greater than we had expected.

Kay moved fluidly between the business cultures of Japan and those of the United States. He was flamboyant, which worked in our favor in Japan, because it bolstered the impression among Japanese businessmen that we were whiz kids. When I was in Japan we'd stay in the same hotel room and he'd be getting phone calls all night long booking millions of dollars of business. It was amazing. One time there were no calls between three and five in the morning, and so when a call came in at five o'clock, Kay reached for the phone and said, "Business is a little slow tonight." It was quite a ride.

For the next eight years, Kay seized every opportunity. Once, in 1981, on a flight from Seattle to Tokyo, Kay found himself sitting next to Kazuo Inamori, the president of the giant $650 million Kyocera Corporation. Kay, who ran ASCII, his Japanese company, confident of Microsoft's cooperation, successfully pitched Inamori on a new idea—a small laptop computer with simple software built in. Kay and I designed the machine. Microsoft was still small enough that I could play a personal role in the software development. In the United States, it was marketed by Radio Shack in 1983 as the Model 100 for as little as $799. It was also sold in Japan as the NEC PC-8200 and in Europe as the Olivetti M-10. Thanks to Kay's enthusiasm, it was the first popular laptop, a favorite of journalists for years.

Years later, in 1986, Kay decided he wanted to take ASCII in a direction different from the one I wanted for Microsoft, so Microsoft set up its own subsidiary in Japan. Kay's company has continued to be a very important distributor of software in the Japanese market. Kay, who is a close friend, is still as flamboyant and committed to making personal computers universal tools.

The global nature of the PC market will also be a vital element in the development of the information highway. Collaborations between American and European and Asian companies will be even more important for the personal computer than they have been in the past. Countries or companies that fail to make their work global will not be able to lead.

In January 1979, Microsoft moved from Albuquerque to a suburb of Seattle, Washington. Paul and I came home, bringing almost all of our dozen employees with us. We concentrated on writing programming languages for the profusion of new machines that appeared as the personal-computer industry took off. People were coming to us with all kinds of interesting projects that had the potential to turn into something big. Demand for Microsoft's services exceeded what we could supply.

I needed help running the business and turned to my old Economics 2010 pal from Harvard, Steve Ballmer. After graduating, Steve worked as an associate product manager for Procter & Gamble in Cincinnati, where his work included a stint paying calls on small grocery stores in New Jersey. After a few years he decided to go to the Stanford Business School. When he got my call he had finished only one year and wanted to complete his degree, but when I offered him part ownership of Microsoft, he became another student on indefinite leave. Shared ownership through the stock options Microsoft offered most of its employees has been more significant and successful than anyone would have predicted. Literally billions of dollars of value have accrued to them. The practice of granting employee stock options, which has been widely and enthusiastically accepted, is one advantage the United States has that will allow it to support a disproportionate number of start-up successes, building on opportunities the forthcoming era will bring.

Within three weeks of Steve's arrival at Microsoft, we had the first of our very few arguments. Microsoft employed about thirty people by this time, and Steve had concluded we needed to add fifty more immediately.

"No way," I said. Many of our early customers had gone bankrupt, and my natural fear of going bust in a boom time had made me extremely conservative financially. I wanted Microsoft to be lean and hungry. But Steve wouldn't relent, so I did. "Just keep hiring smart people as fast as you can," I said, "and I will tell you when you get ahead of what we can afford." I never had to because our income grew as fast as Steve could find great people.

My chief fear in the early years was that some other company would swoop in and win the market from us. There were several small companies making either microprocessor chips or software that had me particularly worried, but luckily for me none of them saw the software market quite the way we did.

There was also always the threat that one of the major computer manufacturers would take the software for their larger machines and scale it down to run on small microprocessor-based computers. IBM and DEC had libraries of powerful software. Again, fortunately for Microsoft the major players never focused on bringing their computer architecture and software to the personal-computer industry. The only close call came in 1979, when DEC offered PDP-11 minicomputer architecture in a personal-computer kit marketed by HeathKit. DEC didn't completely believe in personal computers, though, and wasn't really pushing the product.

Microsoft's goal was to write and supply software for most personal computers without getting directly involved in making or selling computer hardware. Microsoft licensed the software at extremely low prices. It was our belief that money could be made betting on volume. We adapted our programming languages, such as our version of BASIC, to each machine. We were very responsive to all the hardware manufacturers' requests. We didn't want to give anyone a reason to look elsewhere. We wanted choosing Microsoft software to be a no-brainer.

Our strategy worked. Virtually every personal-computer manufacturer licensed a programming language from us. Even though the hardware of two companies' computers was different, the fact that both ran Microsoft BASIC meant they were somewhat compatible. That compatibility became an important part of what people purchased with their computers. Manufacturers frequently advertised that Microsoft programming languages, including BASIC, were available for their computers.

Along the way, Microsoft BASIC became an industry software standard.

Some technologies do not depend upon widespread acceptance for their value. A wonderful nonstick frying pan is useful even if you're the only person who ever buys one. But for communications and other products that involve collaboration, much of the product's value comes from its widespread deployment. Given a choice between a beautiful, handcrafted mailbox with an opening that would accommodate only one size envelope, and an old carton that everyone routinely dropped all mail and messages for you into, you'd choose the one with broader access. You would choose compatibility.

Sometimes governments or committees set standards intended to promote compatibility. These are called "de jure" standards and have the force of law. Many of the most successful standards, however, are "de facto": ones the market discovers. Most analog timepieces operate clockwise. English-language typewriter and computer keyboards use a layout in which the keys across the top letter row, left to right, spell QWERTY. No law says they must. They work, and most customers will stick with those standards unless something dramatically better comes along.

But because de facto standards are supported by the marketplace rather than by law, they are chosen for the right reasons and replaced when something truly better shows up—the way the compact disc has almost replaced the vinyl record.

De facto standards often evolve in the marketplace through an economic mechanism very similar to the concept of the positive spiral that drives successful businesses, in which success reinforces success. This concept, called positive feedback, explains why de facto standards often emerge as people search for compatibility.

A positive-feedback cycle begins when, in a growing market, one way of doing something gets a slight advantage over its competitors. It is most likely to happen with high-technology products that can be made in great volume for very little increase in cost and derive some of their value from compatibility. A home video-game system is one example. It is a special-purpose computer, equipped with a special-purpose operating system that forms a platform for the game's software. Compatibility is important because the more applications—in this case, games—that are available, the more valuable the machine becomes to a consumer. At the same time, the more machines consumers buy, the more applications software developers create for it. A positive-feedback cycle sets in once a machine reaches a high level of popularity and sales grow further.

Perhaps the most famous industry demonstration of the power of positive feedback was the videocassette-recorder format battle of the late 1970s and early 1980s. The persistent myth has been that positive feedback alone caused the VHS format to win out over Beta, even though Beta was technically better. Actually, early Beta tapes only recorded for an hour—compared to three hours for VHS—not enough for a whole movie or football game. Customers care more about a tape's capacity than some engineer's specs. The VHS format got off to a small lead over the Beta format used by Sony in its Betamax player. JVC, which developed the VHS standard, allowed other VCR manufacturers to use the VHS standard for a very low royalty. As VHS-compatible players proliferated, video-rental stores tended to stock more VHS than Beta tapes. This made the owner of a VHS player more likely than a Beta owner to find the movie she wanted at the video store, which made VHS fundamentally more useful to its owners and caused even more people to buy VHS players. This, in turn, further motivated video stores to stock VHS. Beta lost out as people chose VHS in the belief that it represented a durable standard. VHS was the beneficiary of a positive-feedback cycle. Success bred success. But not at the expense of quality.

While the duel between the Betamax and VHS formats was going on, sales of prerecorded videocassettes to U.S. tape-rental dealers were almost flat, just a few million copies a year. Once VHS emerged as the apparent standard, in about 1983, an acceptance threshold was crossed and the use of the machines, as measured by tape sales, turned abruptly upward. That year, over 9.5 million tapes were sold, a more than 50 percent increase over the year before. In 1984, tapes sales reached 22 million. Then, in successive years: 52 million, 84 million, and 110 million units in 1987, by which time renting movies had became one of the most popular forms of home entertainment, and the VHS machine had become ubiquitous.

This is an example of how a quantitative change in the acceptance level of a new technology can lead to a qualitative change in the role the technology plays. Television is another. In 1946, 10,000 television sets were sold in the United States and only 16,000 in the next year. But then a threshold was crossed, and in 1948 the number was 190,000. In successive years it was 1 million units, followed by 4 million, 10 million, and steadily up to 32 million sold in 1955. As more television sets were sold, more was invested in creating programming, which in turn further enticed people to buy television sets.

For the first few years after they were introduced, audio compact disc (CD) players and discs didn't sell well, in part because it was difficult to find music stores that carried many titles. Then, seemingly overnight, enough players were sold and titles were available, and an acceptance threshold was crossed. More people bought players because more titles were available, and record companies made more titles available on CDs. Music lovers preferred the new, high-quality sound and convenience of compact discs, and they became the de facto standard and drove LPs out of the record stores.

One of the most important lessons the computer industry learned is that a great deal of a computer's value to its user depends on the quality and variety of the application software available for it. All of us in the industry learned that lesson—some happily, some unhappily.

In the summer of 1980, two IBM emissaries came to Microsoft to discuss a personal computer they might or might not build.

At the time, IBM's position was unchallenged in the realm of hardware, with a more than 80 percent market share of large computers. It had had only modest success with small computers. IBM was used to selling big, expensive machines to big customers. IBM's management suspected that IBM, which had 340,000 employees, would require the assistance of outsiders if it was going to sell little, inexpensive machines to individuals as well as companies anytime soon.

IBM wanted to bring its personal computer to market in less than a year. In order to meet this schedule it had to abandon its traditional course of doing all the hardware and software itself. So IBM had elected to build its PC mainly from off-the-shelf components available to anyone. This made a platform that was fundamentally open, which made it easy to copy.

Although it generally built the microprocessors used in its products, IBM decided to buy microprocessors for its PCs from Intel. Most important for Microsoft, IBM decided to license the operating system from us, rather than creating software itself.

Working together with the IBM design team, we promoted a plan for IBM to build one of the first personal computers to use a 16-bit microprocessor chip, the 8088. The move from 8 to 16 bits would take personal computers from hobbyist toys to high-volume business tools. The 16-bit generation of computers could support up to one full megabyte of memory—256 times as much as an 8-bit computer. At first this would be just a theoretical advantage because IBM initially intended to offer only 16K of memory, 1/64 of the total memory possible. The benefit of going 16-bit was further lessened by IBM's decision to save money by using a chip that employed only 8-bit connections to the rest of the computer. Consequently, the chip could think much faster than it could communicate. However, the decision to use a 16-bit processor was very smart because it allowed the IBM PC to evolve and remain the standard for PCs to this day.

IBM, with its reputation and its decision to employ an open design that other companies could copy, had a real chance to create a new, broad standard in personal computing. We wanted to be a part of it. So we took on the operating-system challenge. We bought some early work from another Seattle company and hired its top engineer, Tim Paterson. With lots of modifications the system became the Microsoft Disk Operating System, or MS-DOS. Tim became, in effect, the father of MS-DOS.

IBM, our first licensee, called the system PC-DOS; the PC was for personal computer. The IBM Personal Computer hit the market in August 1981 and was a triumph. The company marketed it well and popularized the term "PC." The project had been conceived by Bill Lowe and shepherded to completion by Don Estridge. It is a tribute to the quality of the IBM people involved that they were able to take their personal computer from idea to market in less than a year.

Few remember this now, but the original IBM PC actually shipped with a choice of three operating systems—our PC-DOS, CP/M-86, and the UCSD Pascal P-system. We knew that only one of the three could succeed and become the standard. We wanted the same kinds of forces that were putting VHS cassettes into every video store to push MS-DOS to become the standard. We saw three ways to get MS-DOS out in front.

*1981: The IBM
personal computer*

First was to make MS-DOS the best product. Second was to help other software companies write MS-DOS–based software. Third was to ensure MS-DOS was inexpensive.

We gave IBM a fabulous deal—a low, one-time fee that granted the company the right to use Microsoft's operating system on as many computers as it could sell. This offered IBM an incentive to push MS-DOS, and to sell it inexpensively. Our strategy worked. IBM sold the UCSD Pascal P-System for about $450, CP/M-86 for about $175, and MS-DOS for about $60.

Our goal was not to make money directly from IBM, but to profit from licensing MS-DOS to computer companies that wanted to offer machines more or less compatible with the IBM PC. IBM could use our software for free, but it did not have an exclusive license or control of future enhancements. This put Microsoft in the business of licensing a software platform to the personal-computer industry. Eventually IBM abandoned the UCSD Pascal P-system and CP/M-86 enhancements.

Consumers bought the IBM PC with confidence, and in 1982, software developers began turning out applications to run on it. Each new customer, and each new application, added to the IBM PC's strength as a potential de facto standard for the industry. Soon most of the new and best software, such as Lotus 1-2-3, was being written for it. Mitch Kapor, with Jonathan Sachs, created 1-2-3 and revolutionized spreadsheets. The original inventors of the electronic spreadsheet, Dan Bricklin and Bob Frankston, deserve immense credit for their product, VisiCalc, but 1-2-3 made it obsolete. Mitch is a fascinating person whose eclectic background—in his case as a disc jockey and transcendental meditation instructor—is typical of that of the best software designers.

A positive-feedback cycle began driving the PC market. Once it got going, thousands of software applications appeared, and untold numbers of companies began making add-in or "accessory" cards, which extended the hardware capabilities of the PC. The availability of software and hardware add-ons sold PCs at a far greater rate than IBM had anticipated—by a factor of millions. The positive-feedback cycle spun out billions of dollars for IBM. For a few years, more than half of all personal computers used in business were IBMs and most of the rest were compatible with its machines.

The IBM standard became the platform everybody imitated. A lot of the reason was timing and its use of a 16-bit processor. Both timing and marketing are key to acceptance with technology products. The PC happened to be a good machine, but another company could have set the standard by getting enough desirable applications and selling enough machines.

IBM's early business decisions, caused by its rush to get the PCs out, made it very easy for other companies to build compatible machines. The architecture was for sale. The microprocessor chips from Intel and Microsoft's operating system were available. This openness was a powerful incentive for component builders, software developers, and everyone else in the business to try to copy.

Within three years almost all the competing standards for personal computers disappeared. The only exceptions were Apple's Apple II and Macintosh. Hewlett Packard, DEC, Texas Instruments, and Xerox, despite their technologies, reputations, and customer bases, failed in the personal-computer market in the early 1980s because their machines weren't compatible and didn't offer significant enough improvements over the IBM architecture. A host of start-ups, such as Eagle and Northstar, thought people would buy their hardware because it offered something different and slightly better than the IBM PC. All of the start-ups either changed to building compatible hardware or failed. The IBM PC became the hardware standard. By the mid-1980s, there were dozens of IBM-compatible PCs. Although buyers of a PC might not have articulated it this way, what they were looking for was the hardware that ran the most software, and they wanted the same system the people they knew and worked with had.

It has become popular for certain revisionist historians to conclude that IBM made a mistake working with Intel and Microsoft to create its PC. They argue that IBM should have kept the PC architecture proprietary, and that Intel and Microsoft somehow got the better of IBM. But the revisionists are missing the point. IBM became the central force in the PC industry precisely because it was able to harness an incredible amount of innovative talent and entrepreneurial energy and use it to promote its open architecture. IBM set the standards.

In the mainframe business IBM was king of the hill, and competitors found it hard to match the IBM sales force and high R&D. If a competitor tried climbing the hill, IBM could focus its assets to make the ascent nearly impossible. But in the volatile world of the personal computer, IBM's position was more like that of the leading runner in a marathon. As long as the leader keeps running as fast or faster than the others, he stays in the lead and competitors will have to keep trying to catch up. If, however, he slacks off or stops pushing himself, the rest will pass him by. There weren't many deterrents to the other racers, as would soon become clear.

By 1983, I thought our next step should be to develop a graphical operating system. I didn't believe we would be able to retain our position at the forefront of the software industry if we stuck with MS-DOS, because MS-DOS was character-based. A user had to type in often-obscure commands, which then appeared on the screen. MS-DOS didn't provide pictures and other graphics to help users with applications. The interface is the way the computer and the user communicate. I believed that in the future interfaces would be graphical and that it was essential for Microsoft to move beyond MS-DOS and set a new standard in which pictures and fonts (typefaces) would be part of an easier-to-use interface. In order to realize our vision, PCs had to be made easier to use—not only to help existing customers, but also to attract new ones who wouldn't take the time to learn to work with a complicated interface.

To illustrate the huge difference between a character-based computer program and a graphical one, imagine playing a board game such as chess, checkers, Go, or Monopoly on a computer screen. With a character-based system, you type in your moves using characters. You write "Move the piece on square 11 to square 19," or something slightly more cryptic like "Pawn to QB3." But in a graphical computer system, you see the board game on your screen. You move pieces by pointing at them and actually dragging them to their new locations.

Researchers at Xerox's now-famous Palo Alto Research Center in California explored new paradigms for human–computer interaction. They showed that it was easier to instruct a computer if you could point at things on the screen and see pictures. They used a device called a "mouse," which could be rolled on a tabletop to move a pointer around on the screen. Xerox did a poor job of taking commercial advantage of

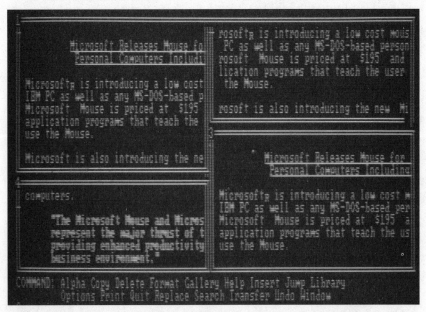

1984: Character user interface in an early version of Microsoft Word for DOS

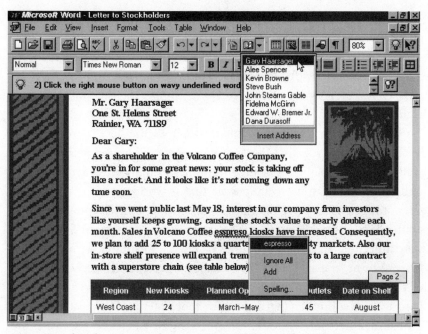

1995: Graphical user interface in Microsoft Word for Windows

this groundbreaking idea, because its machines were expensive and didn't use standard microprocessors. Getting great research to translate into products that sell is still a big problem for many companies.

In 1983, Microsoft announced that we planned to bring graphical computing to the IBM PC, with a product called Windows. Our goal was to create software that would extend MS-DOS and let people use a mouse, employ graphical images on the computer screen, and make available on the screen a number of "windows," each running a different computer program. At that time two of the personal computers on the market had graphical capabilities: the Xerox Star and the Apple Lisa. Both were expensive, limited in capability, and built on proprietary hardware architectures. Other hardware companies couldn't license the operating systems to build compatible systems, and neither computer attracted many software companies to develop applications. Microsoft wanted to create an open standard and bring graphical capabilities to any computer that was running MS-DOS.

The first popular graphical platform came to market in 1984, when

Apple released its Macintosh. Everything about the Macintosh's proprietary operating system was graphical, and it was an enormous success. The initial hardware and operating-system software Apple released were quite limited but vividly demonstrated the potential of the graphical interface. As the hardware and software improved, the potential was realized.

We worked closely with Apple throughout the development of the Macintosh. Steve Jobs led the Macintosh team. Working with him was really fun. Steve has an amazing intuition for engineering and design as well as an ability to motivate people that is world class.

It took a lot of imagination to develop graphical computer programs. What should one look like? How should it behave? Some ideas were inherited from the work done at Xerox and some were original. At first we went to excess with the possibilities. We used nearly every one of the fonts and icons we could. Then we figured out all that made it hard to look at and changed to more sober menus. We created a word processor, Microsoft Word, and a spreadsheet, Microsoft Excel, for the Macintosh. These were Microsoft's first graphical products.

The Macintosh had great system software, but Apple refused (until 1995) to let anyone else make computer hardware that would run it. This was traditional hardware-company thinking: If you wanted the software, you had to buy Apple computers. Microsoft wanted the Macintosh to sell well and be widely accepted, not only because we had invested a lot in creating applications for it, but also because we wanted the public to accept graphical computing.

Mistakes such as Apple's decision to limit the sale of its operating-system software for its own hardware will be repeated often in the years ahead. Some telephone and cable companies are already talking about communicating only with the software they control.

It's increasingly important to be able to compete and cooperate at the same time, but that calls for a lot of maturity.

The separation of hardware and software was a major issue in the collaboration between IBM and Microsoft to create OS/2. The separation of hardware and software standards is still an issue today. Software standards create a level playing field for the hardware companies, but many manufacturers use the tie between their hardware and their soft-

*1984: the Apple
Macintosh computer*

ware to distinguish their systems. Some companies treat hardware and software as separate businesses and some don't. These different approaches will be played out again on the highway.

Throughout the 1980s, IBM was awesome by every measure capitalism knows. In 1984, it set the record for the most money ever made by any firm in a single year—$6.6 billion of profit. In that banner year IBM introduced its second-generation personal computer, a high-performance machine called the PC AT, which incorporated Intel's 80286 microprocessor (colloquially known as the "286"). It was three times faster than the original IBM PC. The AT was a great success, and within a year had more than 70 percent of all business PC sales.

When IBM launched the original PC, it never expected the machine to challenge sales of the company's business systems, although a significant percentage of the PCs were bought by IBM's traditional customers. Company executives thought the smaller machines would find their place only at the low end of the market. As PCs became more powerful, to avoid having them cannibalize its higher-end products, IBM held back on PC development.

In its mainframe business, IBM had always been able to control the adoption of new standards. For example, the company would limit the price/performance of a new line of hardware so it wouldn't steal business from existing, more expensive products. It would encourage the adoption of new versions of its operating systems by releasing hardware that required the new software or vice versa. That kind of strategy might have worked well for mainframes, but it was a disaster in the fast-moving personal-computer market. IBM could still command somewhat higher prices for equivalent performance, but the world had discovered that lots of companies made compatible hardware, and that if IBM couldn't deliver the right value, someone else would.

Three engineers who appreciated the potential offered by IBM's entry into the personal-computer business left their jobs at Texas Instruments and formed a new company—Compaq Computer. They built hardware that would accept the same accessory cards as the IBM PC and licensed MS-DOS so their computers were able to run the same applications as the IBM PC. The company produced machines that did everything the IBM PCs did and were more portable. Compaq quickly became one of the all-time success stories in American business, selling more than $100 million worth of computers its first year in business. IBM was able to collect royalties by licensing its patent portfolio, but its share of market declined as compatible systems came to market and IBM's hardware was not competitive.

The company delayed the release of its PCs with the powerful Intel 386 chip, Intel's successor to the 286. This was done to protect the sales of its low-end minicomputers, which weren't much more powerful than a 386-based PC. IBM's delay allowed Compaq to become the first company to introduce a 386-based computer in 1986. This gave Compaq an aura of prestige and leadership that previously had been IBM's alone.

IBM planned to recover with a one-two punch, the first in hardware and the second in software. It wanted to build computers and write operating systems, each of which would depend exclusively on the other for its new features so competitors would either be frozen out or forced to pay hefty licensing fees. The strategy was to make everyone else's "IBM-compatible" personal computer obsolete.

The IBM strategy included some good ideas. One was to simplify the design of the PC by taking many applications that had formerly been selectable options and building them into the machine. This would both reduce costs and increase the percentage of IBM components in the ultimate sale. The plan also called for substantial changes in the hardware architecture: new connectors and standards for accessory cards, keyboards, mice, and even displays. To give itself a further advantage IBM didn't release specifications on any of these connectors until it had shipped the first systems. This was supposed to redefine compatibility standards. Other PC manufacturers and the makers of peripherals would have to start over—IBM would have the lead again.

By 1984, a significant part of Microsoft's business was providing MS-DOS to manufacturers that built PCs compatible with IBM's systems. We began working with IBM on a replacement for MS-DOS, eventually named OS/2. Our agreement allowed Microsoft to sell other manufacturers the same operating system that IBM was shipping with its machines. We each were allowed to extend the operating system beyond what we developed together. This time it wasn't like when we did MS-DOS. IBM wanted to control the standard to help its PC hardware and mainframe businesses. IBM became directly involved in the design and implementation of OS/2.

OS/2 was central to IBM's corporate software plans. It was to be the first implementation of IBM's Systems Application Architecture, which the company ultimately intended to have as a common development environment across its full line of computers from mainframe to midrange to PC. IBM executives believed that using the company's mainframe technology on the PC would prove irresistible to corporate customers who were moving more and more capabilities from mainframe and minicomputers to PCs. They also thought that it would give IBM a huge advantage over PC competitors who would not have access to mainframe technology. IBM's proprietary extensions of OS/2—called Extended Edition—included communications and database services. And it planned to build a full set of office applications—to be called OfficeVision—to work on top of Extended Edition. The plan predicted these applications, including word processing, would allow IBM to become a major player in PC-application software, and compete with Lotus and WordPerfect. The development of OfficeVision required another team of thousands. OS/2 was not just an operating system, it was part of a corporate crusade.

The development work was burdened by demands that the project meet a variety of conflicting feature requirements as well as by IBM's schedule commitments for Extended Edition and OfficeVision. Microsoft went ahead and developed OS/2 applications to help get the market going, but as time went on, our confidence in OS/2 eroded. We had entered into the project with the belief that IBM would allow OS/2 to be enough like Windows that a software developer would have to make at most only minor modifications to get an application running on both platforms. But after IBM's insistence that the applications be compatible with its mainframe and midrange systems, what we were left with was more like an unwieldy mainframe operating system than a PC one.

Our business relationship with IBM was vital to us. That year, 1986, we had taken Microsoft public to provide liquidity for the employees who had been given stock options. It was about that time Steve Ballmer and I proposed to IBM that they buy up to 30 percent of Microsoft—at a bargain price—so it would share in our fortune, good or bad. We thought this might help the companies work together more amicably and productively. IBM was not interested.

We worked extremely hard to make sure our operating-system work with IBM succeeded. I felt the project would be a ticket to the future for both companies. Instead, it eventually created an enormous rift between us. A new operating system is a big project. We had our team working outside Seattle. IBM had teams in Boca Raton, Florida; Hursley Park, England; and later Austin, Texas.

But the geographical problems were not as bad as those that came from IBM's mainframe legacy. IBM's previous software projects almost never caught on with PC customers precisely because they were designed with a mainframe customer in mind. For instance, it took three minutes for one version of OS/2 to "boot" (to make itself ready for use after it was turned on). That didn't seem bad to them, because in the mainframe world, booting could take fifteen minutes.

IBM, with more than 300,000 employees, was also stymied by its commitment to company-wide consensus. Every part of IBM was invited to submit Design Change Requests, which usually turned out to be demands that the personal-computer-system software be changed to fit the needs of mainframe products better. We got more than 10,000 such requests, and talented people from IBM and Microsoft would sit and discuss them for days.

I remember change request #221: "Remove fonts from product. Reason: Enhancement to product's substance." Someone at IBM didn't want the PC operating system to offer multiple typefaces because a particular IBM mainframe printer couldn't handle them.

Finally it became clear that joint development wasn't going to work. We asked IBM to let us develop the new operating system on our own and license it to them cheaply. We'd make our profit by selling the same thing to other computer companies. But IBM had declared that its own programmers had to be involved in the creation of any software it considered strategic. And operating-system software clearly was that.

IBM was such a great company. Why should it have so much trouble with PC software development? One answer was that IBM tended to promote all their good programmers into management and leave the less talented behind. Even more significant, IBM was haunted by its successful past. Its traditional engineering process was unsuitable for the rapid pace and market requirements of PC software.

In April 1987, IBM unveiled its integrated hardware/software, which was supposed to beat back imitators. The "clone-killer" hardware was called PS/2 and it ran the new operating system, OS/2.

The PS/2 included a number of innovations. The most celebrated was the new "microchannel bus" circuitry, which allowed accessory cards to connect to the system and permitted the PC hardware to be extended to meet such particular customer requirements as sound or mainframe communications capabilities. Every compatible computer included a hardware-connection "bus" to allow these cards to work with the PC. The PS/2's Microchannel was an elegant replacement for the connection bus in the PC AT. But it solved problems that most customers didn't have. It was potentially much faster than the PC AT's bus. But in actual practice the speed of the bus hadn't been holding anyone up, and therefore customers couldn't get much benefit from this newly available speed. More important, the Microchannel didn't work with any of the thousands of add-in cards that worked with the PC AT and compatible PCs.

Ultimately, IBM agreed to license the Microchannel, for a royalty, to manufacturers of add-in cards and PCs. But by then a coalition of manufacturers had already announced a new bus with many of the capabilities of the Microchannel but compatible with the PC AT bus. Customers rejected Microchannel in favor of machines with the old PC AT bus. The complement of accessory cards for the PS/2 never came close to the number available for PC AT–compatible systems. This forced IBM to continue to release machines that supported the old bus. The real casualty was that IBM lost control of personal-computer architecture. Never again would they be able to move the industry singlehanded to a new design.

Despite a great deal of promotion from both IBM and Microsoft, customers thought OS/2 was too unwieldy and complicated. The worse OS/2 looked, the better Windows seemed. Because we'd lost the chances both for compatibility between Windows and OS/2, and for OS/2 to run on modest machines, it still made sense to us to continue to develop Windows. Windows was far "smaller"—meaning it used less hard-disk space and could work in a machine with less memory, so there would be a place for it on machines that could never run OS/2. We called this the "family" strategy. In other words, OS/2 would be the high-end system and Windows would be the junior member of the family, for smaller machines.

IBM was never happy about our family strategy, but it had its own plans. In the spring of 1988, it joined other computer makers in establishing the Open Software Foundation to promote UNIX, an operating system that had originally been developed at AT&T's Bell Labs in 1969 but over the years had splintered into a number of versions. Some of the versions were developed at universities, which used UNIX as a working laboratory for operating-systems theory. Other versions were developed by computer companies. Each company enhanced UNIX for its own computers, which made their operating system incompatible with everyone else's. This meant that UNIX had become not a single open system, but a collection of operating systems competing with one another.

All the differences made software compatibility harder and held back the rise of a strong third-party software market for UNIX. Only a few software companies could afford to develop and test applications for a dozen different versions of UNIX. Also, computer-software stores couldn't afford to stock all the different versions.

The Open Software Foundation was the most promising of several attempts to "unify" UNIX and create a common software architecture that would work on various different manufacturers' hardware. In theory, a unified UNIX could get a positive-feedback cycle going. But despite significant funding, it turned out to be impossible for the Open Software Foundation to mandate cooperation from a committee of vendors who were competing for each sale. Its members, including IBM, DEC, and others, continued to promote the benefits of their particular versions of UNIX. The UNIX companies suggested their systems would benefit customers by offering them more choices. But if you bought a UNIX system from one vendor, your software couldn't automatically run on any other system. This meant you were tied to that vendor, whereas in the PC world you have a choice of where to buy your hardware.

The problems of the Open Software Foundation and similar initiatives point up the difficulty of trying to impose a standard in a field in which innovation is moving rapidly and all the companies that make up the standards committee are competitors. The marketplace (in computers or consumer electronics) adopts standards because customers insist on standards. Standards are to ensure interoperability, minimize user training, and of course foster the largest possible software industry. Any company that wants to create a standard has to price it very reasonably or it won't be adopted. The market effectively chooses a reasonably priced standard and replaces it when it is obsolete or too expensive.

Microsoft operating systems are offered today by more than nine hundred different manufacturers, which gives customers choices and options. Microsoft has been able to provide compatibility because hardware manufacturers have agreed not to allow modifications to our software that introduce incompatibility. This means that hundreds of thousands of software developers don't need to worry about what PCs their software will run on. Although the term "open" is used in many different ways, to me it means offering choice in hardware and software applications to the customer.

Consumer electronics has also benefited from standards managed by private companies. Years ago consumer electronics companies often tried to restrict competitors from using their technology, but now all of the major consumer electronics makers are quite open to licensing their patents and trade secrets. The royalties for their products are typically under 5 percent of the cost of the device. Audiocassettes, VHS tapes, compact discs, televisions, and cellular telephones are all examples of technologies that were created by private companies that receive royalties from everyone who makes the equipment. Dolby Laboratories' algorithms, for example, are the de facto standard for noise reduction.

In May 1990, the last weeks before the release of Windows 3.0, we tried to reach an agreement with IBM for it to license Windows to use on its personal computers. We told IBM we thought that although OS/2 would work out over time, for the moment Windows was going to be a success and OS/2 would find its niche slowly.

In 1992, IBM and Microsoft stopped their joint development of OS/2. IBM continued to develop the operating system alone. The ambitious plan for OfficeVision was eventually canceled.

Analysts estimate that IBM poured more than $2 billion into OS/2, OfficeVision, and related projects. If IBM and Microsoft had found a way to work together, thousands of people-years—the best years of some of the best employees at both companies—would not have been wasted. If OS/2 and Windows had been compatible, graphical computing would have become mainstream years sooner.

The acceptance of graphical interfaces was also held back because most major software-applications companies did not invest in them. They largely ignored the Macintosh and ignored or ridiculed Windows. Lotus and WordPerfect, the market leaders for spreadsheet and word-processing applications, made only modest efforts on OS/2. In retrospect, this was a mistake, and, in the end, a costly one. When Windows finally benefited from a positive-feedback cycle, generated by applications from many of the small software companies, the big companies fell behind because they didn't move to Windows fast enough.

Windows, like the PC, continues to evolve. Microsoft has continued to add new capabilities to various versions. Anyone can develop application software that runs on the Windows platform, without having to notify or get permission from Microsoft. In fact, today there are tens of thousands of commercially available software packages for the platform, including offerings that compete with most Microsoft applications.

Customers express to me their worry that Microsoft, because it is, by definition, the only source for Microsoft operating-system software, could raise prices and slow down or even stop its innovation. Even if we did we wouldn't be able to sell our new versions. Existing users would not upgrade and we wouldn't get any new users. Our revenue would fall and many more companies would compete to take our place. The positive-feedback mechanism helps challengers as well as the incumbent. You can't rest on your laurels, because there is always a competitor coming up behind you.

No product stays on top unless it is improved. Even the VHS standard will be replaced when better formats appear at reasonable prices. In fact, the era of VHS is almost over. Within the next several years we will see new digital tape formats, digital movie discs that put feature films on discs like a music CD, and eventually the information highway will enable new services such as video-on-demand, and VHS will be unnecessary.

MS-DOS is being replaced now. Despite its incredible strength as the leading operating system for personal computers, it is being replaced by a system with a graphical user interface. The Macintosh software might have become the successor to MS-DOS. So might OS/2 or UNIX. It appears that Windows has the lead for the moment. However, in high tech this is no guarantee we'll have it even in the near future.

We have had to improve our software to keep up with hardware advances. Each subsequent version will only be successful with new users if current users adopt it. Microsoft has to do its best to make new versions so attractive in terms of price and features that people will want to change. This is hard because a change involves a big overhead for both developers and customers. Only a major advance is able to convince enough users it is worth their while to change. With enough innovation it can be done. I expect major new generations of Windows to come along every two to three years.

The seeds of new competition are being sown constantly in research environments and garages around the world. For instance, the Internet is becoming so important that Windows will only thrive if it is clearly the best way to gain access to the Internet. All operating-system companies are rushing to find ways to have a competitive edge in providing Internet support. When speech recognition becomes genuinely reliable, this will cause another big change in operating systems.

In our business things move too fast to spend much time looking back. I pay close attention to our mistakes, however, and try to focus on future opportunity. It's important to acknowledge mistakes and make sure you draw some lesson from them. It's also important to make sure no one avoids trying something because he thinks he'll be penalized for what happened or that management is not working to fix the problems. Almost no single mistake is fatal.

Lately, under Lou Gerstner's leadership, IBM has become far more efficient and regained both its profitability and its positive focus on the future. Although the continuing decline in mainframe revenues remains a problem for IBM, it will clearly be one of the major companies providing products for businesses and the information highway.

In recent years, Microsoft has deliberately hired a few managers with experience in failing companies. When you're failing you're forced to be creative, to dig deep and think, night and day. I want some people around who have been through that. Microsoft is bound to have failures in the future, and I want people here who have proved they can do well in tough situations.

Death can come swiftly to a market leader. By the time you have lost the positive-feedback cycle it's often too late to change what you've been doing, and all the elements of a negative spiral come into play. It is difficult to recognize that you're in a crisis and react to it when your business appears extremely healthy. That is going to be one of the paradoxes for companies building the information highway. It keeps me alert. I never anticipated Microsoft's growing so large, and now, at the beginning of this new era, I unexpectedly find myself a part of the establishment. My goal is to prove that a successful corporation can renew itself and stay in the forefront.

4

APPLICATIONS AND APPLIANCES

When I was a kid, *The Ed Sullivan Show* aired at eight o'clock on Sunday nights. Most Americans with television sets tried to be home to watch it because it might be the only time and place to see the Beatles, Elvis Presley, the Temptations, or that guy who could spin ten plates simultaneously on the noses of ten dogs. But if you were driving back from your grandparents' house or were on a Cub Scout camping trip, too bad. Not being home on Sundays at eight meant you also missed out on the Monday-morning conversations about the previous night's broadcast.

Conventional television allows us to decide what we watch, but not when we watch it. The technical term for this sort of broadcasting is "synchronous." Viewers must synchronize their schedules with the time of a broadcast sent to everyone. That's how I watched *The Ed Sullivan Show* three decades ago, and it's still how most of us will watch the news tonight.

In the early 1980s the videocassette recorder gave us more flexibility. If you cared enough about a program to fuss with timers and tapes in advance, you could watch it whenever you liked. You could claim from the broadcasters the freedom and luxury to serve as your own program scheduler—and millions of people do. A telephone conversation is also synchronous, because both parties must be on the line at the same time. When you tape a television show or let an answering machine record an incoming call, you are converting synchronous communications into a more convenient form: "asynchronous" communications.

It is human nature to find ways to convert synchronous communications into asynchronous forms. Before the invention of writing, 5,000 years ago, the only form of communication was the spoken word and audiences had to be in the presence of the speaker or they missed his message. Once the message could be written, it could be stored and read later by anyone, at his or her convenience. I am writing these words at home early in 1995, but I have no idea when or where you'll read them.

One of the benefits bestowed by the information highway will be more control over our schedules. There will be many others. Once you make a form of communication asynchronous, you can also increase the variety and selection possibilities. Even viewers who rarely record television programs routinely rent movies. There are thousands of choices available at local video-rental stores for just a few dollars each, so the home viewer can spend any evening with Elvis, the Beatles—or Greta Garbo.

Television has been around for fewer than sixty years, but in that time it has become a major influence in the life of almost everyone in developed nations. But television, in some ways, was just a replacement for commercial radio, which had been bringing electronic entertainment into homes for twenty years. No broadcast medium is comparable to what the highway will be like.

The highway will enable capabilities that seem magical when they are described, but represent technology at work to make our lives easier and better. Because consumers already understand the value of movies and are used to paying to watch them, video-on-demand will be an important application on the information highway. It won't be the first, however. We already know that PCs will be connected long before television sets and that the quality of movies shown on early systems will not be very high. The systems will be able to offer other applications such as games, electronic mail, and home banking. When high-quality video can be transmitted, there won't be any intermediary VCR; you'll simply request what you want from a long list of available programs. Limited video-on-demand systems are already installed in some higher-priced hotel rooms, replacing or complementing premium movie channels. Hotel rooms, airports, and even airplanes are great laboratories for all the new highway services that will come later into homes. They offer a controlled environment and an upscale audience for experimentation.

Television shows will continue to be broadcast as they are today for synchronous consumption. After they air, these shows—as well as thousands of movies and virtually all other kinds of video—will be available whenever you want to view them. You'll be able to watch the new episode of *Seinfeld* at 9:00 P.M. on Thursday night, or at 9:13 P.M., or at 9:45 P.M., or at 11:00 A.M. on Saturday. If you don't care for his brand of humor, there will be thousands of other choices. Your request for a specific movie or television program episode will register and the bits will be routed to you across the network. The information highway will make it feel as though all the intermediary machinery between you and the object of your interest has been removed. You indicate what you want, and presto! you get it.

Movies, television programs, and all sorts of other digital information will be stored on "servers," which are computers with capacious disks. Servers will provide information for use anywhere on the network. If you ask to see a particular movie, check a fact, or retrieve your electronic mail, your request will be routed by switches to the server or servers storing that information. You won't know whether the material that arrives at your house is stored on a server down the road or on the other side of the country, nor will it matter.

The requested digital data will be retrieved from the server and routed by switches back to your television, personal computer, or telephone—your information appliances. These digital devices will succeed for the same reason their analog precursors did—they will make some aspect of life easier. Unlike the dedicated word processors that brought the first microprocessors to many offices, these information appliances will be general-purpose, programmable computers connected to the information highway.

------------------------------➤

Even if a show is being broadcast live, you'll be able to use your infrared remote control to start, stop, or go to any previous part of the program, at any time. If someone comes to your door, you'll be able to pause the program for as long as you like. You'll be in absolute control. Except, of course, you won't be able to forward past part of a live show as it's taking place.

Delivering movies and television programs is technically one of the simpler things to do. Most viewers can understand video-on-demand and will welcome the freedom it provides. It has the potential to be what in computer parlance is called the "killer application" for the highway. A killer application (or just "killer app") is a use of technology so attractive to consumers that it fuels market forces and makes an invention all but indispensable, even if it wasn't anticipated by the inventor. Skin-So-Soft was just another lotion competing in a crowded market until someone discovered its insect-repelling qualities. Now it may still be sold for its original application—to soften skin—but its sales have increased because of its killer app.

The phrase is new, but the idea isn't. Thomas Edison was as great a business leader as he was an inventor. When he founded the Edison General Electric Company in 1878, he understood that to sell electricity he had to demonstrate its value to consumers—to sell the idea that light could fill a house day or night with just the flick of a switch. Edison lit up the public's imagination with the promise that electric lighting would become so cheap that only the rich would buy candles. He correctly foresaw that people would pay to bring electric power into their homes so that they could enjoy a great application of electric technology—light.

Electricity found a place in most homes as a means of providing lighting, but a number of additional applications were added quite quickly. The Hoover Company greatly improved the early electric sweeping machine. Electric cooking was popularized. Soon there were electric heaters, toasters, refrigerators, washing machines, irons, power tools, hair dryers, and a host of other laborsaving appliances, and electricity became a basic utility.

Killer applications help technological advances change from curiosities into moneymaking essentials. Without killer apps an invention won't catch on—witness such notable consumer-electronics flops as 3-D movies and quadraphonic sound.

In chapter 3, I mentioned that word processing brought microprocessors into corporate offices in the 1970s. At first it was provided by dedicated machines such as Wang's, which were used solely for creating documents. The market for dedicated word processors grew incredibly fast, until it included more than fifty manufacturers, with combined sales of more than $1 billion annually.

Within a couple of years, personal computers appeared. Their ability to run different types of applications was something new. That was their killer app. A PC user could quit WordStar (for years one of the most popular word-processing applications) and start up another application, such as the spreadsheet program VisiCalc or dBASE for database management. Collectively, WordStar, VisiCalc, and dBASE were attractive enough to motivate the purchase of a personal computer. They were the killer applications.

The first killer application for the original IBM PC was Lotus 1-2-3, a spreadsheet tailored to the strengths of that machine. The Apple Macintosh's killer business applications were Aldus PageMaker for designing documents to be printed, Microsoft Word for word processing, and Microsoft Excel for spreadsheets. Early on, more than a third of the Macintoshes used in business and many in the home were purchased for what became known as desktop publishing.

The highway will come about because of a confluence of technological advances in both communications and computers. No single advance would be able to produce the necessary killer applications. But together these will. The highway will be indispensable because it will offer a combination of information, education services, entertainment, shopping, and person-to-person communication. We can't be sure yet exactly when all the necessary components will be ready. Easy-to-use information appliances will be critical components. In the years immediately ahead there will be a proliferation of digital devices that will take on different forms and communicate at different speeds. I'll discuss them at length later. For the moment it's enough to know that a variety of PC-like appliances will allow each of us to stay in touch over the highway with other people as well as with information. These will include digital replacements for many of the analog devices, including televisions and telephones, that surround us today. We can already be sure that the ones that are retained will be those that become indispensable. Although we don't know which forms will be popular, we know they will be general-purpose, programmable computers connected to the information highway.

Many homes are already attached to two dedicated communications infrastructures: telephone lines and television cables. When these specialized communication systems have been generalized into a single digital-information utility, the information highway will have arrived.

Your television set will not look like a computer and won't have a keyboard, but the additional electronics inside or attached will make it architecturally a computer like a PC. Television sets will connect to the highway via a set-top box similar to ones supplied today by most cable TV companies. But these new set-top boxes will include a very powerful general-purpose computer. The box may be located inside a television, behind a television, on top of a television, on a basement wall, or even outside the house. Both the PC and the set-top box will connect to the information highway and conduct a "dialogue" with the switches and servers of the network, retrieving information and programming and relaying the subscriber's choices.

1995: A personal-computer-based interactive media server

However much like a PC the set-top box becomes, there will continue to be a critical difference between the way a PC is used and a television is used: viewing distance. Today, more than a third of U.S. households have personal computers (not counting game machines). Eventually, almost every home will have at least one, connected directly to the information highway. This is the appliance you'll use when details count or when you want to type. It places a high-quality monitor a foot or two from your face, so your eyes focus easily on text and other small images. A big-screen TV across the room doesn't lend itself to the use of a keyboard, nor does it afford privacy, although it is ideal for applications that multiple people watch at the same time.

Set-top boxes and PC-interface equipment will be designed so that even the oldest TV sets and most current personal computers can be used with the highway, but there will be new televisions and PCs with better pictures. The images on today's television sets are quite poor compared to pictures in magazines or on movie theater screens. While U.S. television signals can have 486 lines of picture information, they are not all distinguishable on most sets, and the typical home VCR can record or play back only about 280 lines of resolution. As a result,

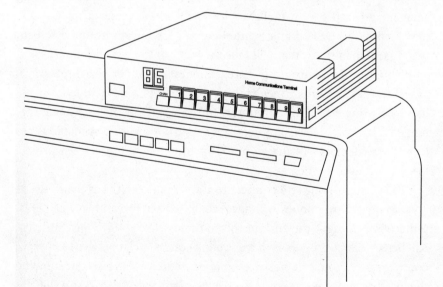

Prototype of a television set-top box

it is difficult to read the credits at the end of a movie on a television set. Conventional television screens are also a different shape from most movie theater screens. Our TVs have an "aspect ratio" (the relationship of picture width to height) of 4 by 3, meaning a picture is a third wider than it is tall. Feature films typically are made with an aspect ratio of about 2 to 1—twice as wide as they are tall.

High-definition television (HDTV) systems that offer more than 1,000 lines of resolution, with a 16-by-9 aspect ratio and better color, have been demonstrated, and they are beautiful to watch. But despite the efforts of the government and industry in Japan, where they were created, HDTV did not catch on, because it required expensive new equipment for both broadcasting and receiving. Advertisers wouldn't pay extra to fund HDTV, because it doesn't make ads measurably more effective. However, HDTV might still catch on, because the highway will allow video to be received at multiple resolutions and aspect ratios. This idea of adjustable resolution is familiar to users of personal computers who can choose the typical resolution of 480 (called VGA) or higher resolutions of 600, 768, 1,024, or 1,200 horizontal lines of resolution, depending on what their monitor and display card can support.

Both TV screens and PC screens will continue to improve—to get smaller and improve in quality. Most will be flat-panel displays. One new form will be the digital white board: a large wall-mounted screen, perhaps an inch thick, that will take the place of today's blackboards and white boards. It will display pictures, movies, and other visual materials, as well as text and other fine details. People will be able to draw or make lists by writing on it. The computer controlling the white board will recognize a handwritten list and convert it into one with a readable typeface. These devices will show up first in conference rooms, then private offices and even homes.

Today's telephone will connect to the same networks as the PCs and TVs. Many future phones will have small, flat screens and tiny cameras. Otherwise, though, they'll look more or less like today's instruments. Kitchens will continue to have wall phones, because they conserve counter space. You'll sit close to the phone and look at a screen showing the person you are speaking to—or at a stock picture he or she has elected to transmit in lieu of live video. Technologically, the phone hanging over a dishwasher tomorrow will have a lot in common with the set-top box in the living room and the personal computer in the den, but it will assume the form of a phone. Under the hood, all information appliances will have pretty much the same computer architecture. Their exterior forms will be different to match their varying functions.

In a mobile society, people need to be able to work efficiently while on the road. Two centuries ago, travelers often carried a "lap desk," a hinged writing board attached to a thin mahogany box with a drawer for pens and ink. When folded, it was reasonably compact, and when opened, it offered an ample writing surface. In fact, the Declaration of Independence was written on a lap desk in Philadelphia, a long way from Thomas Jefferson's Virginia home. The need for a portable writing station is met today by the laptop, a folding, lap-size personal computer. Many people—including me—who work from both office and home, choose a laptop (or a slightly smaller computer, known as a notebook) as their primary computer. These small computers can then be connected to a large monitor and to the corporate network in the office. Notebook computers will continue to get thinner until they are nearly the size of a tablet of paper. Notebooks are the smallest and most portable real computers today, but soon there will be pocket-size computers with snapshot-size color screens. When you whip one out, no one will say, "Wow! You've got a computer!"

1995: Multimedia notebook computer by Digital Equipment Corporation

What do you carry on your person now? Probably at least keys, identification, money, and a watch. Quite possibly you also carry credit cards, a checkbook, traveler's checks, an address book, an appointment book, a notepad, reading material, a camera, a pocket tape recorder, a cellular phone, a pager, concert tickets, a map, a compass, a calculator, an electronic entry card, photographs, and perhaps a loud whistle to summon help.

You'll be able to keep all these and more in another information appliance we call the wallet PC. It will be about the same size as a wallet, which means you'll be able to carry it in your pocket or purse. It will display messages and schedules and also let you read or send electronic mail and faxes, monitor weather and stock reports, and play both simple and sophisticated games. At a meeting you might take notes, check your appointments, browse information if you're bored, or choose from among thousands of easy-to-call-up photos of your kids.

Rather than holding paper currency, the new wallet will store unforgeable digital money. Today when you hand someone a dollar bill, check, gift certificate, or other negotiable instrument, the transfer of paper represents a transfer of funds. But money does not have to be expressed on paper. Credit card charges and wired funds are exchanges of

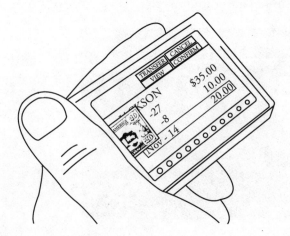

Prototype of a wallet PC

digital financial information. Tomorrow the wallet PC will make it easy for anyone to spend and accept digital funds. Your wallet will link into a store's computer to allow money to be transferred without any physical exchange at a cash register. Digital cash will be used in interpersonal transactions, too. If your son needs money, you might digitally slip five bucks from your wallet PC to his.

When wallet PCs are ubiquitous, we can eliminate the bottlenecks that now plague airport terminals, theaters, and other locations where people queue to show identification or a ticket. As you pass through an airport gate, for example, your wallet PC will connect to the airport's computers and verify that you have paid for a ticket. You won't need a key or magnetic card key to get through doors either. Your wallet PC will identify you to the computer controlling the lock.

As cash and credit cards begin to disappear, criminals may target the wallet PC, so there will have to be safeguards to prevent a wallet PC from being used in the same manner as a stolen charge card. The wallet PC will store the "keys" you'll use to identify yourself. You will be able to invalidate your keys easily, and they will be changed regularly. For some important transactions, just having the key in your wallet PC won't be enough. One solution is to have you enter a password at the time of the transaction. Automatic teller machines ask you to provide a personal identification number, which is just a very short password. Another option, which would eliminate the need for you to remember a password, is the use of biometric measurements. Individual biometric measurements are more secure and almost certainly will be included eventually in some wallet PCs.

A biometric security system records a physical trait, such as a voiceprint or a fingerprint. For example, your wallet PC might demand that you read aloud a random word that it flashes on its screen or that you press your thumb against the side of the device whenever you are about to conduct a transaction with significant financial implications. The wallet will compare what it "heard" or "felt" with its digital record of your voice- or thumbprint.

Wallet PCs with the proper equipment will be able to tell you exactly where you are anyplace on the face of Earth. The Global Positioning System (GPS) satellites in an orbit around Earth broadcast signals that

------------------------->

permit jetliners, oceangoing boats, and cruise missiles, or hikers with handheld GPS receivers, to know their exact location to within a few hundred feet. Such devices are currently available for a few hundred dollars, and they will be built into many wallet PCs.

The wallet PC will connect you to the information highway while you travel a real highway, and tell you where you are. Its built-in speaker will be able to dictate directions to let you know that a freeway exit is coming up or that the next intersection has frequent accidents. It will monitor digital traffic reports and warn you that you'd better leave for an airport early, or suggest an alternate route. The wallet PC's color maps will overlay your location with whatever kinds of information you desire—road and weather conditions, campgrounds, scenic spots, even fast-food outlets. You might ask, "Where's the nearest Chinese restaurant that is still open?" and the information requested will be transmitted to the wallet by wireless network. Off the roads, on a hike in the woods, it will be your compass and as useful as your Swiss Army knife.

In fact, I think of the wallet PC as the new Swiss Army knife. I had one of those knives when I was a kid. Mine was neither the most basic with just two blades nor the one with a workshop's worth of equipment. It had the classic shiny red handle with the white cross and lots of blades and attachments, including a screwdriver, a tiny pair of scissors, and even a corkscrew (although at the time I had no use for that particular accessory). Some wallet PCs will be simple and elegant and offer only the essentials, such as a small screen, a microphone, a secure way to transact business with digital money, and the capability to read or otherwise use basic information. Others will bristle with all kinds of gadgets, including cameras, scanners that will be able to read printed text or handwriting, and receivers with the global-positioning capability. Most will have a panic button for you to press if you need emergency help. Some models will include thermometers, barometers, altimeters, and heart-rate sensors.

Prices will vary accordingly, but generally wallet PCs will be priced about the way cameras are today. Simple, single-purpose "smart cards" for digital currency will cost about what a disposable camera does now, whereas, like an elaborate camera, a really sophisticated wallet PC might cost $1,000 or more, but it will outperform the most exotic computer of just a decade ago. Smart cards, the most basic form of the wallet PC, look like credit cards and are popular now in Europe. Their microprocessors are embedded within the plastic. The smart card of the future will identify its owner and store digital money, tickets, and medical information. It won't have a screen, audio capabilities, or any of the more elaborate options of the more expensive wallet PCs. It will be handy for travel or as a backup, and may be sufficient by itself for some people's uses.

If you aren't carrying a wallet PC, you'll still have access to the highway by using kiosks—some free, some requiring payment of a fee—which will be found in office buildings, shopping malls, and airports in much the same spirit as drinking fountains, rest rooms, and pay phones. In fact, they will replace not only pay phones but also banking machines, because they will offer their capabilities as well as all the other highway applications, from sending and receiving messages to scanning maps and buying tickets. Access to kiosks will be essential, and available everywhere. Some kiosks will display advertising links to specific services when you first log on—a bit like the phones in airports that connect right to hotel and rental-car reservations. Like the cash machines we find in airports today, they will look like rugged devices, but inside they will also be PCs.

No matter what form the PC takes, users will still have to be able to navigate their way through its applications. Think of the way you use your television remote control today to choose what you want to watch. Future systems with more choices will have to do better. They'll have to avoid making you go step-by-step through all the options. Instead of having to remember which channel number to use to find a program, you will be shown a graphical menu and be able to select what you want by pointing to an easy-to-understand image.

You won't necessarily have to point to make your point. Eventually we'll also be able to speak to our televisions, personal computers, or other information appliances. At first we'll have to keep to a limited vocabulary, but eventually our exchanges will become quite conversational. This capability requires powerful hardware and software, because conversation that a human can understand effortlessly is very hard for a computer to interpret. Already, voice recognition works fine for a small set of predefined commands, such as "Call my sister." It's much more difficult for a computer to decipher an arbitrary sentence, but in the next ten years this too will become possible.

Some users will find it convenient to handwrite instructions to a computer, rather than speaking or typing them. Many companies, including Microsoft, have spent some years working on what we call "pen-based computers" capable of reading handwriting. I was overly optimistic about how quickly we would be able to create software that would recognize the handwriting of a broad range of people. The difficulties turned out to be quite subtle. When we tested the system ourselves it worked well, but new users continued to have trouble with it. We discovered we were unconsciously making our handwriting neater and more recognizable than usual. We were adapting to the machine rather than the other way around. Another time, when the team thought they had created a program that worked, they came proudly to demonstrate their achievement to me. It didn't work at the demonstration. Everyone on the project happened to be right-handed, and the computer, which was programmed to look at the strokes in the writing, couldn't interpret the very different ones in my left-handed penmanship. It turned out that getting a computer to recognize handwriting is as difficult as getting one to recognize speech. But I remain optimistic that as computer performance increases we'll have computers able to do this too.

Whether you give the command by voice, in writing, or by pointing, the selections you're going to want to make will involve more complicated choices than just which movie to watch, and you'll want to be able to make them easily. Users won't stand for being confused or frustrated or for having their time wasted. The highway's software platform will have to make it almost infallibly easy to find information, even if users don't know what they're looking for. There will be lots of information. The highway will have access to everything in hundreds of libraries and to all types of merchandise.

One of the worries most often expressed about the highway concerns "information overload." It is usually voiced by someone who imagines, rather aptly, that the fiber-optic cables of the information highway will be like enormous pipes spewing out large quantities of information.

Information overload is not unique to the highway, and it needn't be a problem. We already cope with astonishing amounts of information by relying on an extensive infrastructure that has evolved to help us be selective—everything from library catalogs to movie reviews to the Yellow Pages to recommendations from friends. When people worry about the information-overload problem, ask them to consider how they choose what to read. When we visit a bookstore or a library we don't worry about reading every volume. We get by without reading everything because there are navigational aids that point to information of interest and help us find the print material we want. These pointers include the corner newsstand, the Dewey decimal system in libraries, and book reviews in the local newspaper.

On the information highway, technology and editorial services will combine to offer a number of ways to help us find information. The ideal navigation system will be powerful, expose seemingly limitless information, and yet remain very easy to use. Software will offer queries, filters, spatial navigation, hyperlinks, and agents as the primary selection techniques.

One way to understand the different selection methods is to think of them metaphorically. Imagine specific information—a collection of facts, a breaking news story, a list of movies—all placed in an imaginary warehouse. A query does a search through every item in the warehouse to see if it meets some criterion you have established. A filter is a check on everything new that comes into the warehouse to see if it matches that criterion. Spatial navigation is a way you can walk around inside the warehouse checking on inventory by location. Perhaps the most intriguing approach, and the one that promises to be the easiest of all to use, will be to enlist the aid of a personal agent who will represent you on the highway. The agent will actually be software, but it will have a personality you'll be able to talk to in one form or another. This will be like delegating an assistant to look at the inventory for you.

Here's how the different systems will work. A query, as its name indicates, is a question. You will be able to ask a wide range of questions

-------------------------------➤

and get complete answers. If you can't recall the name of a movie but you remember that it starred Spencer Tracy and Katharine Hepburn and that there is a scene in which he's asking a lot of questions and she's shivering, then you could type in a query that asks for all movies that match: "Spencer Tracy," "Katharine Hepburn," "cold," and "questions." In reply, a server on the highway would list the 1957 romantic comedy *Desk Set*, in which Tracy quizzes a shivering Hepburn on a rooftop terrace in the middle of winter. You could watch the scene, watch the whole film, read the script, examine reviews of the movie, and read any comments that Tracy or Hepburn might have made publicly about the scene. If a dubbed or subtitled print had been made for release outside English-speaking countries, you could watch the foreign versions. They might be stored on servers in various countries but would be instantly available to you.

The system will accommodate straightforward queries such as "Show me all the articles that ran worldwide about the first test-tube baby," or "List all the stores that carry two or more kinds of dog food and will deliver a case within sixty minutes to my home address," or "Which of my relatives have I been out of touch with for more than three months?" It will also be able to deliver answers to much more complex queries. You might ask, "Which major city has the greatest percentage of the people who watch rock videos and regularly read about international trade?" Generally, queries won't require much response time, because most of the questions are likely to have been asked before and the answers will already have been computed and stored.

You'll also be able to set up "filters," which are really just standing queries. Filters will work around the clock, watching for new information that matches an interest of yours, filtering out everything else. You will be able to program a filter to gather information on your particular interests, such as news about local sports teams or particular scientific discoveries. If the most important thing to you is the weather, your filter will put that at the top of your personalized newspaper. Some filters will be created automatically by your computer, based on its information about your background and areas of interest. Such a filter might alert me to an important event regarding a person or institution from my past: "Meteorite crashes into Lakeside School." You will also be able to create an explicit filter. That will be an ongoing request for something particular, such as "Wanted: 1990 Nissan Maxima for parts," or "Tell me about anybody selling memorabilia from the last World Cup," or "Is anyone around here looking for someone to bicycle with on Sunday afternoons, rain or shine?" The filter will keep looking until you call off the search. If a filter finds a potential Sunday bicycling companion, for instance, it will automatically check on any other information the person might have published on the network. It will try to answer the question "What's he like?"—which is the first question you'd be likely to ask about a potential new friend.

Spatial navigation will be modeled on the way we locate information today. When we want to find out about some subject now, it's natural to go to a labeled section of a library or bookstore. Newspapers have sports, real estate, and business sections where people "go" for certain kinds of news. In most newspapers, weather reports appear in the same general location day after day.

Spatial navigation, which is already being used in some software products, will let you go where the information is by enabling you to interact with a visual model of a real or make-believe world. You can think of such a model as a map—an illustrated, three-dimensional table of contents. Spatial navigation will be particularly important for interacting with televisions and small, portable PCs, which are unlikely to have conventional keyboards. To do some banking, you might go to a drawing of a main street, then point, using a mouse or a remote control or even your finger, at the drawing of a bank. You will point to a courthouse to find out which cases are being heard by which judges or what the backlog is. You will point to the ferry terminal to learn the schedule and whether the boats are running on time. If you are considering visiting a hotel, you will be able to find out when rooms are available and look at a floor plan, and if the hotel has a video camera connected to the highway, you might be able to look at its lobby and restaurant and see how crowded it is at the moment.

You'll be able to jump into the map so you can navigate down a street or through the rooms of a building. You'll be able to zoom in and out and pan around to different locations very easily. Let's say you want to buy a lawn mower. If the screen shows the inside of a house, you might move out the back door, where you might see landmarks, including a garage. A click on the garage will take you inside it, where you might see tools, including a lawn mower. A click on the lawn mower will take you to categories of relevant information, including advertisements, reviews, user manuals, and sales showrooms in cyberspace. It will be simple to do some quick comparison shopping, taking advantage of any amount of information you want. When you click on the picture of the garage and seem to move inside it, behind-the-scenes information relating to the objects "inside" the garage will be fed to your screen from servers spread over thousands of miles on the highway.

When you point at an object on the screen to bring up information about the object, you are employing a form of "hyperlinking." Hyperlinks let users leap from informational place to informational place instantly, just as spaceships in science fiction jump from geographic place to geographic place through "hyperspace." Hyperlinks on the information highway will let you find answers to your questions when they occur to you and you're interested. Let's say you're watching the news and you see someone you don't recognize walking with the British prime minister. You want to know who she is. Using your television's remote control, you will point at the person. That action will bring up a biography and a list of other news accounts in which she figured recently. Point at something on the list, and you will be able to read it or watch it, jumping any number of times from topic to topic and gathering video, audio, and text information from all over the world.

Spatial navigation can also be used for touring. If you want to see reproductions of the artwork in a museum or gallery, you'll be able to "walk" through a visual representation, navigating among the works much as if you were physically there. For details about a painting or sculpture, you would use a hyperlink. No crowds, no rush, and you could ask anything without worrying about seeming uninformed. You would bump into interesting things, just as you do in a real gallery. Navigating through a virtual gallery won't be like walking through a real art gallery, but it will be a rewarding approximation—just as watching a ballet or basketball game on television can be entertaining even though you're not in the theater or stadium.

If other people are visiting the same "museum," you will be able to choose to see them and interact with them or not, as you please. Your visits needn't be solitary experiences. Some locations will be used purely for cyberspace socialization; in others no one will be visible. Some will force you to appear to some degree as you are; others won't. The way you look to other users will depend on your choices and the rules of the particular location.

If you are using spatial navigation, the place you're moving around in won't have to be real. You'll be able to set up imaginary places and return to them whenever you want. In your own museum, you'll be able to move walls, add imaginary galleries, and rearrange the art. You might want all still lifes to be displayed together, even if one is a fragment of a Pompeian fresco that hangs in a gallery of ancient Roman art and one is a Cubist Picasso from a twentieth-century gallery. You will be able to play curator and gather images of your favorite artworks from around the world to "hang" in a gallery of your own. Suppose you want to include a warmly remembered painting of a man asleep being nuzzled by a lion, but you can't recall either the artist or where you saw it. The information highway won't make you go looking for the information. You'll be able to describe what you want by posing a query. The query will start your computer or other information appliance sifting through a reservoir of information to deliver those pieces that match your request.

You will even be able to give friends tours, whether they are sitting next to you or watching from the other side of the world. "Here, between the Raphael and the Modigliani," you might say, "is a favorite finger painting I did when I was three years old."

The last type of navigational aid, and in many ways the most useful of all, is an agent. This is a filter that has taken on a personality and seems to show initiative. An agent's job is to assist you. In the Information Age, that means the agent is there to help you find information.

To understand the ways an agent can help with a variety of tasks, consider how it could improve today's PC interface. The present state of the art in user interface is the graphical user interface, such as Apple's Macintosh and Microsoft Windows, which depicts information and relationships on the screen instead of just describing them in text. Graphical interfaces also allow the user to point to and move objects— including pictures—around on the screen.

But the graphical user interface isn't easy enough for future systems. We've put so many options on the screen that programs or features that are not used regularly have become daunting. The features are great and fast for people familiar with the software, but for the average user not enough guidance comes from the machine for him or her to feel comfortable. Agents will remedy that.

Agents will know how to help you partly because the computer will remember your past activities. It will be able to find patterns of use that will help it work more effectively with you. Through the magic of software, information appliances connected to the highway will appear to learn from your interactions and will make suggestions to you. I call this "softer software."

Software allows hardware to perform a number of functions, but once the program is written, it stays the same. Softer software will appear to get smarter as you use it. It will learn about your requirements in pretty much the same way a human assistant does and, like a human assistant, will become more helpful as it learns about you and your work. The first day a new assistant is on the job, you can't simply ask him to format a document like another memo you wrote a few weeks ago. You can't say, "Send a copy to everybody who should know about this." But over the course of months and years, the assistant becomes more valuable as he picks up on what is typical routine and how you like things done.

The computer today is like a first-day assistant. It needs explicit first-day instructions all the time. And it remains a first-day assistant forever. It will never make one iota of adjustment as a response to its experience with you. We're working to perfect softer software. No one should be stuck with an assistant, in this case software, that doesn't learn from experience.

If an agent that could learn were available now, I would want it to take over certain functions for me. For instance, it would be very helpful if it could scan every project schedule, note the changes, and distinguish the ones I had to pay attention to from the ones I didn't. It would learn the criteria for what needed my attention: the size of the project, what other projects are dependent on it, the cause and the length of any delay. It would learn when a two-week slip could be ignored, and when such a slip indicates real trouble and I'd better look into it right away before it gets worse. It will take time to achieve this goal, partly because it's difficult, as with an assistant, to find the right balance between initiative and routine. We don't want to overdo it. If the built-in agent tries to be too smart and anticipates and confidently performs unrequested or undesired services, it will be annoying to users who are accustomed to having explicit control over their computers.

When you use an agent, you will be in a dialogue with a program that behaves to some degree like a person. It could be that the software mimics the behavior of a celebrity or a cartoon character as it assists you. An agent that takes on a personality provides a "social user interface." A number of companies, including Microsoft, are developing agents with social-user-interface capabilities. Agents won't replace the graphical-user-interface software, but, rather, will supplement it by providing a character of your choosing to assist you. The character will disappear when you get to the parts of the product you know very well. But if you hesitate or ask for help, the agent will reappear and offer assistance. You may even come to think of the agent as a collaborator, built right into the software. It will remember what you're good at and what you've done in the past, and try to anticipate problems and suggest solutions. It will bring anything unusual to your attention. If you work on something for a few minutes and then decide to discard the revision, the agent might ask if you're sure you want to throw the work away. Some of today's software already does that. But if you were to work for two hours and then give an instruction to delete what you'd just done, the social interface would recognize that as unusual and possibly a serious mistake on your part. The agent would say, "You've worked on this for two hours. Are you really, really sure you want to delete it?"

Some people, hearing about softer software and social interface, find the idea of a humanized computer creepy. But I believe even they will come to like it, once they have tried it. We humans tend to anthropomorphize. Animated movies take advantage of this tendency. *The Lion King* is not very realistic, nor does it try to be. Anybody could distinguish little Simba from a live lion cub on film. When a car breaks down or a computer crashes, we are apt to yell at it, or curse it, or even ask why it let us down. We know better, of course, but still tend to treat inanimate objects as if they were alive and had free will. Researchers at universities and software companies are exploring how to make computer interfaces more effective, using this human tendency. In programs such as Microsoft Bob, they have demonstrated that people will treat mechanical agents that have personalities with a surprising degree of deference. It has also been found that users' reactions differed depending on whether the agent's voice was female or male. Recently we worked on a project that involved users rating their experience with a computer. When we had the computer the users had worked with ask for an evaluation of its performance, the responses tended to be positive. But when we had a second computer ask the same people to evaluate their encounters with the first machine, the people were significantly more critical. Their reluctance to criticize the first computer "to its face" suggested that they didn't want to hurt its feelings, even though they knew it was only a machine. Social interfaces may not be suitable for all users or all situations, but I think that we'll see lots of them in the future because they "humanize" computers.

We have a fairly clear idea of what sorts of navigation we'll have on the highway. It's less clear what we'll be navigating through, but we can make some good guesses. Many applications available on the highway will be purely for fun. Pleasures will be as simple as playing bridge or a board game with your best friends, even though you are all in several different cities. Televised sporting events will offer you the opportunity to choose the camera angles, the replays, and even the commentators for your version. You'll be able to listen to any song, anytime, anywhere, piped in from the world's largest record store: the information highway. Perhaps you'll hum a little tune of your own invention into a microphone, and then play it back to hear what it could sound like if orchestrated or performed by a rock group. Or you'll watch *Gone With the Wind* with your own face and voice replacing that of Vivien Leigh or Clark Gable. Or see yourself walking down the runway at a fashion show, wearing the latest Paris creations adjusted to fit your body or the one you wish you had.

Users with curiosity will be mesmerized by the abundance of information. Want to know how a mechanical clock works? You'll peer inside one from any vantage point and be able to ask questions. Eventually you may even be able to crawl around inside a clock, using a virtual-reality application. Or you'll be able to assume the role of a heart surgeon or play the drums at a sold-out rock concert, thanks to the information highway's ability to deliver rich simulations to home computers. Some of the choices on the highway will be supersets of today's software, but the graphics and animation will be far, far better.

Other applications will be strictly practical. For example, when you go on vacation a home-management application will be able to turn down the heat, notify the post office to hold your mail and the newspaper carrier not to deliver the printed paper, cycle your indoor lighting so that it appears you are home, and automatically pay routine bills.

Still other applications will be completely serious. My dad broke his finger badly one weekend and went to the nearest emergency room, which happened to be Children's Hospital in Seattle. They refused to do anything for him because he was a few decades too old. Had there been an information highway at the time, it would have saved him some trouble by telling him not to bother trying that hospital. An application, communicating on the highway, would have told him which nearby emergency rooms were in the best position to help him at that particular time.

If my dad were to break another finger a few years from now, he not only would be able to use an information highway application to find an appropriate hospital, he might even be able to register electronically with the hospital while driving there and avoid conventional paperwork entirely. The hospital's computer would match his injury to a suitable doctor, who would be able to retrieve my father's medical records from a server on the information highway. If the doctor called for an X ray, it would be stored in digital form on a server, available for immediate review by any authorized doctor or specialist throughout the hospital or the world. Comments made by anyone reviewing the X ray, whether oral or in text form, would be linked to Dad's medical records. Afterward my father would be able to look at the X rays from home and listen to the professional commentary. He could share the X rays with his family: "Look at the size of that fracture! Listen to what the doctor said about it!"

Most of these applications, from checking a pizza menu to sharing centralized medical records, are already starting to appear on PCs. Interactive information sharing is quickly moving closer to becoming a part of everyday life. However, before that happens, a lot of pieces of the highway still have to be put in place.

5

PATHS TO THE HIGHWAY

Before we can enjoy the benefits of the applications and appliances described in the preceding chapter, the information highway has to exist. It doesn't yet. This may surprise some people, who hear everything from a long-distance telephone network to the Internet described as "the information superhighway." The truth is that the full highway is unlikely to be available in homes for at least a decade.

Personal computers, multimedia CD-ROM software, high-capacity cable television networks, wired and wireless telephone networks, and the Internet are all important precursors of the information highway. Each is suggestive of the future. But none represents the actual information highway.

Constructing the highway will be a big job. It will require the installation not only of physical infrastructure, such as fiber-optic cable and high-speed switches and servers, but also the development of software platforms. In chapter 3, I discussed the evolution of the hardware and the software platform that enabled the PC. Applications for the information highway, such as those I described in chapter 4, will also have to be built on a platform—one that will evolve out of the PC and the Internet. The same sort of competition that took place within the PC industry during the 1980s is taking place now to create the software components that will constitute the information highway platform.

The software that runs the highway will have to offer great navigation and security, electronic mail and bulletin board capabilities, connections to competing software components, and billing and accounting services.

Component providers for the highway will make available tools and user-interface standards so it will be easy for designers to create applications, set up forms, and manage databases of information on the system. To make it possible for applications to work together seamlessly, the platform will have to define a standard for user profiles so that information about user preferences can be passed from one application to another. This sharing of information will enable applications to do their best to meet user needs.

A number of companies, including Microsoft, confident that there will be a profitable business in supplying software for the highway, are competing to develop components of the platform. These components will be the foundation on which information highway applications can be built. There will be more than one successful software provider for the highway, and their software will interconnect.

The highway's platform will also have to support many different kinds of computers, including servers and all the information appliances. The customers for much of this software will be the cable systems, telephone companies, and other network providers, rather than individuals, but consumers will ultimately decide which succeed. The network providers will gravitate toward the software that offers consumers the best applications and the broadest range of information. So the first competition among companies developing platform software will be waged for the hearts and minds of applications developers and information providers, because their work will create most of the value.

As applications develop, they will demonstrate the value of the information highway to potential investors—a crucial step, considering the amount of money building the highway will require. Today's estimates put the cost at about $1,200, give or take a couple of hundred dollars, depending on architecture and equipment choices, to connect one information appliance (such as a TV or a PC) in each U.S. home to the highway. This price includes running the fiber into every neighborhood, the servers, the switches and electronics in the home. With roughly 100 million homes in the United States, this works out to around $120 billion of investment in one country alone.

Nobody is going to spend this kind of money until it is clear that the technology really works and that consumers will pay enough for the new applications. The fees customers will pay for television service, including video-on-demand, won't pay for building the highway. To finance the construction, investors will have to believe new services will generate almost as much revenue again as cable television does today. If the financial return on the highway is not evident, investment money isn't going to materialize and construction of the highway will be delayed. This is just as it should be. It would be ridiculous to do the buildout until private firms see the likelihood of a return on their investment. I think investors will become confident of such a return as innovators bring new ideas to the trials. Once investors begin to understand the new applications and services and the potential financial payback for the highway infrastructure is proven, there will be little trouble raising the necessary capital. The outlay will be no greater than that for other infrastructures we take for granted. The roads, water mains, sewers, and electrical connections that run to a house each costs as much.

I'm optimistic. The growth of the Internet over the past few years suggests that highway applications will quickly become extremely popular and justify large investments. The "Internet" refers to a group of computers connected together, using standard "protocols" (descriptions of technologies) to exchange information. It's a long way from being the highway, but it's the closest approximation we have today, and will evolve into the highway.

The popularity of the Internet is the most important single development in the world of computing since the IBM PC was introduced in 1981. The PC analogy is apt for many reasons. The PC wasn't perfect. Aspects of it were arbitrary or even poor. Despite that, its popularity grew to the point where it became the standard for applications development. Companies that tried to fight the PC standards often had good reasons for doing so, but their efforts failed because so many other companies were continuing to work to try and improve the PC.

---------------------------->

Today's Internet is made up of a loose collection of interconnecting commercial and noncommercial computer networks, including on-line information services to which users subscribe. Servers are scattered around the world, linked to the Internet on a variety of high- and low-capacity paths. Most consumers use personal computers to plug into the system through the telephone network, which has a low bandwidth and so can't carry many bits per second. "Modems" (shorthand for **mo**dulator-**dem**odulators) are the devices that connect phone lines to PCs. Modems, by converting to 0s and 1s into different tones, allow computers to connect over phone lines. In the early days of the IBM PC, modems typically carried data at the rate of 300 or 1,200 bits per seconds (also known as 300 or 1,200 "baud"). Most of the data transmitted through phone lines at these speeds was text, because transmitting pictures was painfully slow when so little information could be transferred each second. Faster modems have gotten much more affordable. Today, many modems that connect PCs to other computers via the phone system can send and receive 14,400 (14.4K) or 28,800 (28.8K) bits per second. From a practical standpoint, this is still insufficient bandwidth for many kinds of transmissions. A page of text is sent in a second, but a complete, screen-sized photograph, even if compressed, requires perhaps ten seconds at these baud rates. It takes minutes to send a color photograph with enough resolution for it to be made into a slide. Motion video would take so much time to transmit it just isn't practical at these speeds.

Already, anyone can send anyone else a message on the Internet—for business, education, or just the fun of it. Students around the world can send messages to one another. Shut-ins can carry on animated conversations with friends they might never get out to meet. Correspondents who might be uncomfortable talking to each other in person have forged bonds across a network. The information highway will add video, which unfortunately will do away with the social, racial, gender, and species blindness that text-only exchanges permit.

The Internet and other information services carried on telephone networks suggest some aspects of how the information highway will operate. When I send you a message, it is transmitted by phone line from my computer to the server that has my "mailbox," and from there it

"On the Internet, nobody knows you're a dog."

passes directly or indirectly to whichever server stores your mailbox. When you connect to your server, via the telephone network or a corporate computer network, you are able to retrieve ("download") the contents of your mailbox, including my message. That's how electronic mail works. You can type a message once and send it to one person or twenty-five, or post it on what is called a "bulletin board."

Like its namesake, an electronic bulletin board is where messages are left for anyone to read. Public conversations result, as people respond to messages. These exchanges are usually asynchronous. Bulletin boards typically are organized by topics to serve specific communities of interest. This makes them effective ways to reach targeted groups. Commercial services offer bulletin boards for pilots, journalists, teachers, and much smaller communities. On the Internet, where the often unedited and unmoderated bulletin boards are called "usenet newsgroups," there are thousands of communities devoted to topics as narrow as caffeine, Ronald Reagan, and neckties. You can download all the messages on a topic, or just recent messages, or all messages from a certain person, or those that respond to a particular other message, or that contain a specific word in their subject line, and so forth.

In addition to electronic mail and file exchange, the Internet supports "Web browsing," one of its most popular applications. The "World Wide Web" (abbreviated as the Web or WWW) refers to those servers connected to the Internet that offer graphical pages of information. When you connect to one of those servers, a screen of information with a number of hyperlinks appears. When you activate a hyperlink by clicking on it with your mouse, you are taken to another page containing additional information and other hyperlinks. That page may be stored on the same server or any other server on the Internet.

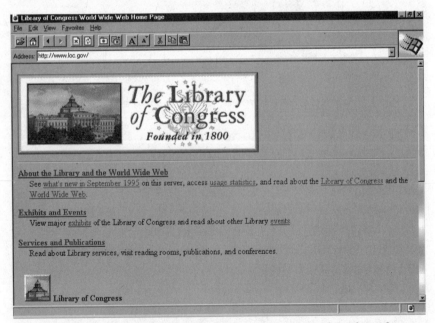

1995: U.S. Library of Congress home page on the World Wide Web, showing hyperlinks

The main page for a company or an individual is called the "home" page. If you create one, you register its electronic address, then Internet users can find you by typing in the address. In advertisements today we are starting to see home page citations as part of the address information. The software to set up a Web server is very cheap and available for almost all computers. The software to browse the Web is also available for all machines, generally for free. You can Web browse using the CD that comes with this book. In the future, operating systems will integrate Internet browsing.

The ease with which companies and individuals can publish information on the Internet is changing the whole idea of what it means to "publish." The Internet has, on its own, established itself as a place to publish content. It has enough users so that it is benefiting from positive feedback: the more subscribers it gets, the more content it gets, and the more content it gets, the more subscribers it gets.

The Internet's unique position arises from a number of elements. The TCP/IP protocols that define its transport level support distributed computing and also scale incredibly well. The protocols that define Web browsing are extremely simple and have allowed servers to handle immense amounts of traffic reasonably well. Many of the predictions about interactive books and hyperlinks—made decades ago by pioneers like Ted Nelson—are coming true on the Web.

Today's Internet is not the information highway I imagine, although you can think of it as the beginning of the highway. An analogy is the Oregon Trail. Between 1841 and the early 1860s, more than 300,000 hardy souls rode wagon trains out of Independence, Missouri, for a dangerous 2,000-mile journey across the wilderness to the Oregon Territories or the gold fields of California. An estimated 20,000 succumbed to marauders, cholera, starvation, or exposure. Their route was named the Oregon Trail. You could easily say the Oregon Trail was the start of today's highway system. It crossed many boundaries and provided two-way traffic to travelers in wheeled vehicles. The modern path of Interstate 84 and several other highways follows the Oregon Trail for much of its length. However, many conclusions drawn from descriptions of the Oregon Trail would be misleading if applied to the future system. Cholera and starvation aren't a problem on Interstate 84. Tailgating and drunk drivers weren't much of a hazard for the wagon trains.

The trail blazed by the Internet will direct many elements of the highway. The Internet is a wonderful, critical development and a very clear element of the final system, but it will change significantly in the years ahead. The current Internet lacks security and needs a billing system. Much of the Internet culture will seem as quaint to future users of the information highway as stories of wagon trains and pioneers on the Oregon Trail do to us today.

In fact, the Internet of today is not the Internet of even a short time ago. The pace of its evolution is so rapid that a description of the Internet as it existed a year or even six months ago might be seriously out-of-date. This adds to the confusion. It is very hard to stay up-to-date with something so dynamic. Many companies, including Microsoft, are working together to define standards in order to extend the Internet and overcome its limitations.

Because the Internet originated as a computer-science project rather than a communications utility, it has always been a magnet for hackers—programmers who turn their talents toward mischief or malice by breaking into the computer systems of others.

On November 2, 1988, thousands of computers connected to the network began to slow down. Many eventually ground to a temporary halt. No data were destroyed, but millions of dollars of computing time were lost as computer system administrators fought to regain control of their machines. Much of the public may have heard of the Internet for the first time when this story was widely covered. The cause turned out to be a mischievous computer program, called a "worm," that was spreading from one computer to another on the network, replicating as it went. (It was designated a worm rather than a virus because it didn't infect other programs.) It used an unnoticed "back door" in the systems' software to access directly the memory of the computers it was attacking. There it hid itself and passed around misleading information that made it harder to detect and counteract. Within a few days *The New York Times* identified the hacker as Robert Morris, Jr., a twenty-three-year-old graduate student at Cornell University. Morris later testified that he had designed and then unleashed the worm to see how many computers it would reach, but a mistake in his programming caused the worm to replicate far faster than he had expected. Morris was convicted of violating the 1986 Computer Fraud and Abuse Act, a federal offense. He was sentenced to three years of probation, a fine of $10,000, and 400 hours of community service.

There have been occasional breakdowns and security problems, but not many, and the Internet has become a reasonably reliable communications channel for millions of people. It provides worldwide connections between servers, facilitating the exchange of electronic mail, bulletin board items, and other data. The exchanges range from short messages of a few dozen characters to multimillion-byte transfers of photographs, software, and other kinds of data. It costs no more to request data from a server that is a mile away than from one that is thousands of miles distant.

Already the Internet's pricing model has changed the notion that communication has to be paid for by time and distance. The same thing happened with computing. If you couldn't afford a big computer you used to pay for computer time by the hour. PCs changed that.

Because the Internet is inexpensive to use, people assume it is government funded. That isn't so. However, the Internet is an outgrowth of a 1960s government project: the ARPANET, as it was called, was initially used solely for computer-science and engineering projects. It became a vital communications link among far-flung project collaborators but was virtually unknown to outsiders.

In 1989, the U.S. government decided to stop funding ARPANET, and plans were laid for a commercial successor, to be called the "Internet." The name was derived from that of the underlying communications protocol. Even when it became a commercial service, the Internet's first customers were mostly scientists at universities and companies in the computer industry, who used it for exchanging e-mail.

The financial model that allows the Internet to be so suspiciously cheap is actually one of its most interesting aspects. If you use a telephone today, you expect to be charged for time and distance. Businesses that call one remote site a great deal avoid these charges by getting a leased line, a special-purpose telephone line dedicated to calls between the two sites. There are no traffic charges on a leased line—the same amount is charged for it each month no matter how much it is used.

The foundation of the Internet consists of a bunch of these leased lines connected by switching systems that route data. The long-distance Internet connections are provided in the United States by five companies, each of which leases lines from telecommunications carriers. Since the breakup of AT&T, the charges for leased lines have become very competitive. Because the volume of traffic on the Internet is so large, these five companies qualify for the lowest possible rates—which means they carry enormous bandwidth quite inexpensively.

The term "bandwidth" deserves further explanation. As I said, it refers to the speed at which a line can carry information to connected devices. The bandwidth depends, in part, on the technology used to transmit and receive the information. Telephone networks are designed for two-way private connections with low bandwidth. Telephones are analog devices that communicate with the telephone company's equipment by means of fluctuating currents—analogs of the sounds of voices. When an analog signal is digitized by a long-distance telephone company, the resulting digital signal contains about 64,000 bits of information per second.

The coaxial cables used to carry cable television broadcasts have much higher bandwidth potential than standard telephone wires because they have to be able to carry higher-frequency video signals. Cable TV systems today, however, don't transmit bits; they use analog technology to transmit thirty to seventy-five channels of video. Coaxial cable can easily carry hundreds of millions or even a billion bits per second, but new switches will have to be added to allow them to support digital-information transmission. A long-distance fiber-optic cable that carries 1.7 billion bits of information from one repeater station (something like an amplifier) to another has sufficient bandwidth for 25,000 simultaneous telephone conversations. The number of possible conversations rises significantly if the conversations are compressed by removing redundant information, such as the pauses between words and sentences, so that each conversation consumes fewer bits.

Most businesses use a special kind of telephone line to connect to the Internet. It is called a T-1 line and carries 1.5 million bits per second, which is relatively high bandwidth. Subscribers pay the local phone company a monthly charge for the T-1 line (which moves their data to the nearest Internet access point) and then pay a flat rate of about $20,000 a year to the company connecting them to the Internet. That yearly charge, based on the capacity of the connection, or "on ramp," covers all of their Internet usage whether they use the Internet constantly or never use it at all, and whether their Internet traffic goes a few miles or across the globe. The sum of these payments funds the entire Internet network.

This works because the costs are based on paying for capacity, and the pricing has simply followed. It would require a lot of technology and effort for the carriers to keep track of time and distance. Why should they bother if they can make a profit without having to? This pricing structure means that once a customer has an Internet connection there is no extra cost for extensive use, which encourages usage. Most individuals can't afford to lease a T-1 line. To connect to the Internet, they contact a local on-line service provider. This is a company that has paid the $20,000 per year to connect via T-1 or other high-speed means to the Internet. Individuals use their regular phone lines to call the local service provider and it connects them to the Internet. A typical monthly charge is $20, for which you get twenty hours of prime-time usage.

Providing access to the Internet will become even more competitive in the next few years. Large phone companies around the world will enter the business. Prices will come down significantly. The on-line service companies such as CompuServe and America Online will be including Internet access as part of their charges. Over the next few years the Internet will improve and provide easy access, wide availability, a consistent user interface, easy navigation, and integration with other commercial on-line services.

One technical challenge still facing the Internet is how to handle "real-time" content—specifically audio (including voice) and video. The underlying technology of the Internet doesn't guarantee that data will move from one point to another at a constant rate. The congestion on the network determines how quickly packets are sent. Various clever approaches do allow high-quality two-way audio and video to be delivered, but full audio and video support will require significant changes in the network and probably won't be available for several years.

When these changes do happen, they will set up the Internet in direct competition with the phone companies' voice networks. Their different pricing approaches will make the competition interesting to watch.

As the Internet is changing the way we pay for communication, it may also change how we pay for information. There are those who think the Internet has shown that information will be free, or largely so. Although a great deal of information, from NASA photos to bulletin board entries donated by users, will continue to be free, I believe the most attractive information, whether Hollywood movies or encyclopedic databases, will continue to be produced with profit in mind.

Software programs are a particular kind of information. There is a lot of free software on the Internet today, some of it quite useful. Often this is software written as a graduate-student project or at a government-funded lab. However, I think that the desire for quality, support, and comprehensiveness for a tool as important as software means that demand for commercial software will continue to grow. Already, many students and faculty members who wrote free software at universities are busy writing business plans for start-up companies to provide commercial versions of their software with more features. Software developers, both those who want to charge for their product and those who want to give it away, will have an easier time getting it distributed than they do now.

All of this bodes well for the future information highway. However, before it becomes a reality, a number of transitional technologies will be used to bring us new applications. While they will fall short of what will be possible once the full-bandwidth highway is available, they will be a step beyond what we can do now. These evolutionary advances are inexpensive enough to be cost-justified with applications that already work and have proven demand.

Some of the transitional technologies will rely on telephone networks. By 1997, most fast modems will support the simultaneous transmission of voice and data across existing phone lines. When you're making travel plans, if you and your travel agent both have PCs, she might show you photos of each of the different hotels you're considering, or display a little grid comparing prices. When you call a friend to ask how he layered his pastry to get it to rise so high, if you both have PCs connected to your phone lines, during the conversation, while your dough is resting, he will be able to transmit a diagram to you.

The technology that will make this possible goes by the acronym DSVD, which stands for **d**igital **s**imultaneous **v**oice **d**ata. It will demonstrate, more clearly than anything has so far, the possibilities of sharing information across a network. I believe it will be adopted widely over the next three years. It is inexpensive because it requires no change to the existing telephone system. The phone companies won't have to modify their switches or increase your phone bill. DSVD works as long as the instruments at both ends of a conversation are equipped with appropriate modems and PC software.

Another interim step for using the phone companies' network does require special telephone lines and switches. The technology is called ISDN (for **i**ntegrated **s**ervices **d**igital **n**etwork). It transfers voice and data starting at 64,000 or 128,000 bits per second, which means it can do everything DSVD does, only five to ten times faster. It's fine for mid-band applications. You get rapid transmission of text and still pictures. Motion video can be transmitted, but the quality is mediocre—not good enough to watch a movie, but reasonable for routine videoconferencing. The full highway requires high-quality video.

Hundreds of Microsoft employees use ISDN every day to connect their home computers to our corporate network. ISDN was invented more than a decade ago, but without PC-application demand almost no one needed it. It's amazing that phone companies invested enormous sums in switches to handle ISDN with very little idea of how it would be used. The good news is that the PC will drive explosive demand. An add-in card for a PC to support ISDN costs $500 in 1995, but the price should drop to less than $200 over the next few years. The line costs vary by location but are generally about $50 per month in the United States. I expect this will drop to less than $20, not much more than a regular phone connection. We are among companies working to convince phone companies all over the world to lower these charges in order to encourage PC owners to connect, using ISDN.

Cable companies have interim technologies and strategies of their own. They want to use their existing coaxial cable networks to compete with the phone companies to provide local telephone service. They have also already demonstrated that special cable modems can connect personal computers to cable networks. This allows cable companies to offer bandwidth somewhat greater than ISDN's.

For cable companies another interim step will be to increase the number of broadcast channels they carry five- to tenfold. They'll do it by using digital-compression technology to squeeze more channels onto existing cables.

This so-called 500-channel approach—which often will really only have 150 channels—makes possible near-video-on-demand, although only for a limited number of television shows and movies. You would choose from a list on-screen rather than selecting a numbered channel. A popular movie might run on twenty of the channels, with the starting time staggered at five-minute intervals so that you could begin watching it within five minutes of whenever you wanted. You would choose from among the available starting times for movies and television programs, and the set-top box would switch to the appropriate channel. The half-hour-long *CNN Headline News* might be offered on six channels instead of one, with the 6:00 P.M. broadcast shown again at 6:05, 6:10, 6:15, 6:20, and 6:25. There would be a new, live broadcast every half hour, just as there is now. Five hundred channels will get used up pretty fast this way.

The cable companies are under pressure to add channels partly as a reaction to competition. Direct-broadcast satellites such as Hughes Electronics' DIRECTV are already beaming hundreds of channels directly into homes. Cable companies want to increase their channel lineup rapidly to avoid losing customers. If the only reason for the information highway were to deliver a limited number of movies, then a 500-channel system would be adequate.

A 500-channel system will still be mostly synchronous, will limit your choices, and will provide only a low-bandwidth back channel, at best. A "back channel" is an information path dedicated to carrying instructions and other information from a consumer's information appliance back up the cable to the network. A back channel on a 500-channel system might let you use your television set-top box to order products or programs, respond to polls or game-show questions, and participate in certain kinds of multiplayer games. But a low-bandwidth back channel can't offer the full flexibility and interactivity the most interesting applications will require. It won't let you send a video of your children to their grandparents, or play truly interactive games.

Cable and phone companies around the world will progress along four parallel paths. First, each will be going after the others' business. Cable companies will offer telephone service, and phone companies will offer video services, including television. Second, both systems will be providing better ways to connect PCs with either ISDN or cable modems. Third, both will be converting to digital technology in order to provide more television channels and higher-quality signals. Fourth, both will be conducting trials of broadband systems connected to television sets and PCs. Each of the four strategies will motivate investment in digital network capacity. There will be intense competition between the telephone companies and cable television networks to be the first network provider in a neighborhood.

Eventually, the Internet and the other transitional technologies will be subsumed within the real information highway. The highway will combine the best qualities of both the telephone and the cable network systems: Like the telephone network, it will offer private connections so that everyone using the network can pursue his or her own interests, on his or her own schedule. It will also be fully two-way like the telephone network, so that rich forms of interaction are possible. Like the cable television network, it will be high capacity, so there will be sufficient bandwidth to allow multiple televisions or personal computers in a single household to connect simultaneously to different video programs or sources of information.

Most of the wires connecting servers with one another, and with the neighborhoods of the world, will be made of incredibly clear fiber-optic cable, the "asphalt" of the information highway. All of the major long-distance trunk lines that carry telephone calls within the United States today use fiber, but the lines that connect our homes to these data thoroughfares are still copper wire. Telephone companies will replace the copper-wire, microwave, and satellite links in their networks with fiber-optic cable so they will have the bandwidth to carry enough bits to de-

--------------------------->

liver high-quality video. Cable television companies will increase the amount of fiber they use. At the same time fiber is being deployed, telephone and cable companies will be incorporating new switches into their networks so that digital video signals and other information can be routed from any point to any other point. The costs of upgrading the existing networks to prepare for the highway will be less than a quarter of what they would be to run new wires into every home.

You can think of a fiber trunk as being like the foot-wide water main that carries water up your street. It doesn't come directly to your house; instead, a smaller pipe at the curb connects the main to your home. At first, the fiber will probably run only to neighborhood distribution points and the signals will be carried from the neighborhood fiber on either the coaxial cable that brings you cable television or on the "twisted-pair" copper-wire connections that provide telephone service. Eventually, though, fiber connections may run directly into your home if you use lots of data.

Switches are the sophisticated computers that shunt streams of data from one track to another, like boxcars in a train yard. Millions of simultaneous streams of communications will flow on large networks, and no matter how many intermediate waypoints are required, all the different bits of information will have to be guided to their destinations, with an assurance they will arrive in the right places and on time. To grasp how big the task will be in the era of the information highway, imagine billions of boxcars that have to be routed along railroad tracks through vast systems of switches and arrive at their destinations on schedule. Because the cars are attached to one another, switchyards get clogged waiting for long, multicar trains to pass through. There would be fewer tie-ups if each boxcar could travel independently and find its own way through the switches, then reassemble as a train at the destination.

Information traversing the information highway will be broken up into tiny packets, and each packet will be routed independently through the network, the way individual automobiles navigate roads. When you order a movie, it will be broken into millions of tiny pieces, each one of which will find its way through the network to your television.

This routing of packets will be accomplished through the use of a communications protocol known as asynchronous transfer mode, or ATM (not to be confused with "automatic teller machine"). It will be one of the building blocks of the information highway. Phone companies around the world are already beginning to rely on ATM, because it takes great advantage of fiber's amazing bandwidth. One strength of ATM is its ability to guarantee timely delivery of information. ATM breaks each digital stream into uniform packets, each of which contains 48 bytes of the information to be transported and 5 bytes of control information that allow the highway's switches to route the packets very quickly to their destinations. At their destinations the packets are recombined into a stream.

ATM delivers streams of information at very high speeds—up to 155 million bits per second at first, later jumping to 622 million bits per second and eventually to 2 billion bits per second. This technology will make it possible to send video as easily as voice calls, and at very low cost. Just as advances in chip technology have driven down the cost of computing, ATM, because it will also be able to carry enormous numbers of old-fashioned voice calls, will drive down the cost of long-distance phone calls.

High-bandwidth cable connections will link most information appliances to the highway, but some devices will connect wirelessly. We already use a number of wireless communication devices—cellular telephones, pagers, and consumer-electronics remote controls. They send radio signals and allow us mobility, but the bandwidth is limited. The wireless networks of the future will be faster, but unless there is a major breakthrough, wired networks will have far greater bandwidth. Mobile devices will be able to send and receive messages, but it will be expensive and unusual to use them to receive an individual video stream.

The wireless networks that will allow us to communicate when we are mobile will grow out of today's cellular-telephone systems and the new alternative wireless phone service, called PCS. When you are on the road and want information from your home or office computer, your portable information appliance will connect to the wireless part of the highway, a switch will connect that to the wired part, and then to the computer/server in your home or office and bring you the information you asked for.

There will also be local, less expensive kinds of wireless networks available inside businesses and most homes. These networks will allow you to connect to the highway or your own computer system without paying time charges so long as you are within a certain range. Local wireless networks will use technology different from the one used by the wide-area wireless networks. However, portable information devices will automatically select the least expensive network they are able to connect to, so the user won't be aware of the technological differences. The indoor wireless networks will allow wallet PCs to be used in place of remote controls.

Wireless service poses obvious concerns about privacy and security, because radio signals can easily be intercepted. Even wired networks can be tapped. The highway software will have to encrypt transmission to avoid eavesdropping.

Governments have long understood the importance of keeping information private, for both economic and military reasons. The need to make personal, commercial, military, or diplomatic messages secure (or to break into them) has attracted powerful intellects through the generations. It is very satisfying to break an encoded message. Charles Babbage, who made dramatic advances in the art of code breaking in the mid-1800s, wrote: "Deciphering is, in my opinion, one of the most fascinating of arts, and I fear I have wasted upon it more time than it deserves." I discovered its fascination as a kid when, like kids everywhere, a bunch of us played with simple ciphers. We would encode messages by substituting one letter of the alphabet for another. If a friend sent me a cipher that began "ULFW NZXX," it would be fairly easy to guess that this represented "DEAR BILL," and that U stood for D, and L for E, and so forth. With those seven letters it wasn't hard to unravel the rest of the cipher fairly quickly.

Past wars have been won or lost because the most powerful governments on earth didn't have the cryptological power any interested junior high school student with a personal computer can harness today. Soon any child old enough to use a computer will be able to transmit encoded messages that no government on earth will find easy to decipher. This is one of the profound implications of the spread of fantastic computing power.

When you send a message across the information highway it will be "signed" by your computer or other information appliance with a digital signature that only you are capable of applying, and it will be encrypted so that only the intended recipient will be able to decipher it. You'll send a message, which could be information of any kind, including voice, video, or digital money. The recipient will be able to be almost positive that the message is really from you, that it was sent at exactly the indicated time, that it has not been tampered with in the slightest, and that others cannot decipher it.

The mechanism that will make this possible is based on mathematical principles, including what are called "one-way functions" and "public-key encryption." These are quite advanced concepts, so I'm only going to touch on them. Keep in mind that regardless of how complicated the system is technically, it will be extremely easy for you to use. You'll just tell your information appliance what you want it to do and it will seem to happen effortlessly.

A one-way function is something that is much easier to do than undo. Breaking a pane of glass is a one-way function, but not one useful for encoding. The sort of one-way function required for cryptography is one that is easy to undo if you know an extra piece of information and very difficult to undo without that information. There are a number of such one-way functions in mathematics. One involves prime numbers. Kids learn about prime numbers in school. A prime number cannot be divided evenly by any number except 1 and itself. Among the first dozen numbers, the primes are 2, 3, 5, 7, and 11. The numbers 4, 6, 8, and 10 are not prime because 2 divides into each of them evenly. The number 9 is not prime because 3 divides into it evenly. There are an infinite number of prime numbers, and there is no known pattern to them except that they are prime. When you multiply two prime numbers together, you get a number that can be divided evenly only by those same two primes. For example, only 5 and 7 can be divided evenly into 35. Finding the primes is called "factoring" the number.

It is easy to multiply the prime numbers 11,927 and 20,903 and get the number 249,310,081, but it is much harder to recover from the product, 249,310,081, the two prime numbers that are its factors. This one-way function, the difficulty of factoring numbers, underlies an ingenious kind of cipher: the most sophisticated encryption system in use today. It takes a long time for even the largest computers to factor a really large product back into its constituent primes. A coding system based on factoring uses two different decoding keys, one to encipher a message and a different but related one to decipher. With only the enciphering key, it's easy to encode a message, but deciphering it within any practical period of time is nearly impossible. Deciphering requires a separate key, available only to the intended recipient of the message—or, rather, to the recipient's computer. The enciphering key is based on the product of two huge prime numbers, whereas the deciphering key is based on the primes themselves. A computer can generate a new pair of unique keys in a flash, because it is easy for a computer to generate two large prime numbers and multiply them together. The enciphering key thus created can be made public without appreciable risk, because of the difficulty even another computer would have factoring it to obtain the deciphering key.

The practical application of this encryption will be at the center of the information highway's security system. The world will become quite reliant on this network, so it is important that security be handled competently. You can think of the information highway as a postal network where everyone has a mailbox that is impervious to tampering and has an unbreakable lock. Each mailbox has a slot that lets anyone slide information in, but only the owner of a mailbox has the key to get information out. (Some governments may insist that each mailbox have a second door with a separate key that the government keeps, but we'll ignore that political consideration for now and concentrate on the security that software will provide.)

Each user's computer or other information appliance will use prime numbers to generate an enciphering key, which will be listed publicly, and a corresponding deciphering key, which only the user will know. This is how it will work in practice: I have information I want to send you. My information appliance/computer system looks up your public key and uses it to encrypt the information before sending it. No one can read the message, even though your key is public knowledge, because your public key does not contain the information needed for decryption. You receive the message and your computer decrypts it with a private key that corresponds to your public key.

You want to answer. Your computer looks up my public key and uses it to encrypt your reply. No one else can read the message, even though it was encrypted with a key that is totally public. Only I can read it because only I have the private deciphering key. This is very practical, because no one has to trade keys in advance.

How big do the prime numbers and their products have to be to ensure an effective one-way function?

The concept of public-key encryption was invented by Whitfield Diffie and Martin Hellman in 1977. Another set of computer scientists, Ron Rivest, Adi Shamir, and Leonard Adelman, soon came up with the notion of using prime factorization as part of what is now known as the RSA cryptosystem, after the initials of their last names. They projected that it would take millions of years to factor a 130-digit number that was the product of two primes, regardless of how much computing power was brought to bear. To prove the point, they challenged the world to find the two factors in this 129-digit number, known to people in the field as RSA 129:

114,381,625,757,888,867,669,235,779,976,146,612,010,218,296,
721,242,362,562,561,842,935,706,935,245,733,897,830,597,123,
563,958,705,058,989,075,147,599,290,026,879,543,541

They were sure that a message they had encrypted using the number as the public key would be totally secure forever. But they hadn't anticipated either the full effects of Moore's Law, as discussed in chapter 2, which has made computers much more powerful, or the success of the personal computer, which has dramatically increased the number of computers and computer users in the world. In 1993 a group of more than 600 academics and hobbyists from around the world began an assault on the 129-digit number, using the Internet to coordinate the work of various computers. In less than a year they factored the number into two primes, one 64 digits long and the other 65. The primes are as follows:

3,490,529,510,847,650,949,147,849,619,903,898,133,417,764,638,
493,387,843,990,820,577

and

32,769,132,993,266,709,549,961,988,190,834,461,413,177,642,
967,992,942,539,798,288,533

And the encoded message says: "The magic words are squeamish and ossifrage."

One lesson that came out of this challenge is that a 129-digit public key is not long enough if the information being encrypted is really important and sensitive. Another is that no one should get too cocksure about the security of encryption.

Increasing the key just a few digits makes it much more difficult to crack. Mathematicians today believe that a 250-digit-long product of two primes would take millions of years to factor with any foreseeable amount of future computing power. But who really knows? This uncertainty—and the unlikely but conceivable possibility that someone could come up with an easy way of factoring big numbers—means that a software platform for the information highway will have to be designed in such a way that its encryption scheme can be changed readily.

One thing we don't have to worry about is running out of prime numbers, or the prospect of two computers' accidentally using the same numbers as keys. There are far more prime numbers of appropriate length than there are atoms in the universe, so the chance of an accidental duplication is vanishingly small.

Key encryption allows more than just privacy. It can also assure the authenticity of a document because a private key can be used to encode a message that only the public key can decode. It works like this: If I have information I want to sign before sending it to you, my computer uses my private key to encipher it. Now the message can be read only if my public key—which you and everyone else knows—is used to decipher it. This message is verifiably from me, because no one else has the private key that could have encrypted it in this way.

My computer takes this enciphered message and enciphers it again, this time using your public key. Then it sends this double-coded message to you across the information highway.

Your computer receives the message and uses your private key to decipher it. This removes the second level of encoding but leaves the level I applied with my private key. Then your computer uses my public key to decipher the message again. Because it really is from me, the message deciphers correctly and you know it is authentic. If even one bit of information was changed, the message would not decode properly and the tampering or communications error would be apparent. This extraordinary security will enable you to transact business with strangers or even people you distrust, because you'll be able to be sure that digital money is valid and signatures and documents are provably authentic.

Security can be increased further by having time stamps incorporated into encrypted messages. If anyone tries to tinker with the time that a document supposedly was written or sent, the tinkering will be detectable. This will rehabilitate the evidentiary value of photographs and videos, which has been under assault because digital retouching has become so easy to do.

My description of public-key encryption oversimplifies the technical details of the system. For one thing, because it is relatively slow, it will not be the only form of encipherment used on the highway. But public-key encryption will be the way that documents are signed, authenticity is established, and the keys to other kinds of encryption are distributed securely.

The major benefit of the PC revolution has been the way it has empowered people. The highway's low-cost communications will empower in an even more fundamental way. The beneficiaries won't just be technology-oriented individuals. As more and more computers are connected to high-bandwidth networks, and as software platforms provide a foundation for great applications, everyone will have access to most of the world's information.

6

THE CONTENT REVOLUTION

For more than 500 years, the bulk of human knowledge and information has been stored as paper documents. You've got one in your hands right now (unless you're reading this from the CD-ROM or a future on-line edition). Paper will be with us indefinitely, but its importance as a means of finding, preserving, and distributing information is already diminishing.

When you think of a "document" you probably visualize pieces of paper with something printed on them, but that is a narrow definition. A document can be any body of information. A newspaper article is a document, but the broadest definition also includes a television show, a song, or an interactive video game. Because all information can be stored in a digital form, documents will be easy to find, store, and send on the highway. Paper is harder to transmit and very limiting if the contents are more than text with drawings and images. Future digitally stored documents will include pictures, audio, programming instructions for interactivity, and animation, or a combination of these and other elements.

On the information highway, rich electronic documents will be able to do things no piece of paper can. The highway's powerful database technology will allow them to be indexed and retrieved using interactive exploration. It will be extremely cheap and easy to distribute them. In short, these new digital documents will replace many printed paper ones because they will be able to help us in new ways.

But not for quite some time. The paper-based book, magazine, or newspaper still has a lot of advantages over its digital counterpart. To read a digital document you need an information appliance such as a personal computer. A book is small, lightweight, high-resolution, and inexpensive compared to the cost of a computer. For at least a decade it won't be as convenient to read a long, sequential document on a computer screen as on paper. The first digital documents to achieve widespread use will do so by offering new functionality rather than simply duplicating the older medium. A television set is also larger, more expensive, more cumbersome, and lower resolution than a book or magazine, but that hasn't limited its popularity. Television brought video entertainment into our homes, and it was so compelling that television sets found their place alongside books and magazines.

Ultimately, incremental improvements in computer and screen technology will give us a lightweight, universal electronic book, or "e-book," which will approximate today's paper book. Inside a case roughly the same size and weight as today's hardcover or paperback book, you'll have a display that can show high-resolution text, pictures, and video. You'll be able to flip pages with your finger or use voice commands to search for the passages you want. Any document on the network will be accessible from such a device.

The real point of electronic documents is not simply that we will read them on hardware devices. Going from paper book to e-book is just the final stage of a process already well under way. The exciting aspect of digital documentation is the redefinition of the document itself.

This will cause dramatic repercussions. We will have to rethink not only what is meant by the term "document," but also by "author," "publisher," "office," "classroom," and "textbook."

Today, if two companies are negotiating a contract, the first draft is probably typed into a computer, then printed on paper. Chances are it

----------------------->

is then faxed to the other party, who edits, amends, and alters it by writing on the paper or by reentering the changed document into another computer, from which it is printed. He then faxes it back; the changes are incorporated; a new paper document is printed and faxed back again; and the editing process is repeated. During this transaction it is hard to tell who made which changes. Coordinating all the alterations and transmittals introduces a lot of overhead. Electronic documents can simplify this process by allowing a version of the contract to be passed back and forth with corrections and annotations and indications who made them and when printed alongside the original text.

Within a few years the digital document, complete with authenticatable digital signatures, will be the original, and paper printouts will be secondary. Already many businesses are advancing beyond paper and fax machines and exchanging editable documents, computer to computer, through electronic mail. This book would have been much harder to write without e-mail. Readers whose opinions I was soliciting were sent drafts electronically, and it was helpful to be able to look at the suggested revisions and see who had made them and when.

By the end of the decade a significant percentage of documents, even in offices, won't even be fully printable on paper. They will be like a movie or a song is today. You will still be able to print a two-dimensional view of its content, but it will be like reading a musical score instead of experiencing an audio recording.

Some documents are so superior in digital form that the paper version is rarely used. Boeing decided to design its new 777 jetliner using a gigantic electronic document to hold all the engineering information. To coordinate collaboration among the design teams, manufacturing groups and outside contractors during development of previous airplanes, Boeing had used blueprints and constructed an expensive full-scale mock-up of the airplane. The mock-up had been necessary to make sure that parts of the airplane, designed by different engineers, actually fit together properly. During development of the 777, Boeing did away with blueprints and the mock-up and from the start used an electronic document that contained digital 3-D models of all the parts and how they fit together. Engineers at computer terminals were able to look at the design and see different views of the content. They could track the progress in any area, search for interesting test results, annotate with cost information, and change any part of the design in ways that would be impossible on paper. Each person, working with the same data, was able to look for what specifically concerned him. Every change could be shared, and everyone could see who made any change, when it was made, and why. Boeing was able to save hundreds of thousands of pieces of paper and many person-years of drafting and copying by using digital documents.

Digital documents can also be faster to work with than paper. You can transmit information instantly and retrieve it almost as quickly. Those using digital documents are already discovering how much simpler it is to search and navigate through them quickly, because their content can be restructured so easily.

The organizational structure of a reservation book at a restaurant is by date and time. A 9:00 P.M. reservation is written farther down the page than an 8:00 P.M. reservation. Saturday-night dinner reservations follow those for Saturday lunch. A maître d' or anyone else can rapidly find out who has a reservation on any date for any time because the book's information is ordered that way. But if, for whatever reason, someone wants to extract information in another way, the simple chronology is useless.

Imagine the plight of a restaurant captain if I called to say, "My name is Gates. My wife made us a reservation for some time next month. Would you mind checking to see when it is?"

"I'm sorry, sir, do you know the date of the reservation?" the captain would be likely to ask.

"No, that's what I'm trying to find out."

"Would that have been on a weekend?" the captain asks.

He knows he's going to be paging through the book by hand, and he's hoping to reduce the task by focusing the dates in any possible way.

A restaurant can use a paper-based reservation book because the total number of reservations isn't large. An airline reservation system is not a book but a database containing an enormous quantity of information—flights, air fares, bookings, seat assignments, and billing information—for hundreds of flights a day worldwide. American Airlines' SABRE reservation system stores the information—4.4 trillion bytes of it, which is more than 4 million million characters—on computer hard disks. If the information in the SABRE system were copied into a hypothetical paper reservation book, it would require more than 2 billion pages.

For as long as we've had paper documents or collections of documents, we have been ordering information linearly, with indexes, tables of contents, and cross-references of various kinds to provide alternate means of navigation. In most offices filing cabinets are organized by customer, vendor, or project in alphabetical order, but to speed access, often a duplicate set of correspondence is filed chronologically. Professional indexers add value to a book by building an alternative way to find information. And before library catalogs were computerized, new books were entered into the paper catalogs on several different cards so a reader could find a book by its title or any one of its authors or topics. This redundancy was to make information easier to find.

When I was young I loved my family's 1960 *World Book Encyclopedia*. Its heavy bound volumes contained just text and pictures. They showed what Edison's phonograph looked like, but didn't let me listen to its scratchy sound. The encyclopedia had photographs of a fuzzy caterpillar changing into a butterfly, but there was no video to bring the transformation to life. It also would have been nice if it had quizzed me on what I had read, or if the information had always been up-to-date. Naturally I wasn't aware of those drawbacks then. When I was eight, I began to read the first volume. I was determined to read straight through every volume. I could have absorbed more if it had been easy to read all the articles about the sixteenth century in sequence or all the articles pertaining to medicine. Instead I read about "Garter Snakes," then "Gary, Indiana," then "Gas." But I had a great time reading the encyclopedia anyway and kept at it for five years until I reached the Ps. Then I discovered the *Encyclopaedia Britannica*, with its greater sophistication and detail. I knew I would never have the patience to read all of it. Also, by then, satisfying my enthusiasm for computers was taking up most of my spare time.

Current print encyclopedias consist of nearly two dozen volumes, with millions of words of text and thousands of illustrations, and cost hundreds or thousands of dollars. That's quite an investment, especially considering how rapidly the information gets out of date. Microsoft *Encarta*, which is outselling print and other multimedia encyclopedias, comes on a single 1-ounce CD-ROM (which stands for **C**ompact **D**isc—**R**ead **O**nly **M**emory). *Encarta* includes 26,000 topics with 9 million words of text, 8 hours of sounds, 7,000 photographs and illustrations, 800 maps, 250 interactive charts and tables, and 100 animations and video clips. It costs less than $100. If you want to know how the Egyptian "ud" (a musical instrument) sounds, hear the 1936 abdication speech of Great Britain's King Edward VIII, or see an animation explaining how a machine works, the information's all there—and no paper-based encyclopedia will ever have it.

Articles in a print encyclopedia often are followed by a list of articles on related subjects. To read them, you have to find the referenced article, which may be in another volume. With a CD-ROM encyclopedia all you have to do is click on the reference and the article will appear. On the information highway, encyclopedia articles will include links to related

1995: Screen from Microsoft Encarta *electronic multimedia encyclopedia*

subjects—not just those covered in the encyclopedia, but those in other sources. There will be no limit to how much detail you will be able to explore on a subject that interests you. In fact, an encyclopedia on the highway will be more than just a specific reference work—it will be, like the library card catalog, a doorway to all knowledge.

Today, printed information is hard to locate. It's almost impossible to find all the best information—including books, news articles, and film clips—on a specific topic. It is extremely time-consuming to assemble the information you can find. For example, if you wanted to read biographies of all the recent Nobel Prize laureates, compiling them could take an entire day. Electronic documents, however, will be interactive. Request a kind of information, and the document responds. Indicate that you've changed your mind, and the document responds again. Once you get used to this sort of system, you find that being able to look at information in different ways makes that information more valuable. The flexibility invites exploration, and the exploration is rewarded with discovery.

You'll be able to get your daily news in a similar way. You'll be able to specify how long you want your newscast to last. This will be possible because you'll be able to have each of the news stories selected individually. The newscast assembled for and delivered only to you might include world news from NBC, the BBC, CNN, or the *Los Angeles Times*, with a weather report from a favorite local TV meteorologist—or from any private meteorologist who wanted to offer his or her own service. You will be able to request longer stories on the subjects that particularly interest you and just highlights on others. If, while you are watching the newscast, you want more than has been put together, you will easily be able to request more background or detail, either from another news broadcast or from file information.

Among all the types of paper documents, narrative fiction is one of the few that will not benefit from electronic organization. Almost every reference book has an index, but novels don't because there is no need to be able to look something up in a novel. Novels are linear. Likewise, we'll continue to watch most movies from start to finish. This isn't a technological judgment—it is an artistic one: Their linearity is intrinsic to the storytelling process. New forms of interactive fiction are being invented that take advantage of the electronic world, but linear novels and movies will still be popular.

The highway will make it easy to distribute digital documents cheaply, whatever their form. Millions of people and companies will be creating documents and publishing them on the network. Some documents will be aimed at paying audiences and some will be free to anyone who wants to pay attention. Digital storage is fantastically inexpensive. Hard-disk drives in personal computers will soon cost about $0.15 for a megabyte (million bytes) of information. To put this in perspective, 1 megabyte will hold about 700 pages of text, so the cost is something like $0.00021 per page—about one two-hundredth what the local copy center would charge at $0.05 a page. And because there is the option of reusing the storage space for something else, the cost is actually the cost of storage per unit time—in other words, of renting the space. If we assume just a three-year average lifetime for the hard-disk drive, the amortized price per page per year is $0.00007. And storage is getting cheaper all the time. Hard-disk prices have been dropping by about 50 percent per year for the last several years.

Text is particularly easy to store because it is very compact in digital form. The old saying that a picture is worth a thousand words is more than true in the digital world. High-quality photographic images take more space than text, and video (which you can think of as a sequence of up to thirty new images appearing every second) takes even more. Nevertheless, the cost of distribution for these kinds of data is still quite low. A feature film takes up about 4 gigabytes (4,000 megabytes) in compressed digital format, which is about $1,600 worth of hard-disk space.

Sixteen hundred dollars to store a single film doesn't sound low-cost. However, consider that the typical local video-rental store usually buys at least eight copies of a hot new movie for about $80 a copy. With these eight copies the store can supply only eight customers per day.

Once the disk and the computer that manages it are connected up to the highway, only one copy of the information will be necessary for everyone to have access. The most popular documents will have copies made on different servers to avoid delays when an unusual number of users want access. With one investment, roughly what a single shop today spends for a popular videotape title, a disk-based server will be able to serve thousands of customers simultaneously. The extra cost for each user is simply the cost of using the disk storage for a short period of time and the communications charge. And that is becoming extremely cheap. So the extra per-user cost will be nearly zero.

This doesn't mean that information will be free, but the cost of distributing it will be very small. When you buy a paper book, a good portion of your money pays for the cost of producing and distributing it, rather than for the author's work. Trees have to be cut down, ground into pulp, and turned into paper. The book must be printed and bound. Most publishers invest capital in a first printing that reflects the largest number of copies they think will sell right away, because the printing technology is efficient only if lots of books are made at once. The capital tied up in this inventory is a financial risk for the publishers: They may never sell all the copies, and even if they do, it will take a while to sell them all. Meanwhile, the publisher has to store the books and ship them to wholesalers and ultimately to retail bookstores. Those folks also invest capital in their inventory and expect a financial return from it.

By the time the consumer selects the book and the cash register rings, the profit for the author can be a pretty small piece of the pie compared to the money that goes to the physical aspect of delivering information on processed wood pulp. I like to call this the "friction" of distribution, because it holds back variety and dissipates money away from the author and to other people.

The information highway will be largely friction free, a theme I will explore further in chapter 8. This lack of friction in information distribution is incredibly important. It will empower more authors, because very little of the customer's dollar will be used to pay for distribution.

Gutenberg's invention of the printing press brought about the first real shift in distribution friction—it allowed information on any subject to be distributed quickly and relatively cheaply. The printing press created a mass medium because it offered low-friction duplication. The proliferation of books motivated the general public to read and write, but once people had the skills there were many other things that could be done with the written word. Businesses could keep track of inventory and write contracts. Lovers could exchange letters. Individuals could

keep notes and diaries. By themselves these applications were not sufficiently compelling to get large numbers of people to make the effort to
learn to read and write. Until there was a real reason to create an "installed base" of literate people, the written word wasn't really useful as a
means for storing information. Books gave literacy critical mass, so you
can almost say that the printing press taught us to read.

The printing press made it easy to make lots of copies of a document, but what about something written for a few people? New technology was required for small-scale publishing. Carbon paper was fine if
you wanted just one or two more copies. Mimeographs and other messy
machines could make dozens, but to use any of these processes you had
to have planned for them when you prepared your original document.

In the 1930s, Chester Carlson, frustrated by how difficult it was to
prepare patent applications (which involved copying drawings and text
by hand), set out to invent a better way to duplicate information in
small quantities. What he came up with was a process he called "xerog-
raphy" when he patented it in 1940. In 1959, the company he had
hooked up with—later known as Xerox—released its first successful
production-line copier. The 914 copier, by making it possible to reproduce modest numbers of documents easily and inexpensively, set off an
explosion in the kinds and amount of information distributed to small
groups. Market research had projected that Xerox would sell at most
3,000 of their first copier model. They actually placed about 200,000. A
year after the copier was introduced, 50 million copies a month were being made. By 1986, more than 200 billion copies were being made each
month, and the number has been rising ever since. Most of these copies
would never be made if the technology wasn't so cheap and easy.

The photocopier and its later cousin, the desktop laser printer—
along with PC desktop publishing software—facilitated newsletters,
memos, maps to parties, flyers, and other documents intended for
modest-sized audiences. Carlson was another who reduced the distribution friction of information. The wild success of his copier demonstrates
that amazing things happen once you reduce distribution friction.

Of course, it's easier to make copies of a document than it is to make
it worth reading. There is no intrinsic limit to the number of books that
can be published in a given year. A typical bookstore has 10,000 differ-

ent titles, and some of the new superstores might carry 100,000. Only a small fraction, under 10 percent, of all trade books published make money for their publishers, but some succeed beyond anybody's wildest expectations.

My favorite recent example is *A Brief History of Time*, by Stephen W. Hawking, a brilliant scientist who has amyotrophic lateral sclerosis (Lou Gehrig's disease), which confines him to a wheelchair and allows him to communicate only with great difficulty. What are the odds that his treatise on the origins of the universe would have been published if there were only a handful of publishers and each of them could produce only a few books a year? Suppose an editor had one spot left on his list and had to choose between publishing Hawking's book and Madonna's *Sex*? The obvious bet would be Madonna's book, because it would likely sell a million copies. It did. But Hawking's book sold 5.5 million copies and is still selling.

Every now and then this sort of sleeper best-seller surprises everyone (but the author). A book I enjoyed greatly, *The Bridges of Madison County*, was the first published novel by a business-school teacher of communications. It wasn't positioned by the publisher to be a best-seller, but nobody really knows what will appeal to the public's taste. Like most examples of central planning trying to outguess a market decision, this is fundamentally a losing proposition. There are almost always a couple of books on *The New York Times* best-seller list that have bubbled up from nowhere, because books cost so relatively little to publish—compared to other media—that publishers can afford to give them a chance.

Costs are much higher in broadcast television or movies, so it's tougher to try something risky. In the early days of TV there were only a few stations in each geographic area and most programming was targeted for the broadest possible audience.

Cable television increased the number of programming choices, although it wasn't started with that intention. It began in the late 1940s as a way of providing better television reception to outlying areas. Community antennas to feed a local cable system were erected by viewers whose broadcast reception was blocked by hills. No one then imagined that communities with perfectly good broadcast television reception would pay to have cable so they could watch a steady stream of music videos or channels that offered nothing but news or weather twenty-four hours a day.

When the number of stations carried went from three or five to twenty-four or thirty-six, the programming dynamic changed. If you were in charge of programming for the thirtieth channel, you wouldn't attract much of an audience if you just tried to imitate channels 1 through 29. Instead, cable channel programmers were forced to specialize. Like special-interest magazines and newsletters, these new channels attract viewers by appealing to strong interests held by a relatively smaller number of enthusiasts. This is in contrast to general programming, which tries to provide something for everyone. But the costs of production and the small number of channels still limit the number of television programs produced.

Although it costs far less to publish a book than to broadcast a TV show, it's still a lot compared to the cost involved in electronic publishing. To get a book into print a publisher has to agree to pay the up-front expense of manufacturing, distribution, and marketing. The information highway will create a medium with entry barriers lower than any we have ever seen. The Internet is the greatest self-publishing vehicle ever. Its bulletin boards have demonstrated some of the changes that will occur when everyone has access to low-friction distribution and individuals can post messages, images, or software of their own creation.

Bulletin boards have contributed a lot to the popularity of the Internet. To be published there all you have to do is type your thoughts and post them someplace. This means that there is a lot of garbage on the Internet, but also a few gems. A typical message is only a page or two long. A single message posted on a popular bulletin board or sent to a mailing list might reach and engage millions of people. Or it might sit there and languish with no impact whatsoever. The reason anyone is willing to risk the latter eventuality is the low distribution friction. The network bandwidth is so great and the other factors that contribute to the cost are so low that nobody thinks about the cost of sending messages. At worst you might be a bit embarrassed if your message just sits there and nobody responds to it. On the other hand, if your message is popular, a lot of people will see it, forward it as e-mail to their friends, and post their own comments on it.

It is amazingly fast and inexpensive to communicate with bulletin boards. Mail or telephone communications are fine for a one-on-one discussion, but they are also pretty expensive if you are trying to communicate with a group. It costs nearly a dollar to print and mail a letter and on average about that much for a long-distance phone call. And to make such a call you have to know the number and have coordinated a time to talk. So it takes considerable time and effort to contact even a modest-size group. On a bulletin board all you have to do is type your message in once and it's available to everyone.

Bulletin boards on the Internet cover a wide range of topics. Some postings are not serious. Somebody will send a message with something humorous in it to a mailing list or post it somewhere. If it seems funny enough, it starts being forwarded as e-mail. In late 1994 this happened with a phony press release about Microsoft buying the Catholic Church. Thousands of copies were distributed inside Microsoft on our e-mail system. I was sent more than twenty copies as various friends and colleagues inside and outside the company chose to forward them.

There are many more serious examples of the networks' being used to mobilize those who share a common concern or interest. During the recent political conflict in Russia, both sides were able to contact people throughout the world through postings on electronic bulletin boards. The networks let you contact people you have never met or heard from who happen to share an interest.

Information published by electronic posting is grouped by topic. Each bulletin board or newsgroup has a name, and anyone interested can "hang out" there. There are lists of interesting newsgroups or you can browse names that sound interesting. If you wanted to communicate about paranormal phenomena, you would go to the newsgroup alt.paranormal. If you wanted to discuss that sort of thing with others who don't believe in it, you would go to sci.skeptic. Or you could connect to copernicus.bbn.com and look in National School Network Testbed for a set of lesson plans used by kindergarten through twelfth-grade teachers. Almost any topic you can name has a group communicating about it on the network.

We have seen that Gutenberg's invention started mass publishing, but the literacy it engendered ultimately led to a great deal more person-to-person correspondence. Electronic communication developed the other way around. It started out as electronic mail, a way to communicate to small groups. Now millions of people are taking advantage of the networks' low-friction distribution to communicate on a wide scale via various forms of posting.

The Internet has enormous potential, but it's important for its continuing credibility that expectations aren't cranked too high. The total number of users of the Internet, and of commercial on-line services such as Prodigy, CompuServe, and America Online, is still a very small portion of the population. Surveys indicate that nearly 50 percent of all PC users in the United States have a modem, but fewer than about 10 percent of those users subscribe to an on-line service. And the attrition rate is very high—many subscribers drop off after less than a year.

Significant investments will be required to develop great on-line content that will delight and excite PC users and raise the number on-line from 10 percent up to 50 percent, or even the 90 percent I believe it will become. Part of the reason this sort of investment isn't happening today is that simple mechanisms for authors and publishers to charge their users or to be paid by advertisers are just being developed.

Commercial on-line services collect revenue, but they have been paying information providers royalties of only 10 percent to 30 percent of what customers pay. Although the provider probably knows the customers and market better, pricing—the way the customer is charged—and marketing are both controlled by the service. The resulting revenue stream is simply not large enough to encourage the information providers to create exciting new on-line information.

Over the next several years the evolution of on-line services will solve these problems and create an incentive for suppliers to furnish great material. There will be new billing options—monthly subscriptions, hourly rates, charges per item accessed, and advertising payments—so that more revenue flows to the information providers.

Once that happens a successful new mass medium will come into existence. This might take several years and a new generation of network technology, such as ISDN and cable modems, but one way or another it will happen. When it does, it will open tremendous opportunities for authors, editors, directors—every creator of intellectual property.

Whenever a new medium is created, the first content offered is brought over from other media. But to take best advantage of the capabilities of the electronic medium, content needs to be specially authored with it in mind. So far the vast majority of content on-line has been "dumped" from another source. Magazine or newspaper publishers are taking text already created for paper editions and simply shoving it on-line, often minus the pictures, charts, and graphics. Plain-text bulletin boards and e-mail are interesting but cannot really compete with the richer forms of information in our lives. On-line content should include lots of graphics, photos, and links to related information. As communications get faster and the commercial opportunity becomes clear, more audio and video elements will be included.

The development of CD-ROMs—multimedia versions of audio compact discs—provides some lessons that can be applied to the creation of on-line content. CD-ROM-based multimedia titles can integrate different types of information—text, graphics, photographic images, animation, music, and video—into a single document. Much of these titles' value today is in the "multi," not in the "media." They are the best approximations of what the rich documents of the future will be like.

The music and audio on CD-ROMs are clear, but rarely as good as on a music CD. You could store CD-quality sound on a CD-ROM, but the format it uses is very bulky, so if you stored too much CD-quality sound, you wouldn't have room for data, graphics, and other material.

Motion video on CD-ROMs still needs improving. If you compare the quality of video a PC can display today with the postage-stamp-size displays of just a few years ago, the progress is amazing. Longtime computer users got very excited when they first encountered video on their computers. On the other hand, the grainy, jerky image is certainly no better than a 1950s television picture. The size and quality of images will improve with faster processors and better compression, and eventually will become far better than today's television picture.

CD-ROM technology has enabled a new category of applications. Shopping catalogs, museum tours, and textbooks are being republished in this new, appealing form. Every subject is being covered. Competition and technology will bring rapid improvements in the quality of the titles. CD-ROMs will be replaced by a new high-capacity disc that will look like today's CD but will hold ten times as much data. The additional capacity of these extended CDs will allow for more than two hours of digital video on a single disc, which means they'll be capable of holding a whole movie. The picture and sound quality will be much higher than those of the best TV signal you can receive on a home set, and new generations of graphics chips will allow multimedia titles to include Hollywood-quality special effects under the interactive control of the user.

Multimedia CD-ROMs are popular today because they offer users interactivity rather than because they have imitated TV. The commercial appeal of interactivity has already been demonstrated by the popularity of CD-ROM games such as Brøderbund's *Myst* and Virgin Interactive Entertainment's *Seventh Guest*, which are whodunits, a blending of narrative fiction and a series of puzzles that allow a player to investigate a mystery, collecting clues in any order.

The success of these games has encouraged authors to begin to create interactive novels and movies in which they introduce the characters and the general outline of the plot, then the reader/player makes decisions that change the outcome of the story. No one suggests that every book or movie should allow the reader or viewer to influence its outcome. A good story that makes you just want to sit there for a few hours and enjoy it is wonderful entertainment. I don't want to choose an ending for *The Great Gatsby* or *La Dolce Vita*. F. Scott Fitzgerald and Federico Fellini have done that for me. The suspension of disbelief essential to the enjoyment of great fiction is fragile and may not hold up under the heavy-handed use of interactivity. You can't simultaneously control the plot and surrender your imagination to it. Interactive fiction is as similar to and different from the older forms as poetry is similar to and different from drama.

There will be interactive stories and games available on the network too. Such applications can share content with CD-ROMs, but at least for a while the software will have to be carefully prepared so the CD-ROMs won't be slow when used on a network. This is because, as discussed earlier, bandwidth, or the speed at which bits are transferred from the CD-ROM to the computer, is far greater than the bandwidth of the existing telephone network. Over time, the networks will meet—then exceed—the speed of the CD-ROM. And when that happens, the content being created for the two forms will be the same. But this will take a number of years, because improvements are also being made in CD-ROM technology. In the meantime the bit rate will differentiate the two forms enough so that they will remain separate technologies.

The technologies underlying the CD-ROM and on-line services have improved dramatically, but very few computer users are creating multimedia documents yet. Too much effort is still required. Millions of people have camcorders and make videos of their kids or their vacations. However, to edit video you have to be a professional with expensive equipment. This will change. Advances in PC word processors and desktop-publishing software have already made professional-quality tools for creating simple paper documents available relatively inexpensively to millions. Desktop-publishing software has progressed to the point that many magazines and newspapers are produced with the same sort of PC and software package you can buy at any local computer store and use to design an invitation to your daughter's birthday party. PC software for editing film and creating special effects will become as commonplace as desktop-publishing software. Then the difference between professionals and amateurs will be one of talent rather than access to tools.

Georges Méliès created one of the first special effects in movies when, in 1899, he turned a woman into feathers on the screen in *The Conjurer*, and moviemakers have been playing cinematic tricks ever since. Recently, special-effects technology has improved dramatically through the use of the digital manipulation of images. First a photograph is converted into binary information, which, as we have seen, software applications are able to manipulate easily. Then the digital information is altered and finally returned to photographic form, as a frame in a movie. The alterations are nearly undetectable if well done, and the results can be spectacular. Computer software gave life to the dinosaurs in *Jurassic Park*, the thundering wildebeest herd in *The Lion King*, and the crazy cartoon effects in *The Mask*. As Moore's Law increases hardware speed, and software becomes increasingly sophisticated, there is virtually no limit to what can be achieved. Hollywood will continue to push the state of the art and create amazing new effects.

It will be possible for a software program to fabricate scenes that will look as real as anything created with a camera. Audiences watching *Forrest Gump* could recognize that the scenes with Presidents Kennedy, Johnson, and Nixon were fabricated. Everyone knew Tom Hanks hadn't really been there. It was a lot harder to spot the digital processing that removed Gary Sinise's two good legs for his role as an amputee. Synthesized figures and digital editing are being used to make movie stunts safer. You'll soon be able to use a standard PC to make the software to create the effects. The ease with which PCs and photo-editing software already manipulate complex images will make it easy to counterfeit photographic documents or alter photographs undetectably. And as synthesis gets cheaper it will be used more and more; if we can bring Tyrannosaurus rex back to life, can Elvis be far behind?

Even those who don't aspire to becoming the next C. B. DeMille or Lina Wertmuller will routinely include multimedia in the documents they construct every day. Someone might start by typing, handwriting, or speaking an electronic mail message: "Lunch in the park may not be such a great idea. Look at the forecast." To make the message more informative, he could then point his cursor at an icon representing a local television weather forecast and drag it across his screen to move the icon inside his document. When his friends get the message, they will be able to look at the forecast right on their screens—a professional-looking communication.

Kids in school will be able to produce their own albums or movies and make them available to friends and family on the information highway. When I have time, I enjoy making special greeting cards and invitations. If I'm making a birthday card for my sister, for instance, to personalize it I sometimes add pictures reminding her of fun events of the past year. In the future I'll be able to include movie clips that I've customized with only a few minutes' work. It will be simple to create an interactive "album" of photographs, videos, or conversations. Businesses of all types and sizes will communicate using multimedia. Lovers will use special effects to blend some text, a video clip from an old movie, and a favorite song to create a personal valentine.

As the fidelity of visual and audio elements improves, reality in all its aspects will be more closely simulated. This "virtual reality," or VR, will allow us to "go" places and "do" things we never would be able to otherwise.

Vehicle simulators for airplanes, race cars, and spacecraft already provide a taste of virtual reality. Some of the most popular rides at Disneyland are simulated voyages. Software vehicle simulators, such as *Microsoft Flight Simulator*, are among the most popular games ever created for PCs, but they force you to use your imagination. Multimillion-dollar flight simulators at companies such as Boeing give you a much better ride. Viewed from the outside, they're boxy, stilt-legged mechanical creatures that would look at home in a *Star Wars* movie. Inside, the cockpit video displays offer sophisticated data. Flight and maintenance instruments are linked to a computer that simulates flight characteristics—including emergencies—with an accuracy pilots say is remarkable.

A couple of friends and I "flew" a 747 simulator a couple years ago. You sit down to a control panel in a cockpit identical to one in a real plane. Outside the windows, you see computer-generated color video images. When you "take off" in the simulator, you see an identifiable airport and its surroundings. The simulation of Boeing Field, for instance, might show a fuel truck on the runway and Mount Rainier in the distance. You hear the rush of air around wings that aren't there, the clunk of nonexistent landing gear retracting. Six hydraulic systems under the simulator tilt and shake the cockpit. It's pretty convincing.

The main purpose of these simulators is to give pilots a chance to gain experience in handling emergencies. When I was using the simulator my friends decided to give me a surprise by having a small plane fly by. While I sat in the pilot's seat the all-too-real-looking image of a Cessna flashed into view. I wasn't prepared for the "emergency," and I crashed into it.

A number of companies, from entertainment giants to small start-ups, are planning to put smaller-scale simulator rides into shopping malls and urban sites. As the price of technology comes down, entertainment simulators may become as common as movie theaters are today. And it won't be too many years until you'll be able to have a high-quality simulation in your own living room.

Want to explore the surface of Mars? It's a lot safer to do it via VR. How about visiting somewhere humans never will be able to go? A cardiologist might be able to swim through the heart of a patient to examine it in a way she never would have been able to with conventional instrumentation. A surgeon could practice a tricky operation many times, including simulated catastrophes, before she ever touches a scalpel to a real patient. Or you could use VR to wander through a fantasy of your own design.

In order to work, VR needs two different sets of technology—software that creates the scene and makes it respond to new information, and devices that allow the computer to transmit the information to our senses. The software will have to figure out how to describe the look, sound, and feel of the artificial world down to the smallest detail. That might sound overwhelmingly difficult, but actually it's the easy part. We could write the software for VR today, but we need a lot more computer power to make it truly believable. At the pace technology is moving, though, that power will be available soon. The really hard part about VR is getting the information to convince the user's senses.

Hearing is the easiest sense to fool; all you have to do is wear headphones. In real life, your two ears hear slightly different things because of their location on your head and the directions they point. Subconsciously you use those differences to tell where a sound is coming from. Software can re-create this by calculating for a given sound what each ear would be hearing. This works amazingly well. You can put on a set of headphones connected to a computer and hear a whisper in your left ear or footsteps walking up behind you.

Your eyes are harder to fool than your ears, but vision is still pretty straightforward to simulate. VR equipment almost always includes a special set of goggles with lenses that focus each eye on its own small computer display. A head-tracking sensor allows the computer to figure out which direction your head is facing, so the computer can synthesize what you would be seeing. Turn your head to the right, and the scene portrayed by the goggles is farther to the right. Lift your face, and the goggles show the ceiling or sky. Today's VR goggles are too heavy, too expensive, and don't have enough resolution. The computer systems that drive them are still a bit too slow. If you turn your head quickly, the scene lags somewhat behind. This is very disorienting and after a short period of time causes most people to get headaches. The good news is that size, speed, weight, and cost are precisely the kinds of things that technology following Moore's Law will correct soon.

Other senses are much more difficult to fool, because there are no good ways of connecting a computer to your nose or tongue, or to the surface of your skin. In the case of touch, the prevailing idea is that a full bodysuit could be made lined with tiny sensor and force feedback devices that would be in contact with the whole surface of your skin. I don't think bodysuits will be common, but they'll be feasible.

There are between 72 and 120 tiny points of color (called pixels) per inch on a typical computer monitor, for a total of between 300,000 and 1 million. A full bodysuit would presumably be lined with little touch sensor points—each of which could poke one specific tiny spot. Let's call these little touch elements "tactels."

If the suit had enough of these tactels, and if they were controlled finely enough, any touch sensation could be duplicated. If a large number of tactels poked all together at precisely the same depth, the resulting "surface" would feel smooth, as if a piece of polished metal were against your skin. If they pushed with a variety of randomly distributed depths, it would feel like a rough texture.

Between 1 million and 10 million tactels—depending on how many different levels of depth a tactel had to convey—would be needed for a VR bodysuit. Studies of the human skin show that a full bodysuit would have to have about 100 tactels per inch—a few more on the fingertips, lips, and a couple of other sensitive spots. Most skin actually has poor touch resolution. I'd guess that 256 tactels would be enough for the highest-quality simulation. That's the same number of colors most computer displays use for each pixel.

The total amount of information a computer would have to calculate to pipe senses into the tactel suit is somewhere between one and ten times the amount required for the video display on a current PC. This really isn't a lot of computer power. I'm confident that as soon as someone makes the first tactel suit, PCs of that era will have no problem driving them.

Sound like science fiction? The best descriptions of VR actually come from so-called cyberpunk science fiction like that written by William Gibson. Rather than putting on a bodysuit, some of his characters "jack in" by plugging a computer cable directly into their central nervous systems. It will take scientists a while to figure out how this can be done, and when they do, it will be long after the highway is established. Some people are horrified by the notion, whereas others are intrigued. It will probably first be used to help people with physical disabilities.

Inevitably, there has been more speculation (and wishful thinking) about virtual sex than about any other use for VR. Sexually explicit content is as old as information itself. It never takes long to figure out how to apply any new technology to the oldest desire. The Babylonians left erotic poems in cuneiform on clay tablets, and pornography was one of the first things the printing press was used for. When VCRs became common home appliances, they provoked a surge in the sales and rentals of X-rated videos, and today pornographic CD-ROMs are popular. On-line bulletin boards such as the Internet and the French Minitel system have lots of subscribers for their sexually oriented services. If historical patterns are a guide, a big early market for advanced virtual-reality documents will be virtual sex. But again, historically, as each of these markets grew, explicit material became a smaller and smaller factor.

Imagination will be a key element for all new applications. It isn't enough just to re-create the real world. Great movies are a lot more than just graphic depictions on film of real events. It took a decade or so for such innovators as D. W. Griffith and Sergei Eisenstein to take the Vitascope and the Lumières' Cinématographe and figure out that motion pictures could do more than record real life or even a play. Moving film was a new and dynamic art form and the way it could engage an audience was very different from the way the theater could. The pioneers saw this and invented movies as we know them today.

Will the next decade bring us the Griffiths and Eisensteins of multimedia? There is every reason to think they are already tinkering with

------------------------->

the existing technology to see what it can do and what they can do with it.

I expect multimedia experimentation will continue into the decade after that, and the one after that, and so on indefinitely. At first, the multimedia components appearing in documents on the information highway will be a synthesis of current media—a clever way to enrich communication. But over time we will start to create new forms and formats that will go significantly beyond what we know now. The exponential expansion of computing power will keep changing the tools and opening new possibilities that will seem as remote and farfetched then as some of the things I've speculated on here might seem today. Talent and creativity have always shaped advances in unpredictable ways.

How many have the talent to become a Steven Spielberg, a Jane Austen, or an Albert Einstein? We know there was at least one of each, and maybe one is all we're allotted. I cannot help but believe, though, that there are many talented people whose aspirations and potential have been thwarted by economics and their lack of tools. New technology will offer people a new means with which to express themselves. The information highway will open undreamed-of artistic and scientific opportunities to a new generation of geniuses.

7

IMPLICATIONS
FOR BUSINESS

As documents become more flexible, richer in multimedia content, and less tethered to paper, the ways in which people collaborate and communicate will become richer and less tied to location. Almost every sphere of activity—business, education, and leisure—will be affected. The information highway will revolutionize communications even more than it will revolutionize computing. This is already starting in the workplace.

Because the most efficient businesses have an advantage over their competitors, companies have an incentive to embrace technologies that make them more productive. Electronic documents and networks offer businesses opportunities to improve their information management, service, and internal and external collaboration. The personal computer has already had a huge effect on business. But its greatest impact won't be felt until the PCs inside and outside a company are intimately interconnected.

Over the next decade, businesses worldwide will be transformed. Software will become friendlier, and companies will base the nervous systems of their organizations on networks that reach every employee and beyond, into the world of suppliers, consultants, and customers. The result will be companies that are more effective and, often, smaller. In the longer run, as the information highway makes physical proximity to urban services less important, many businesses will decentralize and disperse their activities, and cities, like companies, may be downsized.

In just the next five years the communications bandwidth available in urban business areas will grow by a factor of 100, as network providers compete to connect concentrations of high-use customers. Businesses will be the first users of these high-speed networks. Every new computing technology was adopted first by businesses because the financial benefits of advanced information systems can be readily demonstrated.

Managers of both small and large businesses are going to be dazzled by the capabilities information technology has to offer. Before they invest they should remember that a computer is just a tool to help in solving identified problems. It isn't, as people sometimes seem to expect, a magical universal panacea. If I heard a business owner say, "I'm losing money, I'd better get a computer," I'd tell him to rethink his strategy before he invests. Technology will, at best, probably delay the need for more fundamental changes. The first rule of any technology used in a business is that automation applied to an efficient operation will magnify the efficiency. The second is that automation applied to an inefficient operation will magnify the inefficiency.

Instead of rushing out to buy the latest and greatest equipment for every employee, managers in a company of any size should first step back and think about how they would like their business to work. What are its essential processes, and its key databases? Ideally, how should information move?

For example, when a customer calls, does all the information about your dealings—the status of the account, any complaints, a history of who in your organization has worked with the customer—appear immediately on a screen? The technology for doing this is quite straightforward, and, increasingly, customers expect the level of service it affords. If your systems can't provide product-availability information or quote a price immediately, you risk losing out to a competitor who is taking better advantage of technology. For example, some car companies are centralizing service information so that any dealer can easily check a vehicle's entire service history and watch for recurring problems.

A company should also examine all of its internal processes, such as employee reviews, business planning, sales analysis, and product development, and determine how networks and other electronic information tools can make these operations more effective.

There has been quite a shift in the way we think about and use computers as business tools. When I was a kid, my image of computers was that they were very big and powerful. Banks had a bunch. Computers let big airlines keep track of reservations. They were the tools of large organizations and were part of the edge big businesses had over the small guys who used pencils and typewriters.

But today the personal computer, as the name suggests, is a tool for the individual, even in a large company. We think of and use a personal computer very personally to help us get our job done.

Those doing solo work can write, create newsletters, and explore new ideas better with a personal computer. A Luddite might ask, "If Churchill had used a word processor, would his writing have been better? Would Cicero have given better speeches in the Roman Senate?" Such critics have a notion that because great things were achieved without modern tools, it is presumptuous to suggest that better tools might elevate human potential. We can only speculate on how an artist's output might be helped, but it is quite clear that personal computers improve business processes, efficiency, and accuracy. Consider the average reporter. There have been great journalists through history, but today it's much easier to check facts, transmit a story from the field, and stay in touch electronically with news sources, editors, and even readers. Plus, the inclusion of high-quality diagrams and pictures has become easier. Just look at the presentation of science topics. Twenty or thirty years ago it was unusual to find top-quality scientific illustrations anywhere except in science books or a glossy specialized magazine such as *Scientific American*. Today some newspapers present science stories well, in part because they use personal-computer software to produce detailed drawings and illustrations rapidly.

Businesses of all sizes have received different benefits from personal computers. Small businesses arguably have been the greatest beneficiaries, because low-cost hardware and software have permitted tiny outfits to compete better with large multinational corporations. Big organizations tend to be specialized: one department writes brochures, another deals with accounting, yet another handles customer service, and so forth. When you call a large company to talk about your account, you expect a specialist to get you an answer pretty quickly.

Expectations for small-business operators used to be different, because they couldn't hire specialists. When an individual opens a business or a shop, she is the one creating brochures, doing the financial work, and dealing with customers. It's kind of amazing how many different tasks a small-business owner has to master. Someone running a small business can buy one PC and a few software packages, and she will have electronic support for all the different functions she is performing. The result is that a small business can compete more effectively with the big boys.

For a large company, the biggest benefit of personal computers comes from improving the sharing of information. PCs do away with the huge overhead large businesses incur staying coordinated through meetings, policies, and internal processes. Electronic mail has done more for big companies than for small companies.

One of the first ways Microsoft began using information tools internally was by phasing out printed computer reports. In many companies, when you go into a top executive's office you see books of bound computer printouts with monthly financial numbers, dutifully filed away on a shelf. At Microsoft, those numbers are made available only on a computer screen. When someone wants more detail, he or she can examine it by time period, locale, or almost any other way. When we first put the financial reporting system on-line, people started looking at the numbers in new ways. For example, they began analyzing why our market share in one geographic area was different from our share somewhere else. As we all started working with the information, we discovered errors. Our data-processing group apologized. "We're very sorry about these mistakes," they said, "but we've been compiling and distributing these numbers once a month for five years and these same problems were there all along and no one mentioned them." People hadn't really been using the print information enough to discover the mistakes.

The flexibility that comes from having the information available electronically is hard to convey to a nonuser. I rarely look at our financial reports on paper anymore, because I prefer to view them electronically.

When the first electronic spreadsheets appeared in 1978, they were a vast improvement over paper and pencil. What they made possible was putting formulas behind each element in a table of data. These formulas could refer to other elements of the table. Any change in one value would immediately affect the other cells, so projections such as sales, growth, or changes in interest rates could be played with to examine "what if" scenarios, and the impact of every change would be instantly apparent.

Some current spreadsheets let you view tables of data in different ways. Simple commands permit the filtering and sorting of the data. The spreadsheet application I know best, Microsoft Excel, includes a feature called a pivot table that allows you to look at summarized information in nearly countless ways. It's number-crunching made easy. The summarizing criterion can be changed with the click of a mouse on a selector or by using the mouse to drag a column header from one side of the table to another. It's simple to change the information from a high-level summary report to an analysis of any data category or to an examination of the details one by one.

Monthly a pivot table is distributed electronically to all Microsoft managers containing sales data by office, product, and sales channel for current and previous fiscal years. Each manager can quickly construct a personal view of the data for his or her requirements. Sales managers might compare sales in their region to budget or the prior year. Product managers can look at their products' sales by country and sales channel. There are thousands of possibilities just a click and a drag away.

Increases in computer speed will soon allow PCs to display very high quality three-dimensional graphics. These will permit us to show data in a more effective way than today's two-dimensional presentations. Other advances will make it easy to explore databases by posing questions orally. An example might be, "What products are selling best?"

These innovations will first show up in the mainstream in the high-volume office-productivity packages: word processors, spreadsheets, presentation packages, databases, and electronic mail. Some proponents

	A	B	C	D	E	F
1	Year	1995				
2	Salesperson	(All)				
3						
4	Sum of Sales	Region				
5	Product	East	North	South	West	Grand Total
6	Gasoline	1,722	8,019	53,160	71,935	134,836
7	Heating Oil	27,498	11,098	4,891	36,670	80,157
8	Lubricants	2,294	1,531	993	3,527	8,345
9	Grand Total	31,514	20,648	59,044	112,132	223,338

Pivot table showing sales data for 1995 summarized by product type and territory

	A	B	C	D	E	F
1	Year	1995				
2	Salesperson	Adams				
3						
4	Sum of Sales	Region				
5	Product	East	North	South	West	Grand Total
6	Gasoline	1,722	8,019	2,420	15,154	27,315
7	Heating Oil	6,955	11,098	2,516	9,886	30,455
8	Lubricants	-	1,531	436	1,512	3,479
9	Grand Total	8,677	20,648	5,372	26,552	61,249

The same pivot table after one click on the salesperson selector, showing sales data for 1995 for one salesperson by product type and territory

	A	B	C	E	F	H	I	K
1								
2								
3	Region	(All)						
4								
5	Sum of Sales	Product	Year					
6		Gasoline		Heating Oil		Lubricants		Grand Total
7	Salesperson	1994	1995	1994	1995	1994	1995	
8	Adams	40,251	27,315	28,804	30,455	3,435	3,479	133,739
9	Barnes	31,135	56,781	45,045	26,784	622	2,015	162,382
10	Cooper	40,936	50,740	28,770	22,918	1,475	2,851	147,690

The same pivot table after the "product" and "year" labels were dragged to the row header and the "salesperson" label was dragged to the column header, showing sales data for 1994 and 1995 summarized by salesperson and product type claim these tools are so capable already that there will never be a need for newer versions. But there were those who thought that about software five and ten years ago. Over the next few years, as speech recognition, social interfaces, and connections to the information highway are incorporated into core applications, I think individuals and companies will find the productivity enhancements these improved applications will bring extremely attractive.

The greatest improvement in productivity, and the greatest change in work habits, will be brought about because of networking. The original use for the PC was to make it easier to create documents that were printed on paper and shared by passing around the printed output. The first PC networks allowed people to share printers and store files on central servers. Most of these early networks connected fewer than twenty computers together. As networks get larger, they are being connected to one another and to the Internet so that every user is able to communicate with everyone else. Today, communications are mostly short text files, but eventually they will include the full richness of the documents discussed in chapter 6. Increasingly, companies that want to provide the benefits of document-sharing to every employee have installed extensive networks, often at substantial cost. For example, Microsoft's subsidiary in Greece pays more for its connection to our worldwide network than it pays in salaries.

Now electronic mail is becoming the primary tool for exchanging messages. Print conventions have also evolved. If you want a sentence to end with a chuckle to show that its meaning is intended to be humorous, you might add a colon, a dash, and a parenthesis. This composite symbol, :-), if viewed sideways, makes a smiling face. For instance, you might write, "I'm not sure that's a great idea :-)"—the smiley face showing that your words are good-natured. Using the opposite parenthesis turns the smiling face into a frowning face, :-(, an expression of disappointment. These "emoticons," which are half cousins of the exclamation point, probably won't survive the transition of e-mail into a medium that permits audio and video.

Conventionally, businesses share information internally by exchanging paperwork, placing telephone calls, and/or gathering around a conference table or white board. Plenty of time and plenty of expensive face-to-face meetings and presentations are required to reach good decisions this way. The potential for inefficiency is enormous. Companies that continue to rely on these methods exclusively risk losing out to competitors who reach decisions faster while devoting fewer resources, and probably fewer layers of management, to the process.

At Microsoft, because we're in the technology business, we began using electronic communication early. We installed our first e-mail system in the early 1980s. Even when we had only a dozen employees, it made a difference. It quickly became the principal method of internal communication. E-mail was used in place of paper memos, technology discussions, trip reports, and phone messages. It contributed a lot to the efficiency of our little company. Today, with thousands of employees, it is essential.

E-mail is easy to use. To write and send an electronic message, I click on a large button labeled "Compose." This brings to the screen a simple form. First, I type the name of the person or people to whom I am addressing the message or choose the name from an electronic address book. I can even indicate that I want the message sent to a group of recipients. For example, because I frequently send messages to key employees working on the Microsoft Office project, in my address list I have an addressee called "Office." If I choose that entry, the message goes to everyone concerned. When the message is transmitted, my name will appear automatically in the "From" space. Then I type a short heading for the message, so the recipients will have an idea of what it's about. Then I type the message.

An electronic message is often just a sentence or two with no pleasantries. I might send an electronic message to three or four people, saying nothing more than "Let's cancel the 11:00 A.M. Monday meeting and use the time individually to prepare for Tuesday's presentation. Objections?" A reply to my message, in its entirety, might be as succinct as "Fine."

If this exchange seems terse, keep in mind that the average Microsoft employee receives dozens of electronic messages a day. An e-mail message is like a statement or a question at a meeting—one thought or inquiry in an ongoing communication. Microsoft provides e-mail for business purposes, but, like the office telephone, it serves many other purposes, social and personal. For example, hikers can reach all the members of the Microsoft Hiking Club to try to find a ride to the mountain. And certainly a few romances around Microsoft have benefited from e-mail. When my wife, Melinda, and I were first going out, we took advantage of it. For some reason people are less shy about sending e-mail than communicating on the phone or in person. This can be a benefit or a problem, depending on the situation.

I spend several hours a day reading and answering e-mail to and from employees, customers, and partners around the world. Anyone in the company can send me e-mail, and because I am the only person who reads it, no one has to worry about protocol in a message to me.

I probably wouldn't have to spend so long if my e-mail address weren't semipublic. There is actually a book called *E-Mail Addresses of the Rich & Famous*, which includes my e-mail address as well as ones for Rush Limbaugh and Senator Ted Kennedy. When John Seabrook was writing an article about me for *The New Yorker* magazine, he conducted his interview primarily on e-mail. It was a very effective way to have a dialogue, and I enjoyed the piece when it appeared, but it mentioned my e-mail address. The result has been an avalanche of mail ranging from students asking me, in effect, to do their homework assignments, to people asking for money, to mail from a group interested in whales who for some reason added my e-mail name to their list. My address is also a target for both rude and friendly messages from strangers, and provocative ones from the press. ("If you don't answer this by tomorrow I will publish a story about you and that topless waitress!").

We have special e-mail addresses at Microsoft for job applications, product feedback, and other legitimate communications. But a lot of that mail still comes to me and I have to reroute it. There are also three e-mail equivalents of chain letters that keep making the rounds. One threatens general bad luck if it isn't forwarded. Another specifically says the punishment will be that your sex life will suffer. A third, which has been going around for six years, contains a cookie recipe and a story about a company's having overcharged a woman for the recipe, and so she wants you to distribute it for free. In the various versions different companies are named. Apparently it is the idea of getting back at a corporation, any corporation, that has made that one such a perennial favorite. This is all mixed in with mail that really should come to me, often about important issues. Fortunately, e-mail software is improving all the time and it now includes a feature that lets me prioritize mail from senders I have designated.

When I travel, I connect my portable computer back into Microsoft's electronic mail system every night to retrieve new messages and send off the ones I've written over the course of the day to people in the company. Most recipients will not even be aware that I am out of the office. When I'm connected to our corporate network from a remote site, I can also click on a single icon to see how sales are doing, to check the status of projects, or to access any other management databases. It is reassuring to check my electronic in-box when I'm thousands of miles and a dozen time zones away, because bad news almost always comes through on e-mail. So if nothing bad is waiting there, I don't need to worry.

We now use e-mail in all sorts of ways we hadn't anticipated. For example, at the beginning of the annual Microsoft Giving Campaign, which raises money for charity, employees receive an e-mail message encouraging them to participate. The e-mail message contains an electronic pledge-card program. When the icon in the message is clicked, the pledge card appears on the employee's screen and he or she can pledge a cash gift or sign up for a payroll deduction. If the latter option is chosen, the information is automatically entered into Microsoft's payroll database. From the electronic form employees can direct their gift to their local United Way or to another nonprofit organization. If they want to, they can choose to have their donation go to one or more of the charities the United Way supports, and can even access a server to obtain information about those organizations or about volunteering in their community. From start to finish it's completely electronic. As the leader of the company, I can analyze summary information day by day to find out if we are getting good participation or if we need to have a few more rallies to get out the message about how important we think the giving campaign is.

Today, besides company-operated, text-based e-mail systems, the kind Microsoft operates for its own use, there are commercial services such as MCI Mail and B.T. Gold (operated by British Telecom). There are also offerings from all of the commercial on-line systems such as CompuServe, Prodigy, and the Microsoft Network. These perform some of the same functions that telegrams and, later, telex systems once did. Users connected to these e-mail systems can send a message to virtually anyone who has a standard Internet e-mail address. Both private and commercial e-mail systems include "gateways" that transfer messages sent by a user of one mail system to a recipient on another. You can get a message to almost anyone who has a PC and a modem, although for certain communications privacy is a problem because transmissions across the Internet are not very secure. Some commercial services, such as MCI, will also deliver a message by fax, telex, or traditional mail if the recipient doesn't have an electronic mailbox.

Future advances in electronic mail will streamline lots of activities we may not even realize are inefficient. For example, think about how you pay bills. More often than not, a company prints out a bill on a piece of paper and puts it in an envelope that is physically carried to your house. You open the bill, check your records to see if the amount and details seem appropriate, write a check, and then try to time when you mail it back so that it arrives shortly before the due date. We're so used to this process we don't even think about how wasteful it is. Let's say you disagree with a bill. You call the company up, wait on hold, and try to get through to the right person—who may not really be the right person at all. In which case you have to wait for someone else to call you back.

Very soon you'll check your PC, wallet, or television set—the information appliance of your choice—for e-mail, including bills. When a bill comes in, the device will show your payment history. If you want to inquire about the bill, you'll do it asynchronously—at your convenience—by sending e-mail: "Hey how come this charge is so high?"

Tens of thousands of businesses in the United States already exchange information via an electronic system called Electronic Document Interchange, or EDI. It allows companies that have contractual relationships to execute specific kinds of transactions automatically. Dealings are highly structured—reordering products or checking the status of a shipment—which makes conventional EDI unsuitable for ad hoc communications, although many companies are working to combine the benefits of EDI and e-mail into a single system.

The asynchronicity of e-mail and EDI is one of their advantages, but there is still a place for synchronous communications. Sometimes you want to call someone up, talk directly, and get an immediate response rather than leaving a message.

Within a few years there will be hybrid communications systems that combine elements of synchronous and asynchronous communications. These systems will use DSVD (and later ISDN) telephone connections to permit the simultaneous transfer of voice and data, even before the full information highway is in place.

It will work this way: When companies post information about their products on the Internet, part of that information will include instructions for how a customer can connect synchronously with a sales representative who will be able to answer questions through a voice-data connection. For example, if you're shopping for boots on Eddie Bauer's home page (an electronic catalog) and you want to know if the boots you like are appropriate for use in Florida's Everglades or on a glacier, you'll be able to click a button to get a representative to come on the line and talk to you. The representative will see immediately that you are looking at the boots and will have whatever other information about yourself you have decided to make available, not just your clothing and shoe sizes, style and color preferences, but your athletic interests, your past purchases from other companies, and even your price range. Some people will choose not to make any information about themselves available. Eddie Bauer's computer may route your inquiry to the same person you spoke to last time, or it may route you to someone who has expertise in the product displayed on your screen, in this case, boots. Without preamble, you will be able to ask, "Do these boots work well in swamps like the Everglades?" or whatever your question is. The representative doesn't have to be in an office. He can be anywhere as long as he has access to a PC and has indicated he is available. If he speaks the right language and has the right expertise, he can help out.

Or if you decided to change your will, you'd phone your lawyer, and she might say, "Let's take a quick look at that." She would then call your will up on her PC, and it would appear on your screen as well as hers—courtesy of DSVD, ISDN, or similar technology. As she scrolls through the document, the two of you would discuss your needs. Then, if she was particularly adept, you might even watch her do the editing. However, if you wanted a hand in editing the document instead of just watching it run on your lawyer's computer, you could join in and work together. You would be able not only to talk to each other but also to see the same image on your computer screens.

You won't need to have the same software. The application just has to run on one end of the connection, the lawyer's end in this case. On your end, you would need only an appropriate modem and DSVD software.

Another important use of voice/data connections will be to improve product support. Microsoft has thousands of employees whose job is to answer product-support questions about Microsoft software. In fact, we have as many product-support people answering questions about our software as we have engineers building it. This is wonderful, because we log all that feedback and use it to improve our products. We get lots of these questions by e-mail, but most of our customers still telephone us. These phone conversations are inefficient. A customer calls in to say his particular computer is configured in a specific way and is giving a certain error message. The product-support specialist listens to this description, and then suggests something, which it takes the caller a few minutes to do. Then the conversation resumes. The average call takes fifteen minutes, and some take an hour. But once everyone is using DSVD, the product-support specialist will be able to see what's on the caller's computer screen (with the caller's explicit permission, of course) and examine the caller's computer directly rather than having to rely on the caller to explain what he is seeing. This will have to be done carefully, to ensure that no one's privacy is invaded. The process will reduce the length of the average call by 30 or 40 percent, which will make customers a lot happier and will cut costs and product prices.

The picture transmitted during a DSVD (or ISDN) telephone connection won't necessarily have to be of a document. One or both people participating will also be able to transmit still images of themselves. If you are calling in to buy a product, you might expect the company's service representative to be there, smiling. But you, as the customer, might choose to transmit only your voice. You can select images of yourself dressed appropriately for the occasion, so it won't matter what you are actually wearing. Or you might decide to have available several pictures of yourself, one smiling, one laughing, one contemplative, and maybe one that is angry. During the course of the conversation, you could change the image to suit your mood or the point you were making.

Electronic mail and shared screens will eliminate the need for many meetings. Presentation meetings, called primarily so participants can listen and learn, can be replaced with e-mail messages with spreadsheets and other exhibits enclosed as attachments. When face-to-face meetings do take place, they will be more efficient because participants will already have exchanged background information by e-mail.

It will also be easier to schedule meetings because software will handle it. For example, if you want to sit down face-to-face with your lawyer, your scheduling program and hers will be able to communicate across the network—even the phone network—and pick a date and time that you both have free. Then the appointment would just show up on your respective electronic calendars.

This will also be an efficient way to schedule restaurant or theater reservations, but it raises an interesting issue. Let's say a restaurant isn't getting much business, or tickets to a show aren't selling well, or your lawyer doesn't want you to know that you're her only client. Such companies and individuals might instruct their scheduling programs just to respond to meeting requests. Your scheduling program wouldn't be able to ask your lawyer's program to list all the times she is free. However, if it asked for a specific two-hour block, the response would be: "Yes, we can schedule you for Tuesday at eleven o'clock."

Clients will expect their lawyers, dentists, accountants, and other professionals to be able to schedule appointments and exchange documents electronically. You might have a quick follow-up question for your doctor—for instance, whether a generic version of a drug is acceptable. It is hard to interrupt a doctor, but you'll expect to be able to trade e-mail with all of the professionals you work with. We're going to see competition based on how effectively one professional group has adopted these communications tools and how much more accessible and efficient this makes them. I'm sure we'll then begin seeing ads in which a firm will tout how much more advanced it has become in the use of PC communications.

When the information highway is available, people won't be limited to audio and still images, because the highway will also transmit high-quality video. The meetings they schedule will more and more often be conducted electronically, using shared-screen videoconferencing. Each electronic participant, wherever he or she is, will look at a different physical screen: a video white board, a television set, or a PC, but each screen will show much the same image. Part of the screen might show someone's face, while another part might display a document. If anyone modifies the document, the change will appear almost immediately on all the screens. Geographically distant collaborators will be able to work together in rich ways. This is synchronous or real-time sharing, which means that the computer screens will keep up with the people using them.

If a group were to meet electronically to collaborate on a press release, each member would be able to use his or her PC or notebook computer to move paragraphs around and drop in a photograph or a video. The rest of the group would be able to look at the result on their individual screens and see each contributor's work as it is actually happening.

We're already accustomed to watching video meetings. Anyone who tunes in to television news shows, such as *Nightline,* which feature long-distance debates, is seeing a videoconference. The host and guests may be separated by continents, yet they engage in give-and-take as if they were in the same room, and to viewers it almost appears that they are.

Today, in order to videoconference, it is necessary to go to a specially equipped facility with special phone lines. Microsoft has at least one dedicated videoconference room in each of its sales offices around the world. They're used quite a bit, but the setting is fairly formal. These facilities have saved us lots of traveling. Employees in other offices "sit in" on staff meetings, and customers and vendors have "visited" us without traveling to our headquarters outside Seattle. Such meetings will become very popular because they save time and money and are often more productive than audio-only phone conferences or even face-to-face meetings, because people seem to be more attentive if they know they are on-camera.

I've noticed that it does take some getting used to, though. If one person is on a videoconference screen, he or she tends to get much more attention than others in the meeting. I first noticed this when a bunch of us in Seattle were videoconferencing with Steve Ballmer, who was in Europe. It was as if we were all glued to The Steve Ballmer Show. If Steve took off his shoes, we'd all look at each other's reactions. When the meeting was over I could have told you all about Steve's new haircut but I might not have been able to name the other people who'd been in the room with me. I think this distortion will go away as videoconferences become commonplace.

It's currently fairly expensive to set up a videoconference room—it costs at least $40,000. However, desktop systems that attach to PCs are coming, and they will reduce the cost—and the formality— dramatically. Our facilities are generally connected with ISDN lines operating at 384,000 bits per second, which provide reasonable picture and sound quality for about $20 to $35 an hour for connections within the United States and about $250 to $300 an hour for an international connection.

The cost of videoconferencing, like that of almost every other computer-driven service, is going to drop as technology and communications costs do. Small video devices using cameras attached to personal computers or television sets will allow us to meet readily across the information highway with much higher quality pictures and sound for lower prices. As ISDN connected to PCs becomes popular, videoconferences will be as standard a business procedure as using a copier to duplicate a document for distribution is now.

Some people worry that, by eliminating the subtlety of human dynamics in a meeting, videoconferences and shared screens will give corporate gatherings all the spontaneity of a congressional photo opportunity. How will people whisper, roll their eyes at a tedious speaker, or pass notes? Actually, clandestine communication will be simpler at a video meeting because the network will facilitate individual communications on the side. Meetings have always had unwritten rules, but when the network is mediating videoconferences, some rules will have to become explicit. Will people be able to signal, publicly or privately, individually or collectively, that they are bored? To what degree should a participant be allowed to block his or her video or audio from others? Should private side conversations, one PC to another, be permitted? Over time, as we use these facilities, new rules of meeting etiquette will emerge.

Home videoconferences will naturally be somewhat different. If the conference has only two participants, it will amount to a video phone call. That will be great for saying hello to your kids when you're out of town or showing your veterinarian the way your dog or cat limps. But when you're at home, chances are you'll keep cameras off during most calls, especially with strangers. You may choose to transmit a canned photograph of yourself, your family, or something else you believe expresses your individuality yet protects your visual privacy. It will be something like choosing a message for your answering machine. Live video could be switched on for a friend or when business required it.

All of the synchronous and asynchronous images I have discussed up to this point—photographs, videos, or documents—have been pictures of real things. As computers become more powerful, it will be possible for a standard PC to fabricate realistic synthetic images. Your phone or computer will be able to generate a lifelike digital image of your face, showing you listening or even talking. You really will be talking—it's just that you've taken the call at home and are dripping wet from the shower. As you talk, your phone will synthesize an image of you in your most businesslike suit. Your facial expressions will match your words (remember, small computers are going to get very powerful). Just as easily, your phone will be able to transmit an image of your words issuing from the mouth of someone else, or from an idealized version of you. If you are talking to someone you've never met, and you don't want to show a mole or a flabby chin, your caller won't be able to tell if you really look so much like Cary Grant (or Meg Ryan) or whether you're getting a little help from your computer.

All of these electronic innovations—e-mail, shared screens, videoconferencing, and video phone calls—are ways of overcoming physical separation. By the time they become commonplace, they will have changed not just the way we work together but also distinctions now made between the workplace and everywhere else.

In 1994 in the United States there were more than 7 million "telecommuters" who didn't travel daily to offices but instead "commuted" via fax machines, telephones, and e-mail. Some writers, engineers, attorneys, and others whose jobs are relatively autonomous already stay at home for a portion of their work hours. Salespersons are judged on results; so as long as a professional salesperson is productive, it doesn't much matter whether he or she is working in the office, at home, or on the road somewhere. Many people who telecommute find it liberating and convenient, but some find it claustrophobic to be at home all the time. Others discover they don't have the self-discipline to make it effective. In the years ahead, millions of additional people will telecommute at least part-time, using the information highway.

Employees who do most of their work on the telephone are strong candidates for telecommuting because calls can be routed to them. Telemarketers, customer-service representatives, reservation agents, and product-support specialists will have access to as much information on a screen at home as they would on a screen at an office. A decade from now, advertisements for many jobs will list how many hours a week of work are expected and how many of those hours, if any, are "inside" hours at a designated location such as an office. Some jobs will require that the employee already have a PC so he can work at home. Customer-service organizations will be able to use part-time labor very easily.

When employees and supervisors are physically apart, management will have to adapt, and each individual will have to learn to be a productive employee on his or her own. New feedback mechanisms will have to evolve too, so that both employer and employee can determine the quality of work being done.

An employee in an office is assumed to be working the whole time, but the same employee working at home might be credited (perhaps at a different rate) only for the time he or she is actually performing work. If the baby starts crying, Dad or Mom would click "Not Available," and take care of the child with unpaid minutes away from the job. When the employee was ready once again to focus on the job, he or she would signal availability, and the network would start delivering work that needed attention. Part-time work and job sharing will take on new meanings.

The number of offices a company needs might be reduced. A single office or cubicle could serve several people whose inside hours were staggered or irregular. Already, the major accounting firms Arthur Andersen and Ernst & Young are among the companies that have replaced large numbers of expensive private offices with a smaller number of generic offices, which can be reserved by accountants who are in from the field. Tomorrow, a shared office's computers, phones, and digital white boards could be configured for that day's occupant. For part of a day an office's white-board walls would display one employee's calendar, family photos, and favorite cartoons, and later on the same whiteboard walls would feature the personal photos or artwork of a different employee. Wherever a worker logged on, his or her familiar office surroundings could follow, courtesy of digital white boards and the information highway.

Information technology will affect much more than the physical location and supervision of employees. The very nature of almost every business organization will have to be reexamined. This should include its structure and the balance between inside, full-time staff and outside consultants and firms.

The corporate reengineering movement starts with the premise that there are better ways to design companies. To date, most reengineering has focused on moving information inside the company in new ways. The next movement will be to redefine the boundary between the company and its customers and suppliers. Key questions to reexamine include: How will customers find out about products? How will customers order? What new competitors will emerge as geography becomes less of a barrier? How can the company do the best job of keeping customers happy after the sale?

Corporate structures will evolve. E-mail is a powerful force for flattening the hierarchies common to large companies. If communications systems are good enough, companies don't need as many levels of management. Intermediaries in middle management, who once passed information up and down the chain of command, already aren't as important today as they once were. Microsoft was born an Information

Age company, and its hierarchy has always been relatively flat. Our goal is to have no more than six levels of management between me and anyone in the company. In a sense, because of e-mail, there are no levels between me and anyone in the company.

As technology makes it easier for a business to find and collaborate with outside expertise, a huge and competitive market for consultants will arise. If you want someone to help design a piece of direct-response advertising, you'll ask a software application running on the information highway to list consultants with certain qualifications who are willing to work for no more than a certain rate and have an appropriate time period free. Software will check references for you preliminarily and help you filter out people who aren't qualified. You'll be able to ask, "Have any of these candidates worked for us before and gotten a rating above eight?" This system will become so inexpensive to use that you'll eventually rely on it to find baby-sitters and people to cut your lawn. If you're looking for work as an employee or contractor, the system will match you with potential employers and be able to send your résumé electronically with the click of a button.

Companies will reevaluate such employment issues as how extensive a legal or finance department they should keep, based on the relative benefits of having expertise inside an organization versus outside it. For particularly busy periods a company will be able to get more help easily without adding more employees and the associated office space. Businesses that successfully draw on the resources available across the network will be more efficient, which will challenge others to do the same.

Lots of companies will eventually be far smaller because using the information highway will make it easy to find and work with outside resources. Big is not necessarily good when it comes to business. Hollywood studios are surprisingly small in terms of permanent employees, because they contract for services—including actors and often facilities—on a movie-by-movie basis. Some software companies follow a similar model, hiring programmers as needed. Of course, companies will still reserve many functions for full-time employees. It would be immensely inefficient to have to bid for the time of an outside professional whenever a company needed something done, especially if the outside consultant had to come up to speed. But a number of functions will be dispersed, both structurally and geographically.

Geographic dispersion will affect much more than corporate structure. Many of today's major social problems have arisen because the population has been crowded into urban areas. The drawbacks of city life are obvious and substantial—traffic, cost of living, crime, and limited access to the outdoors, among others. The advantages of city life include access to work, services, education, entertainment, and friends. Over the past hundred years most of the population of the industrialized world has chosen to live in urban areas, after consciously or unconsciously balancing the pluses and minuses.

The information highway changes that balance. For those who have a connection to it, the highway will substantially reduce the drawbacks of living outside a big city. As a consultant or employee involved in a service-related field, you will be able to collaborate easily from virtually anywhere. As a consumer, you will be able to get advice—financial, legal, even some medical—without leaving your house. Flexibility is going to be increasingly important as everyone tries to balance family life with work life. You won't always have to travel to see friends and family or to play games. Cultural attractions will be available via the information highway, although I'm not suggesting that a Broadway or West End musical will be the same experience in your living room as it is in a New York or London theater. However, improvements in screen sizes and resolutions will enhance all video, including movies, in the home. Educational programming will be extensive. All of this will liberate those who would like to abandon city living.

The opening of the interstate highway system had a substantial effect on where in the United States people chose to settle. It made new suburbs accessible and contributed to the culture of the automobile. There will be significant implications for city planners, real estate developers, and school districts if the opening of the information highway also encourages people to move away from city centers. If large pools of talent disperse, companies will feel even more pressure to be creative about how to work with consultants and employees not located near their operations. This could set off a positive-feedback cycle, encouraging rural living.

----------------------------->

If the population of a city were reduced by even 10 percent, the result would be a major difference in property values and wear and tear on transportation and other urban systems. If the average office worker in any major city stayed home one or two days a week, the decreases in gasoline consumption, air pollution, and traffic congestion would be significant. The net effect, however, is hard to foresee. If those who moved out of cities were mostly the affluent knowledge workers, the urban tax base would be reduced. This would aggravate the inner city's woes and encourage other affluent people to leave. But at the same time, the urban infrastructure might be less heavily loaded. Rents would fall, creating opportunities for a better standard of living for some of those remaining in the cities.

It will take decades to implement all the major changes, because most people remain comfortable with whatever they learn early and are reluctant to alter familiar patterns. However, new generations will bring new perspectives. Our children will grow up comfortable with the idea of working with information tools across distances. These tools will be as natural to them as a telephone or a ballpoint pen is to us. But technology isn't going to wait until people are ready for it. Within the next ten years we will start to see substantial shifts in how and where we work, the companies we work for, and the places we choose to live. My advice is to try to find out as much as possible about the technology that will touch you. The more you know about it, the less disconcerting it will seem. Technology's role is to provide more flexibility and efficiency. Forward-looking business managers will have lots of opportunities to perform better in the years ahead.

8

FRICTION-FREE CAPITALISM

When Adam Smith described the concept of markets in *The Wealth of Nations* in 1776, he theorized that if every buyer knew every seller's price, and every seller knew what every buyer was willing to pay, everyone in the "market" would be able to make fully informed decisions and society's resources would be distributed efficiently. To date we haven't achieved Smith's ideal because would-be buyers and would-be sellers seldom have complete information about one another.

Not many consumers looking to buy a car stereo have the time or patience to canvass every dealer and thus are acting on imperfect and limited information. If you've bought a product for $500 and see it advertised in the paper for $300 a week or two later, you feel foolish for overpaying. But you feel a lot worse if you end up in the wrong job because you haven't done thorough enough research.

A few markets are already working fairly close to Smith's ideal. Investors buying and selling currency and certain other commodities participate in efficient electronic markets that provide nearly complete instantaneous information about worldwide supply, demand, and prices. Everyone gets pretty much the same deal because news about all offers, bids, and transactions speeds across wires to trading desks everywhere. However, most marketplaces are very inefficient. For instance, if you are trying to find a doctor, lawyer, accountant, or similar professional, or are buying a house, information is incomplete and comparisons are difficult to make.

The information highway will extend the electronic marketplace and make it the ultimate go-between, the universal middleman. Often the only humans involved in a transaction will be the actual buyer and seller. All the goods for sale in the world will be available for you to examine, compare, and, often, customize. When you want to buy something you'll be able to tell your computer to find it for you at the best price offered by any acceptable source or ask your computer to "haggle" with the computers of various sellers. Information about vendors and their products and services will be available to any computer connected to the highway. Servers distributed worldwide will accept bids, resolve offers into completed transactions, control authentication and security, and handle all other aspects of the marketplace, including the transfer of funds. This will carry us into a new world of low-friction, low-overhead capitalism, in which market information will be plentiful and transaction costs low. It will be a shopper's heaven.

Every market, from a bazaar to the highway, facilitates competitive pricing and allows goods to move from seller to buyer efficiently with modest friction. This is thanks to the market makers—those whose job it is to bring buyers and sellers together. As the information highway assumes the role of market maker in realm after realm, traditional middlemen will have to contribute real value to a transaction to justify a commission. For example, stores and services that until now have profited just because they are "there"—in a particular geographic location—may find they have lost that advantage. But those who provide added value will not only survive, they will thrive, because the information highway will let them make their services available to customers everywhere.

This idea will scare a lot of people. Most change feels a bit threatening, and I expect dramatic changes in the business of retailing as commerce flows across the highway. But, as with so many changes, I think once we get used to it we'll wonder how we did without it. The consumer will get not only competitive cost savings, but also a much wider variety of products and services to choose from. Although there may be fewer stores, if people continue to enjoy shopping in today's outlets, as many stores as their demand justifies will remain available. And because the highway will simplify and standardize shopping, it will also save time. If you are buying a gift for a loved one, you will be able to consider more choices and often you will find something more imaginative. You could use the time saved from shopping to think up a fun clue to put on the package, or create a personalized card. Or you could spend the time you save with the recipient.

We all recognize the value of a knowledgeable salesperson when we are shopping for insurance, clothes, investments, jewelry, a camera, a home appliance, or a home. We also know the salesperson's advice is sometimes biased because he or she is ultimately hoping to make a sale from a particular inventory.

On the information highway lots of product information will be available directly from manufacturers. As they do today, vendors will use a variety of entertaining and provocative techniques to attract us. Advertising will evolve into a hybrid, combining today's television commercials, magazine ads, and a detailed sales brochure. If an ad catches your attention, you'll be able to request additional information directly and very easily. Links will let you navigate through whatever information the advertiser has made available, which might be product manuals consisting of video, audio, and text. Vendors will make getting information about their products as simple as possible.

At Microsoft, we're looking forward to using the highway to get information out about our products. Today we print millions of pages of product brochures and data sheets, and mail them out to people who ask for them. But we never know how much information to put onto a data sheet; we don't want to intimidate casual inquirers, and yet there are people out there who want to know all the detailed product specifications. Also, since the information changes fairly rapidly, we are often in the position of having just printed tens of thousands of copies of some brochure, and then having to throw them out because they de-

-------------------------->

scribe a version of a product we're replacing. We expect a high percentage of our information dissemination will shift to electronic inquiry, particularly because we serve computer users. We have already eliminated the printing of millions of pages of paper by sending quarterly CD-ROMs and using on-line services to reach professional software developers, some of Microsoft's most sophisticated customers.

But you won't have to depend only on what we or any other manufacturer tells you. You'll be able to examine product reviews in search of less biased information. After you've seen the advertising, reviews, and multimedia manuals, you might ask for relevant government regulatory data. You'll check to see if the vendor has surveyed owners. Then you might dig deeper into one area of particular interest to you—for instance, durability. Or you could seek the advice of sales consultants, human or electronic, who will create and publish specialized reviews for all kinds of products, from drill bits to ballet slippers. Of course you will still ask people you know for recommendations, but efficiently, by electronic mail.

If you're thinking of doing business with a company or buying a product, you'll be able to check what others say about it. If you want to buy a refrigerator, you will look for the electronic bulletin boards containing formal and informal reviews of refrigerators and their manufacturers and retailers. You'll get into the habit of checking these bulletin boards before you make any significant purchase. When you have a compliment or complaint about a record club, a doctor, or even a computer chip, it will be easy to find the place on the network where that company or product is discussed and add your opinion. Ultimately, companies that don't serve their customers well will see their reputations and their sales decline, while those that do a great job will attract sizable followings through this new form of word of "mouth."

But the various endorsements and especially the negative comments will have to be examined carefully. They may be motivated more by fanaticism than a genuine desire to share pertinent information.

Let's say a company is selling an air conditioner that 99.9 percent of its customers are very happy with. One angry consumer in the remaining 0.1 percent can post horrible insults about a brand of air conditioner, the company that manufactures it, and individuals in the company, and keep sending the messages over and over and over. The effect could be compared to sitting in a meeting where everyone has a volume control that could be set from 0 to 1,000, and the normal level of conversation is, say, 3. Then a few people decide to crank their volume up to 1,000 and start shouting. This means that if I happen to look in on the bulletin board because I'm buying an air conditioner, my visit may be a waste of time because all I find there is the shouting. It is unfair to me and to the company selling the air conditioners.

Already, a network etiquette, or "netiquette," is evolving. As the information highway becomes society's town square, we will come to expect it to conform to our culture's mores. There are vast cultural differences around the world, so the highway will be divided into different parts, some dedicated to various cultures, and some specified for global usage. So far, a frontier mentality has prevailed, and participants in electronic forums have been known to lapse into behavior that is antisocial and even illegal. Illegal copies of copyrighted intellectual property, including articles, books, and software applications, are distributed freely. Get-rich-quick scams pop up here and there. Pornography flourishes within the easy reach of children. Single-minded voices rant, sometimes almost incessantly, about products, companies, and people they have come to dislike. Forum participants get horrible insults hurled at them because of some comment they have made. The ease with which an individual, any individual, can share his opinions with the members of a huge electronic community is unprecedented. And the ones who are yelling are able, because the electronic community is so efficient, to take a piece of hate mail and post it on twenty bulletin boards. I've seen bulletin boards collapse into foolishness after people start getting shrill. Other participants in the discussion don't know what to do. Some people yell back; a few try to say rational things. But the shrill comments continue, and that destroys the sense of community.

The Internet, true to its roots as an academic cooperative, has relied on peer pressure for regulation. For example, if someone in a discussion group posts an extraneous comment or, worse, tries to sell something in an electronic forum that is seen by others as a noncommercial setting, the would-be diverger or merchant may get a withering barrage of insults. The enforcement so far has been mostly by self-appointed censors who "flame" those they believe have crossed the line into antisocial behavior.

The commercial on-line services employ volunteers and professional moderators to monitor conduct on their bulletin boards. Forums that have moderators can filter out some antisocial behavior by refusing to allow insults or copyrighted information to remain on a system's servers. Most Internet forums remain unmoderated, however. Anything goes, and because people can post messages and information anonymously, little accountability exists. We need a more sophisticated process to gather consensus opinions without depending on the Attorney General's Consumer Complaints Division to act as a filter. We will have to find some way to force people to turn their volume down so the highway doesn't become an amplifier for libel or slander or an outlet for venting irritation.

Many providers of Internet access are beginning to restrict entry to forums containing sexually explicit material, and there has been a crackdown on the illegal traffic of copyrighted materials. Some universities are getting students and staff to remove objectionable postings. This rubs some the wrong way, because they see cyberspace as a place where anything goes. The commercial services have had similar problems. There have been complaints about restriction of free speech. And parents were outraged when their family account was closed after their eleven-year-old made an objectionable comment to a moderator. Companies will create special communities on the Internet and will "compete" by having rules about how they are going to deal with these issues.

Politicians are already wrestling with the question of when an on-line service should be treated as a common carrier and when it should be treated as a publisher. Telephone companies are legally considered common carriers. They transport messages without assuming any responsibility for them. If an obscene caller bothers you, the telephone company will cooperate with the police, but nobody thinks it is the phone company's fault that some creep is calling you and talking dirty. Magazines and newspapers, on the other hand, are publishers. They are legally responsible for their content and can be sued for libel. They also have a strong interest in maintaining their reputation and editorial integrity because that is an important part of their business. Any responsible newspaper checks very carefully before making a previously unpublished allegation about someone—in part because it doesn't want a libel suit, but also because inaccuracy would hurt its reputation.

On-line services function simultaneously as common carriers and publishers, which is where the problem lies. When they act as publishers, and offer content they have acquired, authored, or edited, it makes sense that the rules of libel and the self-governing incentive of editorial reputation would apply. But we also expect them to deliver our e-mail like a common carrier without examining or taking responsibility for its contents. Likewise, chat lines, bulletin boards, and forums that encourage users to interact without editorial supervision are a new means of communication, and shouldn't be treated the same way as material published on the service. A New York judge, however, recently cleared the way for a libel lawsuit by ruling that the on-line service involved was a publisher of information, not just a distributor. Perhaps by the time you read this things will have been clarified. The stakes in the resolution of this issue are high. If network providers are treated entirely as publishers, they will have to monitor and preapprove the content of all information they transmit. This could create an unwelcome atmosphere of censorship and curtail spontaneous exchange, so important in the electronic world.

Ideally, the industry will develop some standards so that when you go into a bulletin board or article, you get an indication of whether or not some "publisher" has looked it over, edited it, and stands behind its content. The question will be what standards and who will oversee them? A bulletin board for lesbians should not be forced to accept antilesbian comments, nor should a bulletin board about some product be overwhelmed by messages from a competitor. It would be a shame to have to keep children away from all bulletin boards, but it would also be unrealistic, and possibly an abridgment of free expression, to force all bulletin boards to undergo review by someone willing to accept liability for everything they contain. What we will most likely end up with is a series of categories, like the ratings given movies, that will indicate whether shrill voices have been controlled and whether an "editor" has deleted messages he thought were out of line with the policies of the group involved.

The bulletin boards I've been discussing are the free, public ones, but there will also be places where professional information and advice will be offered for a fee. You might wonder why you would need an expert when so much information will be available. For the same reasons you might need one now. All sorts of consumer data can be had now. *Consumer Reports* offers objective evaluations of a lot of products, but the reviews are aimed at a broad audience—they don't necessarily discuss your particular requirements. If you can't find exactly the advice you need on the highway, you will be able to hire a knowledgeable sales consultant, for five minutes or an afternoon, via videoconference. She will help you choose products, which your computer will then buy for you from the cheapest reliable source.

I expect the traditional binding together of advice and sales to be much less prevalent, because although the advice appears free to the customer, it is paid for by the stores and services that offer it. This cost then gets added on to the price of the goods. Stores that are charging more because they offer advice will have increasing difficulty competing with the discounters who will operate on the information highway. There will continue to be some modest price variations in products from one outlet to another. These will reflect differences in return policies, delivery times, and whatever limited customer assistance is available.

Some merchants will offer "consultants" as part of the sales price, but for important purchases you are likely to welcome a truly independent guide. The cost of the consultation will be offset to an extent by the lower price you'll end up paying at the outlet the consultant will guide you to. The prices consultants charge will also be very competitive. Suppose you use a service on the highway to obtain information about where to buy an expensive car at the best price, and then you buy it. The price for using the service—which has acted as the middleman in the transaction—might be charged at a low hourly rate, or it could be a small percentage of the purchase price. It will depend on the uniqueness of the service. Electronic competition will determine the fee.

Over time, more advice will be offered by software applications that have been programmed to analyze your requirements and make appropriate suggestions. A number of large banks have already developed "expert" computer systems to analyze routine loan and credit applications, with great success. As software agents become common, and voice-simulation-and-recognition software improves, it will begin to feel as though you're talking to a real person when you consult a multimedia document with a personality. You'll be able to interrupt, request more detail, or ask to have an explanation repeated. The experience will be like chatting with a personable expert. Eventually it won't matter much whether you are talking to a human being or a very good simulation, as long as you get the answers you need to make an appropriate purchase.

A step toward the discount electronic commerce of the highway is today's home-shopping television networks. In 1994 they sold nearly $3 billion worth of goods despite the fact that they are synchronous, which means you may have to sit through pitches for countless other items until they offer one you're interested in. On the information highway you'll be able to amble globally at your own pace among goods and services. If you're looking for sweaters, you'll choose a basic style and see as many variations as you like, in every price range. Perhaps you'll watch a fashion show or a product demonstration. Interactivity will marry convenience with entertainment.

Today, branded products often appear in feature films and television programs. A character who once would have ordered a beer now asks for a Budweiser. In the 1993 movie *Demolition Man,* Taco Bell restaurants seem to be the only fast-food survivors. Taco Bell's corporate parent, PepsiCo, paid for the privilege. Microsoft paid a fee to have Arnold Schwarzenegger discover the Arabic version of Windows running on a computer screen during *True Lies.* In the future, companies may pay not only to have their products on-screen, but also to make them available for you to buy. You will have the option of inquiring about any image you see. This will be another choice the highway will make available un-obtrusively. If you are watching the movie *Top Gun* and think Tom Cruise's aviator sunglasses look really cool, you'll be able to pause the movie and learn about the glasses or even buy them on the spot—if the film has been tagged with commercial information. Or you could mark the scene and return to it later. If a movie has a scene filmed in a resort hotel, you'll be able to find out where it's located, check room rates, and make reservations. If the movie's star carries a handsome leather briefcase or handbag, the highway will let you browse the manufacturer's entire line of leather goods and either order one or be directed to a convenient retailer.

Because the information highway will carry video, you'll often be able to see exactly what you've ordered. This will help prevent the sort of mistake my grandmother once made. I was at summer camp and she ordered lemon drops to be sent to me. She ordered one hundred, thinking I would get one hundred pieces of candy. Instead I got one hundred bags. I gave them out to everyone and was especially popular until we all began to have canker sores. On the highway you will be able to take a video tour of that hotel before you make your reservation. You won't have to wonder whether the flowers you ordered for your mother by telephone really were as stunning as you'd hoped. You'll be able to watch the florist arrange the bouquet, change your mind if you want, and replace wilting roses with fresh anemones. When you're shopping for clothing, it will be displayed in your size. In fact, you'll be able to see it paired with other items you have purchased or are considering.

Once you know exactly what you want, you'll be able to get it just that way. Computers will enable goods that today are mass-produced to be both mass-produced and custom made for particular customers. Customization will become an important way for a manufacturer to add value. Increasing numbers of products—from shoes to chairs, from newspapers and magazines to music albums—will be created on the spot to match the exact desires of a particular person. And often the item will cost no more than a mass-produced one would. In many product categories mass customization will replace mass production, just as a few generations ago mass production largely replaced made-to-order.

Before mass production, everything was made one piece at a time, using labor-intensive methods that hampered productivity and the standard of living. Until the first practical sewing machine was built, every shirt was handmade with needle and thread. The average person didn't have many shirts, because they were expensive. In the 1860s, when mass-production techniques began to be used to make clothing, machines turned out large quantities of identical shirts, the prices dropped, and even laborers could afford to own a number of them.

Soon there will be computerized shirt-making machines that will obey a different set of instructions for every shirt. When you order you'll indicate your measurements as well as your choices for fabric, fit, collar, and every other variable. The information will be communicated across the information highway to a manufacturing plant that will produce the garment for prompt delivery. Delivering goods ordered over the highway will become a big business. There will be amazing competition, and as volume becomes enormous, delivery will get very inexpensive and fast.

Levi Strauss & Co. is already experimenting with custom-made jeans for women. At a growing number of their outlets, customers pay about $10 extra to have jeans made to their exact specifications—any of 8,448 different combinations of hip, waist, inseam, and rise measurements and styles. The information is relayed from a PC in the store to a Levi's factory in Tennessee, where the denim is cut by computer-driven machines, tagged with bar codes, and then washed and sewn. The completed jeans are sent back to the store where the order was placed, or shipped overnight directly to the customer.

It is conceivable that within a few years everyone will have measurements registered electronically so it will be easy to find out how well a ready-made item will fit, or to place a custom order. If you give friends and relatives access to this information, they will find it a lot easier to buy for you.

Customized information is a natural extension of the tailored consultation capabilities of the highway. Individuals who have achieved eminence in some field may publish their opinions, recommendations, or even worldview, in much the same way that successful investors publish newsletters. Arnold Palmer or Nancy Lopez might offer golfers the chance to read or look at whatever golf material they have found helpful. An editor who today works at *The Economist* might start his or her own service, and offer a digest of the news with links to text and video news accounts from a variety of sources. Someone using this review service, instead of paying 60 cents for a newspaper, might pay the expert a few cents a day for performing the middleman function of assembling the day's news, and pay the publisher of each story selected a little bit too. The customer would decide how many articles he wanted to read and how much to spend. For your own daily dose of news, you might subscribe to several review services and let a software agent or a human one pick and choose from them to compile your completely customized "newspaper."

These subscription services, whether human or electronic, will gather information that conforms to a particular philosophy and set of interests. They will compete on the basis of their talents and reputations. Magazines fill a similar role today. Many are narrowly focused and serve as customized realities of a sort. A reader who is politically engaged knows that what he or she is reading in *National Review* is not "the news." It is a bulletin from the world of conservative politics where little of what the reader believes is challenged. At the other end of the political scale, *The Nation* is a magazine that knows its readers' liberal views and biases and sets out to confirm and massage them.

In the same ways that movie studios try to sell you their newest release by showing previews in theaters, print advertising, and various kinds of promotional activities, the providers of information will use all sorts of techniques to convince you to sample their wares. A lot of information will be local—from neighborhood schools, hospitals, merchants, and even pizza joints. Connecting a business to the highway won't be expensive. Once the infrastructure is in place and a critical number of users adopt it, every business will want to reach out to its customers over the highway.

The potential for electronic efficiency is causing some people to worry that if they use the information highway to shop or get their news, they will miss out on the serendipity of running into a surprisingly interesting article in the newspapers or finding an unexpected treat at the mall. Of course, these "surprises" are hardly random. Newspapers are constructed by editors who know from experience a lot about their readers' interests. Once in a while *The New York Times* publishes a front-page article about an advance in mathematics. The somewhat specialized information is presented with an angle that makes it interesting to a good number of readers, including some who didn't think they cared about math. In the same way, buyers for stores think about what is new and might intrigue their type of customer. Stores fill their window displays with products they hope will catch those customers' eyes and lure them inside.

There will be plenty of opportunities for calculated surprise on the information highway. From time to time your software agent will try to entice you to fill out a questionnaire indicating your tastes. The questionnaire will incorporate all sorts of images in an effort to draw subtle reactions out of you. Your agent will be able to make the process fun by giving you feedback on how you compare with the norm. That information will be used to create a profile of your tastes, which will guide the agent. As you use the system for reading news or shopping, an agent will also be able to add information to your profile. It will keep track of what you have indicated interest in, as well as what you "happened upon" and then pursued. The agent will use this information to help prepare various surprises to attract and hold your attention. Whenever you want something offbeat and appealing, it will be waiting for you. Needless to say, there will be lots of controversy and negotiation about who can get access to your profile information. It will be crucial that *you* have such access.

Why would you want to create such a profile? I certainly don't want to reveal everything about myself, but it would be helpful if an agent knew I wanted to see any safety features the new model Lexus might have added. Or, it could alert me to the publication of a new book by Philip Roth, John Irving, Ernest J. Gaines, Donald Knuth, David Halberstam, or any of my other longtime favorite writers. I would also like to have it signal me when a new book appears on some topic that interests me: economics and technology, learning theories, Franklin Delano Roosevelt, and biotechnology, to name a few. I was quite stimulated by a book called *The Language Instinct*, written by Steven Pinker, a professor at MIT, and I'd like to know about new books or articles on its ideas.

You'll also be able to find surprises by following links other people have set up. Today, users like to browse the Internet's World Wide Web, checking the display pages or home pages that include links to other pages with information about a company or links to other companies' pages. These links are indicated by hot spots, those pictures or buttons that, when clicked with a mouse, cause the requested page to be called to the screen.

Some individuals are creating their own home pages. Personal home pages are interesting to consider. What data or thoughts would you want to publish to the whole world? Will your page have links, and, if so, to what? Who will want to look at your home page?

The electronic world will allow companies to sell directly to customers. Certainly every company will provide a home page to facilitate access to information about its products. Any company that has a successful distribution strategy—in our case, software retailers—has to make a choice about whether to take advantage of this. Putting up the latest information, including the names of your distributors, will be very easy, but it's also important to protect retailers. Even Rolls-Royce, which has an extremely exclusive distribution system, will probably have a home page where you can see its latest models and find out where to buy them.

Retailers have done a very good job for Microsoft, and we like the fact that customers can go into stores and see most of our products and the salespeople can give them advice. Microsoft's plan is to continue to sell through retailers, but some of them will be electronic.

Consider an insurance company that has worked effectively through agents. Will the company decide it wants customers to buy directly from the central office? Will it let its agents, who used to sell locally only, sell electronically nationwide? Sales requirements will be tough to define. Each company will have to determine what factors matter most to it. Competition will show which approach works best.

Home pages are an electronic form of advertising. The information highway's software platform will allow companies total control over how information is presented. Advertisers on the information highway will have to be creative to capture viewers who will have grown accustomed to watching whatever they want, whenever they want, and to being able to skip through almost any program.

Today, advertising subsidizes nearly all of the programs we watch on television and articles we enjoy in magazines. Advertisers place their messages in the programs and publications that attract the largest appropriate audience. Companies placing ads spend a lot of money trying to make sure their advertising strategy is working. On the highway, advertisers will also want some sort of assurance that their messages are reaching their targeted audiences. Advertising doesn't pay if everyone chooses to skip by the ad. The highway will offer alternatives. One might be software that lets the customer fast-forward past everything except for the advertising, which will play at normal speed. The highway will possibly offer the viewer the option of asking to see a group of commercials. In France, when commercials were grouped and aired together, that five-minute block was one of the most popular time segments.

Today, television viewers are targeted on a cluster basis. Advertisers know that a television newsmagazine tends to attract one kind of viewer and professional wrestling another. Television commercials are purchased with audience size and demographics in mind. Ads aimed at kids subsidize children's shows; those aimed at homemakers subsidize daytime soap operas; car and beer ads subsidize sports coverage. The broadcast advertiser is dealing with aggregated information about the viewers of a show, based on a statistical sample. Broadcast advertising reaches many people who aren't interested in the products.

Magazines, because they can be and often are narrowly focused editorially, are able to aim their advertising at somewhat more targeted audiences—car enthusiasts, musicians, women interested in fitness, even groups as narrow as teddy bear fans. People buying a teddy bear magazine want to see the ads for teddy bears and their accessories. In fact, people often buy special-interest magazines as much for the advertising as for the articles. Fashion magazines, for instance, if they're doing well, are more than half advertising. They offer readers the experience of window-shopping without the walking. The advertiser doesn't know the specific identities of the magazine's readers, but it knows something about the readership in general.

The information highway will be able to sort consumers according to much finer individual distinctions, and to deliver each a different stream of advertising. This will benefit all parties: the viewers, because ads will be better tailored to their specific interests, and therefore more interesting; producers and on-line publications, because they will be able to sell advertisers focused blocks of viewers and readers. Advertisers will be able to spend their ad dollars more efficiently. Preference data can be gathered and disseminated without violating anyone's privacy, because the interactive network will be able to use information about consumers to route advertising without revealing which specific households received it. A restaurant chain would know only that a certain number of middle-income families with small children received their ad.

A middle-aged executive and her husband might see an advertisement for retirement property at the beginning of an episode of *Home Improvement*, while the young couple next door might see a family vacation advertisement at the opening of the same show, regardless of whether they watched the show at the same or a different time. These closely targeted advertisements will be of more value to the advertiser, so a viewer could subsidize an entire evening of television by watching a small number of them.

Some advertisers—Coca-Cola, for example—want to reach everyone. But even Coca-Cola might decide to direct diet cola ads to households that have expressed an interest in diet books. The Ford Motor Company might want affluent people to be shown a Lincoln Continental ad, young people to see a Ford Escort ad, rural residents to watch an ad for full-size pickup trucks, and everyone else to be sent a Taurus ad. Or a company might advertise the same product for everyone but vary the actors by gender or race or age. They will certainly want to revise the copy to target particular purchasers. To maximize the value of the advertising, complex algorithms will be required to allocate ad space within a show for each viewer. This will take more effort, but because it will make the messages more effective, it will be a good investment.

Even corner groceries and the local dry cleaner will be able to advertise in ways they never could before. Because individually targeted ad streams will be flowing through the network all the time, video advertising is likely to become cost-effective even for small advertisers. A store's ads might target only a few blocks and address very specific neighborhoods or community interests.

Today, the most effective way to reach a narrow audience is with a classified ad. Each classification represents a small community of interest: people who want to buy or sell a rug, for example. Tomorrow, the classified ad won't be tied to paper or limited to text. If you're looking for a used car, you will send out a query specifying the price range, model, and features that interest you and will be shown a list of the available cars that match your preferences. Or you will ask a software agent to notify you when a suitable car comes on the market. Car sellers' ads might include links to a picture or a video of the car or even the car's maintenance records, so you can get a sense of what shape it is in. You'll be able to learn the mileage the same way, and whether the engine has ever been replaced, and if the car has air bags. Perhaps you will want to cross-link to police records, which are public, to see whether it has been in a wreck.

If you put your house on the market, you will be able to describe it fully and include photographs, video, floor plans, tax records, utility and repair bills, even a little mood music. The chances that a potential buyer for your house will see your ad are improved because the information highway will make it easy for anyone to look it up. The whole system of real estate agencies and commissions may be changed by the principals' having direct access to so much information.

At first, on-line classified ads won't be very attractive, because not many people will be using them. But then word-of-mouth from a few satisfied customers will entice more and more users to the service. There will be a positive-feedback loop created as more sellers attract more buyers and vice versa. When a critical mass is achieved, which might be only a year or two after the service is first offered, the information highway's classified advertising service will be transformed from a curiosity to the primary way private sellers and buyers get together.

Direct-response advertising—the junk-mail business—is in for even bigger changes. Today, a lot of it really is junk, because we cut down a lot of trees in order to mail out material, much of which is discarded unopened. Direct-response advertising on the information highway will come in the form of an interactive multimedia document rather than a piece of paper. Although it won't waste natural resources, there will have to be some way to make sure you don't get thousands of these almost-free communications a day.

You won't be drowned by the deluge of unimportant information because you'll use software to filter incoming advertising and other extraneous messages and spend your valuable time looking at those messages that interest you. Most people will block e-mail ads except for those about product areas of particular concern. One way for the advertiser to capture your attention will be to offer a small amount of money—a nickel or a dollar, perhaps—if you will look at an ad. When you have watched it, or as you're interacting with it, your electronic account gets credited and the advertiser's electronic account is debited. In effect, some of the billions of dollars now spent annually on media advertising, and on the printing and postage of direct-mail advertising, will instead be divvied up among consumers who agree to watch or read ads sent directly to them as messages.

Mailings offering this sort of paying advertisement could be extremely effective because they can be carefully targeted. Advertisers will be smart about sending messages worth money only to people who meet appropriate demographics. A company such as Ferrari or Porsche might send $1 messages to car enthusiasts, on the chance that seeing a cool new car and hearing the sound of its engine will generate interest. If the ad led to even one in 1,000 people's buying a new car as a result, it would be worthwhile to the company. They could adjust the amount they offer according to the customer's profile. Such ads will be available to those not on the advertiser's A-list. For instance, if a sixteen-year-old car-crazy kid wants to experience a Ferrari, and is willing to do it for nothing, he'll get the message too.

This may sound a little strange, but it is just another use of the market mechanism for friction-free capitalism. The advertiser decides how much money it is willing to bid for your time, and you decide what your time is worth.

Advertising messages, like the rest of your incoming mail, will be stored in various folders. You will instruct your computer how to do the sorting for you. Unread mail from friends and family members might be in one folder. Messages and documents that relate to a personal or business interest would be in other folders. And advertisements and messages from unknown people could be sorted by how much money was attached to them. There would be a group of 1-cent messages, a group of 10-cent messages, and so forth. If there was no fee attached, they could be refused. You will be able to scan each message and dispose of it if it isn't of interest. Some days you might not look into any of the advertising message folders. But if someone sent you a $10 message, you would probably take a look—if not for the money, then just to see who thought reaching you was worth $10.

You won't have to take the money someone bids, of course. When you accept the message, you'll be able to cancel the payment, so it's really just the amount the person puts at risk to get your attention. The sender's credit will be checked in advance. If a man sends you a $100 message suggesting that he is your long-lost brother, you might forgive him the money if, in fact, he turned out to be your brother. On the other hand, if he was just someone trying to get your attention to sell you something, you would probably keep the money, thank you very much.

In the United States, advertisers currently spend more than $20 a month per American family to subsidize free broadcast and cable television. Ads in general are so familiar they don't really bother us when we watch television or listen to the radio. We understand that programs are "free" because of the commercials. Customers pay for them indirectly because advertising costs are built into the prices of cornflakes, shampoo, and diamonds. We also pay for entertainment and information directly when we buy a book or a movie ticket, or order a pay-per-view movie. The average American household pays a total of $100 a month for movie tickets, subscriptions to newspapers and magazines, books, cable television fees, compact discs and tapes, video rentals, and the like.

When you pay for entertainment by buying a tape or a disc, your rights to reuse or resell it are restricted. If you buy a copy of *Abbey Road* by the Beatles, you're actually purchasing the physical disc or tape and a license to replay, any number of times, for noncommercial purposes, the music stored on it. If you buy a paperback book, what you're really buying is the paper and ink and the right to read, and allow others to read, the words printed on that particular paper with that particular ink. You don't own the words and you can't reprint them, except in narrowly defined circumstances. When you watch a television show, you don't own it, either. In fact, it took a United States Supreme Court decision to confirm that people in this country can legally videotape a television show for their personal use.

The information highway will enable innovations in the way that intellectual property, such as music and software, is licensed. Record companies, or even individual recording artists, might choose to sell music a new way. You, the consumer, won't need compact discs, tapes, or any other kinds of physical apparatus. The music will be stored as bits of information on a server on the highway. "Buying" a song or album will really mean buying the right to access the appropriate bits. You will be able to listen at home, at work, or on vacation, without carrying around a collection of titles. Anyplace you go where there are audio speakers connected to the highway, you'll be able to identify yourself and take advantage of your rights. You won't be allowed to rent a concert hall and play that recording of the music or create an advertisement that incorporated it. But in any noncommercial setting, anywhere you go, you'll have the right to play the song without additional payment to the copyright holder. In the same way, the information highway could keep track of whether you had bought the right to read a particular book or see a movie. If you had, you'd be able to call it up at any time, from any information appliance anywhere.

This personal, lifetime buyout of rights is similar to what we do today when we buy a music disc or tape, or book, except that there is no physical medium involved. It sounds comfortingly familiar. However, there are lots of other ways to sell the enjoyment of music or other information.

For example, a song could be made available on a pay-per-hearing basis. Each time you listened to it, your account would be charged some small amount, such as 5 cents. At that rate, it would cost 60 cents to listen to a twelve-song "album." You would have to play the whole album twenty-five times to spend $15, which is roughly what a compact disc sells for today. If you found that you liked only one song on the album, you could play it three hundred times, at a nickel each time, for your $15. Because digital information is so flexible, as the audio quality improves you won't have to pay for the same music again the way people did when they bought CDs to replace the LPs in their personal libraries.

All kinds of pricing schemes will be tried. We may see digital entertainment that has an expiration date or that allows only a certain number of plays before it has to be purchased again. A record company might offer a very low price for a song but let you play it only ten or twenty times. Or they might let you play a song—or an addictive game—ten times free before asking if you want to buy it. This kind of "demo" usage might replace part of the function served by radio stations today. An author could allow you to mail a new song to a friend, but she will only be able to listen to it a few times before getting charged. A musical group could have a special price, far lower than if every album was bought individually, for a buyer who wanted all their work.

Even today, paying for entertainment information isn't without nuances. The limited time value of entertainment information affects the way publishers and film studios market their products. The book publisher often does this by having two release windows, hardcover and paperback. If a customer wants a book and can comfortably afford it, he or she pays $25 to $30. Or the customer can wait for between six months and two years and buy the same book, in a somewhat less expensive and long-lasting format, for $5 to $10.

Successful movies are progressively shown in first-run theaters, secondary theaters, hotel rooms, on pay-per-view TV, and on airplanes. Then they are available as video rentals, on premium channels such as HBO, and eventually on network TV. Still later they appear on local television or basic cable channels. Each new form brings the movie to a different audience as customers who missed the previous forms of release (accidentally or on purpose) take advantage of the new opportunity.

On the information highway various release windows for content will almost certainly be tried. When a hot movie, multimedia title, or electronic book is released, there may be an initial period during which it is priced at a premium. Some will be willing to pay a high fee, perhaps as much as $30, to see a movie at the same time it appears in the first-run theaters. After a week, a month, or a season, the price will drop to the $3 or $4 we are charged today for pay-per-view movies. Marketers may try some wild things. Perhaps a movie will come along that you won't be able to see at all in its first month of release unless you're one of the top 1,000 bidders in an electronic auction on the highway. At the other extreme, if you have a track record of buying movie posters and merchandise related to what you watch, you may find you can get certain movies for next to nothing or with few, if any, commercial interruptions. Purchases of *The Little Mermaid* and *Aladdin* videotapes and associated merchandise might justify Disney's allowing every child in the world one free viewing.

The transferability of information will be another big pricing issue. The information highway will allow the transfer of intellectual property

-------------------------------▶

rights from one person to another at the speed of light. Almost all the music, writing, or other intellectual properties stored on disks or in books sits unused most of the time. When you're not consuming your particular copy of *Thriller* or *Bonfire of the Vanities*, most likely no one else is, either. Publishers count on this. If the average buyer lent his or her albums and books frequently, fewer would be sold and prices would be higher. If we assume that an album is in use, say, 0.1 percent of the time, "light speed" lending might cut the number of copies sold by a factor of 1,000. Lending will probably be restricted so users will only be allowed to lend a copy out perhaps up to ten times a year.

Public libraries will become places where anyone can sit down and use high-quality equipment to gain access to the information highway's resources. Library committees might use the budgets that today pay for buying books, albums, movies, and subscriptions to fund the royalties for using educational electronic materials. Authors may decide to forfeit some or all of their royalties if their work is to be used in a library.

New copyright laws will be required to clarify the purchaser's rights to the content under different schemes. The highway will force us to think more explicitly about what rights users have to intellectual property.

Videos, which tend to be watched only once, will continue to be rented, but probably not from stores. Instead, consumers will shop on the information highway to find movies and other programs deliverable on demand. Neighborhood video-rental stores and music stores will face a dwindling market. Bookstores will continue to stock printed books for a long time, but nonfiction and especially reference material will probably be used much more often in electronic rather than print form.

Efficient electronic markets are going to change a lot more than just the ratio of renting to buying for entertainment. Almost any person or business that serves as a middleman will feel the heat of electronic competition.

A small-town lawyer will face new competition when legal services are available by videoconference over the network. A person buying a piece of property might choose to consult with a sharp real estate attorney from the other side of the county rather than using a local lawyer who is a generalist. The resources of the highway, however, will allow the local lawyer to retrain and become an expert in any specialty of her choice. She will be able to compete in this specialty because of her lower overhead. Clients will benefit as well. The prices for executing routine legal tasks, such as the drafting of wills, will be driven down by the efficiency and specialization of the electronic marketplace. The information highway will also be able to deliver complicated medical, financial, and other video consulting services. These will be convenient and popular, especially when they are short. It will be much easier to make an appointment and turn on your television or computer screen for a fifteen-minute meeting than it will be to drive somewhere, park, sit in a waiting room, and then drive back to your home or office.

Videoconferences of all sorts will increasingly become alternatives to having to drive or fly to a meeting. When you do go somewhere, it will be because it is important that a particular meeting be face-to-face, or because something fun requires that you be there physically. Business travel may fall off, but leisure travel will rise because people will be able to take working vacations, knowing they can stay connected to their offices and homes through the information highway.

The travel industry will change even though the total amount of traveling may stay the same. Travel agents, like all professionals whose service has been to offer specialized access to information, will have to add value in new ways. Travel agents now search for the availability of travel arrangements using databases and reference books customers don't have access to. Once they become familiar with the power of the highway and all the information that will be on it, many travelers will prefer to conduct searches themselves.

Smart, experienced, and creative travel agents will prosper, but they will specialize and do more than book reservations. Say you want to visit Africa. You will be able to find the cheapest tickets to Kenya, so the travel agency will have to be able to provide something else. Perhaps the agency books nothing but trips to East Africa—hence, they'll be able to tell you what other customers especially liked, or that the Tsavo National Park is too crowded, or that if you're really interested in seeing herds of zebra, you are better off visiting Tanzania. Some other travel agents may decide to specialize in selling travel to, rather than from, their own cities. An agent in Chicago might offer services across the network to people around the world who want to visit his hometown, rather than selling services to Chicagoans who want to visit other places. Customers wouldn't know the travel agent, but the travel agent certainly would know Chicago, which might be more important.

Although today's newspapers will be around for a long, long time, the newspaper business will be fundamentally altered when the consumer has access to the information highway. In the United States, daily newspapers are dependent on local advertising for most of their revenue. In 1950, when television sets were still novelties, national advertising contributed 25 percent of the advertising revenue of American newspapers. By 1993, national advertising contributed only 12 percent, in large measure because of competition from television. The number of daily newspapers in the United States has declined dramatically and the burden of financing those that remain has shifted to local retail and classified advertising. Classifieds don't really work on radio or television. In 1950, only 18 percent of the advertising revenue of daily newspapers in the United States came from classifieds, but by 1993 that had risen to 35 percent and represented billions of dollars.

The information highway will provide alternative, more efficient ways for individual buyers and sellers to get together. Once the majority of customers in a market use electronic access to shop, classified revenues will be threatened. That means much of the newspaper advertising base could be in jeopardy.

It does not, however, mean that newspapers will disappear overnight, or that newspaper companies can't continue to be important and profitable players in the delivery of news and advertising. But, like all companies that have a middleman or brokering role, they'll have to be alert to change and take advantage of their unique qualities to succeed in the electronic world.

Banking is another industry destined for change. There are about 14,000 banks in the United States that cater to retail customers. Most people bank with a firm that has a branch office near their home or on their commuting path. Although minor differences in interest rates and services might shift people from one local bank to another, few customers would consider switching to a branch ten miles out of their way. Today, moving your bank records is time-consuming.

But when the information highway makes geography less important, we will see electronic, on-line banks that have no branches—no bricks, no mortar, and low fees. These low-overhead electronic banks will be extremely competitive and transactions will be made through computer appliances. There will be less need for cash because most purchases will be handled with a wallet PC or an electronic "smart card" that will combine the features of a credit card, automatic teller machine card, and checkbook. This is all coming at a time when the U.S. banking industry is already consolidating and becoming more efficient.

A lot of the interest-rate differential between large and small deposits will disappear. With the communications available on the highway, a new kind of middleman will be able to aggregate small customers efficiently and get them a rate very close to what large depositors are offered. Financial institutions will be able to specialize; one bank may choose only to make automobile loans, whereas another concentrates on boat loans. Fees will be generated for all of these services, but the fee structure will be based on broad, efficient competition.

It wasn't so long ago that a small investor who wanted to put his money in anything beyond a passbook savings account was stymied. The world of stocks and beyond—mutual funds, penny stocks, commercial paper, debentures, and other arcane instruments—was simply off-limits to anyone who wasn't a Wall Street insider.

But that was before computers changed things. Today, "discount" stockbroker listings are plentiful in the Yellow Pages, and quite a few investors make their stock purchases from a machine at a local bank or over the telephone. As the information highway gains in efficiency, investment choices will proliferate. Stockbrokers, like other middlemen whose job has been merely to chaperon a transaction, will probably have to offer something beyond just purchasing securities. They'll add value by being knowledgeable. Financial services companies will still thrive. The basic economics of the industry will change, but the volume of transactions will skyrocket as the information highway gives the average consumer direct access to financial markets. Investors with relatively small amounts of money to commit will get better advice and have opportunities to make profits from the sorts of investments now available only to institutions.

When I prognosticate about the future changes in an industry, people often wonder if Microsoft plans to go into that field. Microsoft's competence is in building great software products and the information services that go with them. We will not become a bank or a store.

Once, when I referred to a bank's back-end databases as "dinosaurs," a reporter wrote an article saying I thought banks themselves were dinosaurs and we wanted to compete with them. I have now spent more than a year going around the world telling banks I was misquoted. Microsoft faces plenty of challenges and opportunities in the business we know— whether it's enterprise support, making computer software, groupware for the Internet servers, or any other part of our business.

Our success in the PC world has come from working in partnership with such great companies as Intel, Compaq, Hewlett Packard, DEC, NEC, and dozens of others. Even IBM and Apple, with whom we have occasionally been in competition, have had an immense amount of our cooperation and support. We created a company that was dependent on partners. We bet that somebody other than us would do great chips, somebody other than us would build great PCs, somebody other than us would do great distribution and integration. We took a narrow slice and focused on that. In this new world, we want to work with companies from every industry to help them make the most of the opportunities the information revolution will bring.

Industry after industry will be changed, and change is unsettling. Some middlemen who handle information or product distribution will find they no longer add value and change fields, whereas others will rise to the competitive challenge. There is a nearly infinite number of tasks left undone in services, education, and urban affairs, to say nothing of the workforce the highway itself will require. So this new efficiency will create all sorts of exciting employment opportunities. And the highway, which will put an immense amount of information at anyone's fingertips, will be an invaluable training tool. Someone who decides to change careers and go into computer consulting will have access to the best texts, the greatest lectures, and information about course requirements, exams, and accreditation. There will be dislocations. However, overall, society will benefit from these changes.

Capitalism, demonstrably the greatest of the constructed economic systems, has in the past decade clearly proved its advantages over the alternative systems. The information highway will magnify those advantages. It will allow those who produce goods to see, a lot more efficiently than ever before, what buyers want, and will allow potential consumers to buy those goods more efficiently. Adam Smith would be pleased. More important, consumers everywhere will enjoy the benefits.

9

EDUCATION:
THE BEST INVESTMENT

Great educators have always known that learning is not something you do only in classrooms, or only under the supervision of teachers. Today it is sometimes difficult for someone who wants to satisfy his curiosity or end his confusion to find the appropriate information. The highway is going to give us all access to seemingly unlimited information, anytime and anyplace we care to use it. It's an exhilarating prospect, because putting this technology to use to improve education will lead to downstream benefits in every area of society.

Some fear that technology will dehumanize formal education. But anyone who has seen kids working together around a computer, the way my friends and I first did in 1968, or watched exchanges between students in classrooms separated by oceans, knows that technology can humanize the educational environment. The same technological forces that will make learning so necessary will also make it practical and enjoyable. Corporations are reinventing themselves around the flexible opportunities afforded by information technology; classrooms will have to change as well.

Howard Gardner, a professor at the Harvard Graduate School of Education, argues that different children must be taught differently, because individuals understand the world in different ways. Mass-produced education can't take into account children's various approaches to the world. Gardner recommends that schools be "filled with apprenticeships, projects, and technologies" so that every kind of learner can be accommodated. We will discover all sorts of different approaches to teaching because the highway's tools will make it easy to try various methods and to measure their effectiveness.

Just as information technology now allows Levi Strauss & Co. to offer jeans that are both mass-produced and custom fitted, information technology will bring mass customization to learning. Multimedia documents and easy-to-use authoring tools will enable teachers to "mass-customize" a curriculum. As with blue jeans, the mass customization of learning will be possible because computers will fine-tune the product—educational material, in this case—to allow students to follow somewhat divergent paths and learn at their own rates. This won't happen only in classrooms. Any student will be able to enjoy the custom fit of a tailor-made education at mass-production prices. Workers will be able to keep up-to-date on techniques in their fields.

Every member of society, including every child, will have more information easily at hand than anyone has today. I believe that just the availability of information will spark the curiosity and imagination of many. Education will become a very individual matter.

There is an often-expressed fear that technology will replace teachers. I can say emphatically and unequivocally, IT WON'T. The information highway won't replace or devalue any of the human educational talent needed for the challenges ahead: committed teachers, creative administrators, involved parents, and, of course, diligent students. However, technology will be pivotal in the future role of teachers.

The highway will bring together the best work of countless teachers and authors for everyone to share. Teachers will be able to draw on this material, and students will have the opportunity to explore it interactively. In time, this access will help spread educational and personal opportunities even to students who aren't fortunate enough to enjoy the best schools or the greatest family support. It will encourage a child to make the most of his or her native talents.

Before the benefits of these advances can be realized, though, the way computers in the classroom are thought about will have to change. A lot of people are cynical about educational technology because it has been overhyped and has failed to deliver on its promises. Many of the PCs in schools today are not powerful enough to be easy to use, and they don't have the storage capacity or network connections to permit them to respond to a child's curiosity with much information. So far, education remains largely unchanged by computers.

The slowness of schools to embrace technology partly reflects conservatism in many corners of the educational establishment. It reflects discomfort or even apprehension on the part of teachers and administrators, who as a group are older than the average worker. It also reflects the minuscule amounts city school budgets have allotted for educational technology.

The average primary or secondary school in the United States lags considerably behind the average American business in the availability of new information technology. Preschoolers familiar with cellular telephones, pagers, and personal computers enter kindergartens where chalkboards and overhead projectors represent the state of the art.

Reed Hundt, chairman of the U.S. Federal Communications Commission, commented on this. "There are thousands of buildings in this country with millions of people in them who have no telephones, no cable television and no reasonable prospect of broadband services," he said. "They are called schools."

Despite these constraints, genuine change is going to come. It won't happen abruptly. On the face of it, the basic patterns of education will remain the same. Students will continue to attend classes, listen to teachers, ask questions, participate in individual and group work (including hands-on experiments), and do homework.

There seems to be a universal commitment to having more computers in schools, but the rate at which they are being supplied varies from country to country. Only a few countries, such as the Netherlands, already have computers in nearly every school. In France and many other places, although few installations have taken place, governments have pledged to equip all their classrooms with computers. Britain, Japan, and the People's Republic of China have begun the process of incorporating information technology into their national curricula, with a focus on vocational training. I believe most countries will decide to make increased investments in education, and computer use in schools will catch up to its use in homes and businesses. Over time—longer in less developed countries—we are likely to see computers installed in every classroom in the world.

The cost of computer hardware gets cheaper almost by the month, and educational software will become quite affordable when purchased in quantity. Already many cable and telephone companies in the United States have promised free or reduced-price network connections to schools and libraries in their areas. For example, Pacific Bell has announced a plan to provide free ISDN service to every school in California for one year, and TCI and Viacom offer free cable to schools in every community they serve.

Although a classroom will still be a classroom, technology will transform a lot of the details. Classroom learning will include multimedia presentations, and homework will involve exploring electronic documents as much as textbooks, perhaps even more. Students will be encouraged to pursue areas of particular interest, and it will be easy for them to do so. Each pupil will be able to have his own question answered simultaneously with the other students' queries. A class will spend part of a day at a personal computer exploring information individually or in groups. Then the students will bring back their thoughts and questions about the information they have discovered to the teacher, who will be able to decide which questions should be brought to the attention of the full class. While students are at their computers, the teacher will be free to work with individuals or small groups and focus less on lecturing and more on problem solving.

Educators, like so many in today's economy, are, among other things, facilitators. Like many other, similar workers, they will have to adapt and readapt to changing conditions. Unlike some professions, however, the future of teaching looks extremely bright. As innovation has improved the standard of living, there has always been an increase in the portion of the workforce dedicated to education. Educators who bring energy and creativity to a classroom will thrive. So will teachers who build strong relationships with children, because kids love classes taught by adults they know genuinely care about them.

We've all had teachers who made a difference. I had a great chemistry teacher in high school who made his subject immensely interesting. Chemistry seemed enthralling compared to biology. In biology, we were dissecting frogs—just hacking them to pieces, actually—and our teacher didn't explain why. My chemistry teacher sensationalized his subject a bit and promised that it would help us understand the world. When I was in my twenties, I read James D. Watson's *Molecular Biology of the Gene* and decided my high school experience had misled me. The understanding of life is a great subject. Biological information is the most important information we can discover, because over the next several decades it will revolutionize medicine. Human DNA is like a computer program but far, far more advanced than any software ever created. It seems amazing to me now that one great teacher made chemistry endlessly fascinating while I found biology totally boring.

When teachers do excellent work and prepare wonderful materials, only their few dozen students benefit each year. It's difficult for teachers in different locations to build on one another's work. The network will enable teachers to share lessons and materials, so that the best educational practices can spread. In most cases watching a lecture on video is much less interesting than actually being in the room with the teacher. But sometimes the value of being able to hear a particular teacher outweighs the loss of interactivity. A few years ago, a friend and I discovered in the University of Washington's catalog videotapes of a series of lectures by the distinguished physicist Richard Feynman. We were able to watch the lectures on vacation ten years after Feynman gave the talks at Cornell. We might have gotten more from the lectures if we had been in the lecture hall or been able to ask him questions via a videoconference. But the clarity of his thinking explained many of the concepts of physics better than any book or any instructor I've ever had. He brought the subject to life. I think anyone studying physics should have these lectures easily accessible. With the information highway there will be lots of such uniquely valuable resources available to teachers and students.

If a teacher in Providence, Rhode Island, happened to have a particularly good way of explaining photosynthesis, her lecture notes and multimedia demonstrations could be obtained by educators around the world. Some teachers will use material exactly as it comes off the highway, but others will take advantage of easy-to-use authoring software to adapt and combine bits and pieces of what they find. Feedback from other interested instructors will be easy to get and will help refine the lesson. In a short time the improved material could be in thousands of classrooms all over the world. It will be easy to tell what materials are popular, because the network will be able to count the number of times they are accessed, or to poll teachers electronically. Corporations wanting to help with education could provide recognition and cash awards to teachers whose materials are making a difference.

It is hard for a teacher to prepare in-depth, interesting material for twenty-five students, six hours a day, 180 days a year. This is particularly true if students' extensive television watching has raised their entertainment expectations. I can imagine a middle-school science teacher a decade or so from now, working on a lecture about the sun, explaining not only the science but also the history of discoveries that made it possible. When a teacher wants to select a picture, still or video, whether it's a piece of art or a portrait of a great solar scientist, the highway will allow her to select from a comprehensive catalog of images. Snippets of video and narrated animations from countless sources will be available. It will only take minutes to pull together a visual show that would now require days of work to organize. As she lectures about the sun, she will have images and diagrams appear at appropriate times. If a student asks her about the source of the sun's power, she can answer using animated graphics of hydrogen and helium atoms, she'll be able to show solar flares or sunspots or other phenomena, or she might call up a brief video on fusion energy to the white board. The teacher will have organized the links to servers on the information highway in advance. She will make the list of links available to her students, so that during study times in the library or at home, they will be able to review the material from as many perspectives as they find helpful.

Think of a high school art teacher using a digital white board to display a high-quality digital reproduction of Seurat's *Bathers at Asnières*, which shows young men relaxing on the bank of the Seine River in the

-------------------------->

1880s against a background of sailboats and smokestacks. The white board will pronounce the name of the painting in the original French— *Une Baignade à Asnières*—and show a map of the outskirts of Paris, with the town of Asnières highlighted. The teacher might use the painting, which presaged Pointillism, to illustrate the end of Impressionism. Or she will use it to get into broader topics, such as life in France at the end of the nineteenth century, the Industrial Revolution, or even the way the eye sees complementary colors.

She might point to the orangish-red hat of a figure standing on the far right side of the composition and say: "Look at the vibrancy of the hat. Seurat has tricked the eye. The hat is red, but he has added tiny dots of orange and blue. You don't really notice the blue unless you look closely." As the teacher says this, the picture will zoom in on the hat, until the texture of the canvas is apparent. At this magnification, specks of blue will be obvious, and the teacher will explain that blue is the complement of orange. A color wheel will appear on the white board, and either the teacher or the multimedia document itself will explain: "Every color on this wheel is arranged opposite its complement. Red is opposite green, yellow is opposite purple, and blue is opposite orange. It is a quirk of the eye that staring at a color creates an afterimage of its complementary color. Seurat used this trick to make the red and orange hues of the hat more vivid by sneaking in dots of blue."

Computers connected to the highway will help teachers monitor, evaluate, and guide student performance. Teachers will continue to give homework, but soon their assignments will include hypertext references to electronic resource material. Students will create their own links and use multimedia elements in their homework, which will then be submitted electronically on a diskette or across the highway. Teachers will be able to keep a cumulative record of a student's work, which can be reviewed at any time or shared with other instructors.

Special software programs will help summarize information on the skills, progress, interests, and expectations of students. Once teachers have enough information on a student and are relieved of a lot of tedious paperwork, they will have more energy and time to meet the revealed individual needs of that student. This information will be used to tailor classroom materials and homework assignments. Teachers and parents will also be able to review and discuss the particulars of a child's progress easily. As a result of this—and of the common availability of videoconferences—the potential for strong parent-teacher collaboration will grow. Parents will be in a better position to help their children, whether by creating informal study groups with other parents or by seeking additional assistance for their children.

Parents may also help their children at school by teaching them to use the software they use in their work. Some teachers and staff are already using popular business software to administer their activities and to give students experience with the tools of the modern workplace. Most college students and an increasing number of high schoolers now prepare reports on PCs with word processors instead of using typewriters or writing by hand. Spreadsheets and charting applications are routinely used to explain mathematics and economic theories and have become a standard part of most accounting courses. Students and faculty have also discovered new uses for popular business applications. For example, students studying a foreign language can take advantage of the major word-processor programs' ability to work in different languages. Such programs include supplemental tools for checking spellings and looking up synonyms in multilingual documents.

In some families, children are probably introducing their parents to computing. Kids and computers get along just great, partly because kids aren't invested in established ways of doing things. Children like to provoke a reaction, and computers are reactive. Parents are sometimes surprised by how taken with computers even their preschoolers are, but the fascination makes sense if you think about how much a young child enjoys interaction—whether it is playing peek-a-boo with a parent or stabbing at a remote control and watching channels change.

I like to watch my three-year-old niece play with *Just Grandma and Me*, a Brøderbund CD-ROM based on a children's book. She has memorized the dialogue in this cartoon story and talks along with the characters, much as she does when her mother reads her a book. If my niece uses the computer's mouse to click on a mailbox, the mailbox opens and a frog jumps out or sometimes a hand appears and pulls the mailbox door shut. Her ability to influence what she sees on the screen—to answer the question "What happens if I click here?"—keeps her curiosity high. The interactivity, combined with the underlying quality of the storyline, keeps her involved.

I've always believed most people have more intelligence and curiosity than current information tools encourage them to use. Most people have had the experience of getting interested in a topic and feeling the gratifying sense of accomplishment that comes from finding good material on it, and the pleasure of mastering the topic. But if a search for information brings you up against a blank wall, you become discouraged. You begin to think you're never going to understand the subject. And if you experience that natural reaction too often, especially when you're a child, your impulse to try again is diminshed.

I was fortunate to be raised in a family that encouraged kids to ask questions. And I was lucky in my early teens to become friends with Paul Allen. Soon after I had met Paul, I asked him where gasoline came from. I wanted to know what it meant to "refine" gasoline. I wanted to know exactly how it was that gasoline could power a car. I had found a book on the subject, but it was confusing. Gasoline, however, was one of the many subjects that Paul understood, and he explained it in a way that made it interesting and understandable to me. You might say my curiosity about gasoline is what fueled our friendship.

Paul had lots of answers to things I was curious about (and a great collection of science fiction books too). I was more of a math person than Paul, and I understood software better than anyone he knew. We were interactive resources for each other. We asked or answered questions, drew diagrams, or brought each other's attention to related information. We liked to challenge and test each other. This is exactly the way the highway will interact with users. Let's say another teenager wants to find out about gasoline—not in 1970, but three or four years from now. He may not be lucky enough to have a Paul Allen around, but if his school or library has a computer linked to rich multimedia information, he'll be able to delve as deeply into the topic as he likes.

He'll see photos, videos, and animations explaining how oil is drilled, transported, and refined. He'll learn the difference between automobile fuel and aviation fuel—and if he wants to know the difference between a car's internal-combustion engine and a jetliner's turbine engine, all he'll have to do is ask.

He'll be able to explore the complex molecular structure of gasoline, which is a combination of hundreds of distinct hydrocarbons, and learn about hydrocarbons too. With all of the links to additional knowledge, who knows what fascinating topics this exploration will lead him to.

At first, new information technology will just provide incremental improvements over today's tools. Wall-mounted video white boards will replace a teacher's chalkboard handwriting with readable fonts and colorful graphics drawn from millions of educational illustrations, animations, photographs, and videos. Multimedia documents will assume some of the roles now played by textbooks, movies, tests, and other educational materials. And because multimedia documents will be linked to servers on the information highway, they will be kept thoroughly up-to-date.

CD-ROMs available today offer a taste of the interactive experience. The software responds to instructions by presenting information in text, audio, and video forms. CD-ROMs are already being used in schools and by kids doing their assignments at home, but they have limitations the highway won't. CD-ROMs can offer either a little information about a broad range of topics the way an encyclopedia does, or a lot of information about a single topic, such as dinosaurs, but the total amount of information available at one time is limited by the capacity of the disc. And, of course, you can use only the discs you have available. Nevertheless, they're a great advance over just-paper texts. Multimedia encyclopedias provide not only a research tool, but all sorts of material that can be incorporated into homework documents. These encyclopedias are available with teacher's guides that include suggestions for ways to use the encyclopedias in the classroom or as part of assignments. I have been excited to hear from teachers and students about the ways they have used our products—only a few of which we had anticipated.

CD-ROMs are one clear precursor to the highway. The Internet's World Wide Web is another. The Web offers access to interesting, educational information, although most of it is still plain text. Creative teachers are already using on-line services to devise exciting new kinds of lessons.

Fourth-graders in California have done on-line searches of newspapers to read about the challenges Asian immigrants face. Boston University has created interactive software for high school students that shows detailed visual simulations of chemical phenomena, such as salt molecules dissolving in water.

Christopher Columbus Middle School in Union City, New Jersey, was a school created out of crisis. In the late 1980s, the state test scores were so low and the absentee and dropout rates were so high among the children of the school district that the state was considering taking it over. The school system, the teachers, and the parents (well over 90 percent of whom were of Hispanic extraction and didn't speak English as a first language) came up with an innovative five-year plan to rescue their schools.

Bell Atlantic (the local telephone company) agreed to help find a special networked, multimedia system of PCs linking the students' homes with the classrooms, teachers, and school administrators. The corporation initially provided 140 multimedia PCs, enough for the homes of the seventh-graders, the homes of all seventh-grade teachers, and at least four per classroom. The computers were networked and linked with high-speed lines and connected to the Internet, and the teachers were trained in using the PCs. The teachers set up weekend training courses for the parents, over half of whom attended, and encouraged the students to use e-mail and the Internet.

Two years later, parents are actively involved with their children's use of the home PCs and employ them themselves to keep in touch with teachers and administrators; the dropout rate and absenteeism are both almost zero, and the students are scoring nearly three times higher than the average for all New Jersey inner-city schools on standardized tests. And the program has been expanded to include the entire middle school.

Raymond W. Smith, chairman of the board and CEO of Bell Atlantic, comments, "I believe a combination of a school system ready for fundamental change in teaching methods, a parent body that was supportive and wanted to be involved, and the careful but intensive integration of technology into both the homes and classrooms . . . created a true learning community in which the home and school reinforce and support each other."

At Lester B. Pearson School, a Canadian high school serving an ethnically diverse neighborhood, computers are an integral part of every course in the daily curriculum. For the 1,200 students there are more than 300 personal computers, and more than 100 different software titles are in use. The school says its dropout rate, 4 percent, when compared with a national average of 30 percent, is Canada's lowest. Thirty-five hundred people a year visit to see how a high school can "incorporate technology in every aspect of school life."

When the information highway is in operation, the texts of millions of books will be available. A reader will be able to ask questions, print the text, read it on-screen, or even have it read in his choice of voices. He'll be able to ask questions. It will be his tutor.

Computers with social interfaces will figure out how to present information so that it is customized for the particular user. Many educational software programs will have distinct personalities, and the student and the computer will get to know each other. A student will ask, perhaps orally, "What caused the American Civil War?" His or her computer will reply, describing the conflicting contentions: that it was primarily a battle over economics or human rights. The length and approach of the answer will vary depending on the student and the circumstances. A student will be able to interrupt at any time to ask the computer for more or less detail or to request a different approach altogether. The computer will know what information the student has read or watched and will point out connections or correlations and offer appropriate links. If the computer knows the student likes historical fiction, war stories, folk music, or sports, it may try to use that knowledge to present the information. But this will be only an attention-getting device. The machine, like a good human teacher, won't give in to a child who has lopsided interests. Instead it will use the child's predilections to teach a broader curriculum.

Different learning rates will be accommodated, because computers will be able to pay individual attention to independent learners. Children with learning disabilities will be particularly well served. Regardless of his or her ability or disability, every student will be able to work at an individual pace.

Another benefit of computer-aided learning will be the way many students come to view tests. Today, tests are pretty depressing for many kids. They are associated with falling short: "I got a bad grade," or "I ran out of time," or "I wasn't ready." After a while, many kids who haven't done well on tests may think to themselves, I'd better pretend tests aren't important to me, because I can never succeed at them. Tests can cause a student to develop a negative attitude toward all education.

The interactive network will allow students to quiz themselves anytime, in a risk-free environment. A self-administered quiz is a form of self-exploration, like the tests Paul Allen and I used to give each other. Testing will become a positive part of the learning process. A mistake won't call forth a reprimand; it will trigger the system to help the student overcome his misunderstanding. If someone really gets stuck, the system will offer to explain the circumstances to a teacher. There should be less apprehension about formal tests and fewer surprises, because ongoing self-quizzing will give each student a better sense of where he or she stands.

Many educational software and textbook companies are already delivering interactive computer products in mathematics, languages, economics, and biology that build basic skills this way. For example, Academic Systems of Palo Alto, California, is working on an interactive multimedia instructional system for colleges, to help teach basic math and English courses. The concept is called "mediated learning," and it blends traditional instruction with computer-based learning. Each student begins by taking a placement test to determine which topics he or she understands and where instruction is required. The system then creates a personalized lesson plan for the student. Periodic tests monitor the student's progress, and the lesson plan can be modified as the student masters concepts. The program can also report problems to the instructor, who can then give the student individual help. So far, the company has found that students in pilot programs like the new learning materials, but the most successful classes are those in which an instructor is more available. These results underscore the point that new technology, by itself, is not sufficient to improve education.

Some parents resist the use of computers because they believe they can't monitor what their child is doing and can't exert any control. Most parents are delighted when a child curls up with an engrossing book, but less enthusiastic when he spends hours at the computer. They're probably thinking of video games. A kid can spend a great deal of time using a video game without learning much. So far, a great deal more has been invested in computer software meant to entertain than in software to educate. It's easier to create an addictive game than it is to expose a child to a world of information in an appealing way.

However, as textbook budgets and parental spending shift to interactive material, there will be thousands of new software companies working with teachers to create entertainment-quality interactive learning materials. The Lightspan Partnership, for example, is using Hollywood talent to create live action and animated programs. Lightspan hopes its sophisticated production techniques will capture and retain the interest of the young viewers—ages five through eleven—and encourage them to spend more hours learning. Animated characters lead students through lessons that explain basic concepts, then into games that put them to use. The Lightspan lessons are grouped by two-year age spans and organized into series intended to complement elementary school curricula in mathematics, reading, and language arts. These programs will be available on televisions in homes and community centers as well as in classrooms. Until interactive television is widely available, this kind of programming will be offered on CD-ROMs or across the Internet to PC users.

All this information, however, is not going to solve the serious problems facing many public schools today: budget cuts, violence, drugs, high dropout rates, dangerous neighborhoods, teachers more concerned about survival than education. Offering new technology won't suffice. Society will also have to fix the fundamental problems.

But while some public schools face major challenges, they are also our greatest hope. Imagine a situation in which most of the kids in inner-city public schools are on the dole, are barely able to speak the national language, have few skills and an uncertain future. This was America in the early 1900s, when tens of millions of immigrants had overwhelmed the schools and social services of our big cities.

Yet that generation and the next achieved a standard of living unequaled in the world. The problems of America's schools are not insurmountable, just extremely complicated. Even today, for every disastrous public school there are dozens of successful ones you don't read

------------------------->

about. I've mentioned several examples here. It is outside the scope of this book to go deeply into this subject, but communities can, and have, won back their streets and schools. It's always taken an intense local effort. One street at a time, one school at a time. Then parents must insist that their kids come to school ready to learn. If the attitude is "Let the school (or government) do it," kids will fail.

Once even the most modest positive atmosphere for education is established, the information highway will help raise the educational standards for everyone in future generations. The highway will allow new methods of teaching and much more *choice*. Quality curriculums can be created with government funding and made available for free. Private vendors will compete to enhance the free material. The new vendors might be other public schools; public-school teachers or retired teachers going into business for themselves; or some privately run, highway-based school service program wanting to prove its capabilities. The highway would be a way for schools to try out new teachers or use their services at a distance.

The highway will also make home schooling easier. It will allow parents to select some classes from a range of quality possibilities and still maintain control over content.

Learning with a computer will be a springboard for learning away from the computer. Young children will still need to touch toys and tools with their hands. Seeing chemical reactions on a computer screen can be a good supplement to hands-on work in a chemistry lab, but it can't replace the real experience. Children need personal interaction with each other, and with adults, to learn social and interpersonal skills, such as how to work cooperatively.

The good teachers of the future will be doing much more than showing kids where to find information on the highway. They will still have to understand when to probe, observe, stimulate, or agitate. They'll still have to build kids' skills in written and oral communications, and will use technology as a starting point or an aid. Successful teachers will act as coaches, partners, creative outlets, and communications bridges to the world.

Computers on the information highway will be able to simulate the world as well as explain it. Creating or using a computer model can be a great educational tool. Several years ago, a teacher at Sunnyside High School in Tucson, Arizona, organized a club of students to create computer simulations of real-world behaviors. The students discovered the grim consequences of gang behavior by modeling it for themselves mathematically. The success of the club led eventually to a complete reorganization of the mathematics curriculum around the idea that education is not about making kids give the "right" answer, but about giving kids methods by which to decide whether an answer is "right."

The teaching of science lends itself particularly well to using models. Kids now learn trigonometry by measuring the height of real mountains. They triangulate from two points rather than just doing abstract exercises. There are already a number of computer models that teach biology. *SimLife*, a popular software program, simulates evolution, so kids get to experience the process instead of just getting facts about it. You don't have to be a child to enjoy this program, which lets you design plants and animals and then watch how they interact and evolve in an ecosystem that you also design. Maxis Software, the publisher of *SimLife*, also produces another program, *SimCity*, which lets you design a city with all of its interrelated systems, such as roads and public transportation. As a player, you get to be the mayor or city planner of a virtual community and to challenge yourself to meet your own goals for the community, rather than goals artificially imposed by the software's design. You build farms, factories, homes, schools, universities, libraries, museums, zoos, hospitals, prisons, marinas, freeways, bridges, even subways. You cope with urban growth or natural disasters, such as fires. You change the terrain too. When you modify your simulated city by building an airport or raising taxes, the changes can have a predictable or unexpected effect on the simulated society. It is a great, fast way to find out how the real world works.

Or use a simulation to find out about what goes on out of this world. Kids can navigate the solar system or galaxy in a simulated spaceship by playing with a space simulator. Kids who may think they aren't interested in biology or urban design or outer space can discover they are by exploring and experimenting with computer simulations. When science is made more interesting in these ways, it should appeal to a broader set of students.

------------------------->

In the future, students of all ages and capabilities will be able to visualize and interact with information. For example, a class studying weather will be able to view simulated satellite images based on a model of hypothetical meteorological conditions. Students will propose "what if?" questions, such as "What would happen to the next day's weather if the wind speed increased by 15 MPH?" The computer will model the predicted results, displaying the simulated weather system as it would appear from space. Simulation games will get much better, but even now the best of them are fascinating and highly educational.

When simulations get completely realistic, we enter the realm of virtual reality. I'm sure that at some point schools will have virtual-reality equipment—or maybe even VR rooms, the way some now have music rooms and theaters—to allow students to explore a place, an object, or a subject in this engrossing, interactive way.

Technology will not, however, isolate students. One of the most important educational experiences is collaboration. In some of the world's most creative classrooms, computers and communications networks are already beginning to change the conventional relationships among students themselves, and between students and teachers, by facilitating collaborative learning.

Teachers at the Ralph Bunche school (P.S. 125) in Harlem created a computer-assisted teaching unit to show New York inner-city students how to use the Internet for research, to communicate with electronic pen pals worldwide, and to collaborate with volunteer tutors at nearby Columbia University. Ralph Bunche was one of the first elementary schools in the nation to put its own home page on the Internet's World Wide Web. Its Web home page, the work of a student, includes links to such things as the school newspaper, student artwork, and a lesson on the Spanish alphabet illustrated.

Especially at the college level, academic research has been aided enormously by the Internet, which has made it easier for far-flung institutions and individuals to collaborate. Computer innovation has always taken place at universities. Several universities are centers for advanced research into new computer technologies, and many others maintain large computer labs that students use for collaboration and homework. Also, today some of the most interesting home pages on the Internet's World Wide Web are posted on behalf of universities around the world.

Some universities put the network to less global uses. At the University of Washington, lesson plans and assignments for some classes are posted on the World Wide Web. Lecture notes are often published on the Web too, a free service I would have loved in my college days. Elsewhere, an English teacher requires all his students to have e-mail addresses and use e-mail to participate in after-hours electronic discussions. Class members are graded on their e-mail contributions, just as they are on classroom contributions and homework.

College students everywhere already understand the joys of e-mail, both for educational purposes and to keep in touch inexpensively with family and friends, including high school friends who have gone to other universities. A growing number of parents of college students have become regular e-mail users because it seems to be the best way to contact their kids. Even some elementary schools allow older students to have Internet accounts. At Lakeside, my old school, the school's network

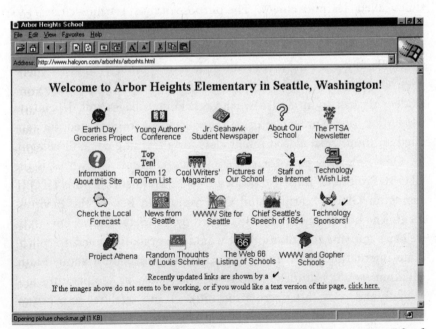

1995: World Wide Web home page from Arbor Heights Elementary School

is now connected to the Internet, which permits kids to browse for on-line information and exchange national and international e-mail. Nearly all Lakeside students requested e-mail accounts, and in one typical twelve-week period they received a total of 259,587 messages—an average of about 30 messages per student each week. About 49,000 messages were from the Internet during the twelve-week period, and the students sent about 7,200 messages.

Lakeside doesn't know how many messages each student sends, and it doesn't know what the messages are about. Some e-mail relates to school studies and activities, but doubtless a lot of it, including much of Lakeside's traffic on the Internet, concerns students' outside interests. Lakeside doesn't view this as an abuse of the electronic mail system, but as another way to learn.

A number of secondary school students, like those at New York's P.S. 125, are discovering how the long-distance access afforded by computer networks can help them learn from students from other cultures, and participate in discussions all over the world. Many classrooms, in different states and countries, are already linking up in what are sometimes called "learning circles." The purpose of most learning circles is to let students study a specific topic, in collaboration with faraway counterparts. In 1989, as the Berlin Wall was falling, West German students were able to discuss the event with their contemporaries in other countries. One learning circle that was studying the whaling industry included Alaskan Inuit students, whose Eskimo villages still depend on whales for food. Students outside the village got so interested, they invited an Inuit tribal elder to their class for a learning circle discussion.

One ambitious plan for students using computer networks is the GLOBE Project, an initiative pushed by Vice President Al Gore. GLOBE stands for Global Learning and Observations to Benefit the Environment. The hope is that it will be funded by a variety of governments as well as by private contributions. It would ask grade-schoolers to collaborate internationally on collecting scientific information about Earth. Children would routinely collect statistics, such as temperature and rainfall, and relay them across the Internet and satellites to a central database at the National Oceanic and Atmospheric Administration in Maryland, where the information would be used to create composite

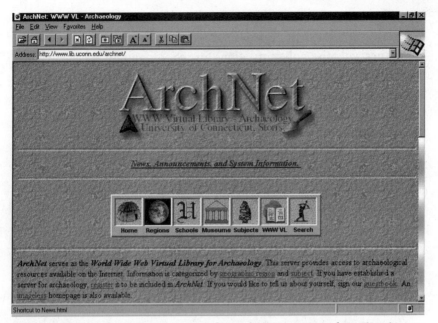

1995: World Wide Web home page from the University of Connecticut, featuring archeological resources drawn from many sources

pictures of the planet. The composites would be relayed back to the students, as well as to scientists and the general public. No one knows how much scientific value the data would have, especially the data collected by the very young, but gathering the facts and seeing the composite pictures would be a fine way for large numbers of children from many nations to learn about global cooperation, communication, and environmental issues.

The highway's educational possibilities will also be open to the world's unofficial students. People anywhere will be able to take the best courses taught by great teachers. The highway will make adult education, including job training and career-enhancement courses, more readily available.

A lot of parents, professionals, and community or political leaders will have the opportunity to participate in the teaching process, even if only for an hour here or there. It will be practical, inexpensive, and, I think, commonplace for knowledgeable guests to lead or join discussions, via videoconferences, from their homes or offices.

Having students connected directly to limitless information and to each other will raise policy questions for schools and for society at large. I discussed the issue of regulation of the Internet. Will students routinely be allowed to bring their portable PCs with them into every classroom? Will they be allowed to explore independently during group discussions? If so, how much freedom should they have? Should they be able to look up a word they don't understand? Should they have access to information that their parents find objectionable on moral, social, or political grounds? Be allowed to do homework for an unrelated class? Be permitted to send notes to each other during class? Should the teacher be able to monitor what is on every student's screen or to record it for later spot-checking?

Whatever problems direct access to unlimited information may cause, the benefits it will bring will more than compensate. I enjoyed school but I pursued my strongest interests outside the classroom. I can only imagine how access to this much information would have changed my own school experience. The highway will alter the focus of education from the institution to the individual. The ultimate goal will be changed from getting a diploma to enjoying lifelong learning.

10

PLUGGED IN
AT HOME

One of the many fears expressed about the information highway is that it will reduce the time people spend socializing. Some worry that homes will become such cozy entertainment providers that we'll never leave them, and that, safe in our private sanctuaries, we'll become isolated. I don't think that's going to happen, and later in this chapter, when I describe the house I'm building, I think I make my case.

The house, which has been under construction for what seems like most of my life (and it seems I've been reading about the construction even longer), is full of advanced entertainment equipment, such as a small movie theater and a video-on-demand system. It should be an interesting place to live, but I certainly don't plan to stay home all the time. Other people, when they have entertainment flowing into their homes, will also continue to go to theaters, just as they'll visit parks, museums, and shops. As behaviorists keep reminding us, we're social animals. We will have the option of staying home more because the highway will create so many new options for home-based entertainment, for communications—both personal and professional—and for employment. Although the mix of activities will change, I think people will decide to spend almost as much time out of their homes.

In chapter 1, I mentioned dire anticultural predictions from the past that didn't come about. More recently, in the 1950s, there were those who said movie theaters would disappear and everyone would stay home watching the new invention, television. Pay TV and, later, movie video rentals provoked similar fears. Why would anyone spend money for parking and baby-sitters, buy the most expensive soft drinks and candy bars in the world, to sit in a dark room with strangers? But popular movies continue to fill theaters. Personally, I love movies and enjoy the experience of going out to see them. I do it almost every week, and I don't think the information highway will change that.

The new communications capabilities will make it far easier than it is today to stay in touch with friends and relatives who are geographically distant. Many of us have struggled to keep alive a friendship with someone far away. I used to date a woman who lived in a different city. We spent a lot of time together on e-mail. And we figured out a way we could sort of go to the movies together. We'd find a film that was playing at about the same time in both our cities. We'd drive to our respective theaters, chatting on our cellular phones. We'd watch the movie, and on the way home we'd use our cellular phones again to discuss the show. In the future this sort of "virtual dating" will be better because the movie watching could be combined with a videoconference.

I already play bridge on an on-line system that allows the players to see who else is interested in joining a game because it has a waiting room. Players have a primitive ability to choose the way they want to appear to the other players: their sex, hairstyle, body build, etc. The first time I connected to the system, I was in a rush to keep a bridge appointment, and I didn't spend any time setting up my electronic appearance. After my friends and I had started playing, they all began to send me messages about how I was bald and naked (from the waist up, the only part of the body it showed). Even though this system didn't allow video or voice communication the way future systems will, the ability to send text messages to each other while we were playing made it a real blast.

The highway will not only make it easier to keep up with distant friends, it will also enable us to find new companions. Friendships formed across the network will lead naturally to getting together in person. Right now our methods for linking up with people we might like are pretty limited, but the network will change that. We will be meeting some of our new friends in different ways from the ones we use today. This alone will make life more interesting. Suppose you want to reach someone to play bridge with. The information highway will let you find cardplayers with the right skill level and availability in your neighborhood, or in other cities or nations. The idea of interactive games played by far-flung participants is hardly new. Chess players have been carrying on games by mail, one move at a time, for generations. The difference will be that applications running on the network will make it easy to find others who share similar interests and also to play together at the same pace you would face-to-face.

Another difference will be that while you are playing a game—say, bridge or *Starfighter*—you will be able to chat with the other players. The new DSVD modems I discussed earlier will let you use a normal phone line to carry on a voice conversation with the other players while watching the play unfold on your computer screen.

The experience of playing a friendly group game, as you do at the traditional card table, is pleasurable as much for the fellowship as for the competition. The game is more fun when you are enjoying the conversation. A number of companies are taking this multiplayer-game concept to a new level. You'll be able to play alone, with a few friends, or with thousands of people, and it will eventually be possible to see the people you are playing with—if they choose to permit you to. It will be easy to locate an expert and watch him play or take lessons from him. On the highway, you and your friends will not only be able to gather around a game table, you'll also be able to "meet" at a real place, such as Kensington Gardens, or in an imaginary setting. You'll be able to play a conventional game in a remarkable location, or play a new kind of game in which exploring the virtual setting is part of the action.

Warren Buffett, who is famous for his investment savvy, is a good friend of mine. For years I kept trying to think of how to entice him to use a personal computer. I even offered to fly out and get him started. He wasn't interested until he found out he could play bridge with friends all over the country through an on-line service. For the first six months he would come home and play for hours on end. Despite the fact that he had studiously stayed away from technology and technology investing, once he tried the computer, he was hooked. Now, many weeks Warren uses on-line services more than I do. The present system doesn't require you to enter your true appearance, or name, age, or sex. However, it seems that most of the users are either kids or retirees—neither of which describes Warren. One feature that had to be added into the system was a limit that permits parents to restrict the amount of time (and money) their kids spend on-line.

I think on-line computer-game playing will catch on in a big way. We'll be able to choose from a rich set of games, including all the classic board and card games as well as action adventure and role-playing games. New styles of games will be invented specifically for this medium. There will be contests with prizes awarded. From time to time, celebrities and experts will come onto the system and everyone else will be able to watch as the celebrities play, or sign up to play against them.

TV game shows will evolve to a new level when viewer feedback is added. Viewers will be able to vote and see the results immediately—sort of like the applause meter used on the live audience in old shows such as *Queen for a Day*. This format will also allow for prizes to be given to players. Some entrepreneurial companies, Answer TV for one, have already designed and tested systems specifically for interactive TV games, but because the system has only one application, so far it hasn't caught on enough to make money. On the information highway, you won't have to buy special hardware or software to interact with a television show. Imagine the future *Password* or *Jeopardy!* show that will let viewers at home participate and win either cash or credits of some sort. Shows will even be able to keep track of and reward their regular audience members by giving them special prizes or mentioning them by name if they choose to join the game.

Gambling is going to be another way to play on the highway. It's a huge business in Las Vegas, Reno, and Atlantic City, and it nearly supports Monaco. The profits garnered by the casinos are incredible. Gamblers continue to believe that even though the odds are against them, they're going to win. When I was in college I enjoyed playing poker. I think of poker as mostly a game of skill. Although I play blackjack sometimes when I'm in Las Vegas, the gambling games that are mostly luck don't have a strong appeal for me. Perhaps it's because I am so much more limited by time than money. If they had a form of gambling that would award the winners a few more hours in the day, I might be drawn in.

Advances in technology have already had an impact on gambling. One of the early uses of the telegraph and, later, ticker services was to deliver racetrack results. Satellite television broadcasts contributed to off-track betting. Slot machine designs have always tracked the progress in mechanical calculators and, more recently, computers. The information highway will have an even more significant effect on both legal and illegal gambling. We are sure to see current odds posted on servers, and e-mail as a way to make bets. Electronic currency will be used to place bets and make payoffs.

Gambling is a highly regulated business, so it's difficult to predict what forms will be allowed on the highway. Maybe air travelers who are stuck on a plane with nothing else to do will be able to gamble with each other. Perhaps gambling games will have to provide full disclosure of the odds against you. The technology will allow people to bet on anything they choose to, and if it's legal someone is sure to set up a service. It will be possible to bring horse races, dog races, or any other kind of live sports event into your home in real-time, so some of the excitement of the track or stadium will be made available. Many governments raise revenue with lotteries and in the future could provide plug-into electronic lotteries. The highway will make gambling far more difficult to control than it is today.

We can be sure we'll use the highway's unique capabilities to help us find communities of others with common interests. Today you may belong to the local ski club so you can meet other people who like to ski. You may also subscribe to *Recreational Skier* so you can get information about new ski products. Tomorrow you will be able to join such a community on the information highway. It will not only provide you with up-to-date information about weather conditions instantly, but will also be a way for you to stay in touch with other enthusiasts.

The greater the number of people who join an electronic community, the more valuable it will be to everyone who uses it. Most of the world's skiing enthusiasts will participate, at least occasionally. In time, the world's best information about skis and skiing will be available electronically. If you join, you will find the best slopes near Munich, the lowest price anywhere for a particular set of poles, and the latest news and advertising about all ski-related products. If people have taken photos or made videos of a race or a trip, they can share them. Books about skiing will be reviewed by anyone who has an opinion. Laws and safety practices will be debated. Instructional videos will be available on a moment's notice. These multimedia documents will be available free or for a charge, to one person or to hundreds of thousands. This community on the information highway will become the place to go if you are interested in skiing.

If you want to get yourself in better physical condition before trying a hard slope, you might find training more fun if you are in close electronic touch with a dozen other people who are your size, weight, and age, and who share your specific goals for exercise and weight reduction. You would have less to be self-conscious about in an exercise program in which everyone else is like you. And if you still were uncomfortable, you could turn your video camera off. Members of this community could get together to encourage each other and even work out at the same time.

The community of skiers is quite large and easy to define. On the information highway there will be applications to help you find people and information that intersect with your interests, no matter how specific. If you're thinking of visiting Berlin, the highway will make vast amounts of historical, touristic, and sociological information available. But there will also be applications to let you find fellow enthusiasts there. You'll be invited to register your interests in databases that can be analyzed by the applications. These applications will even suggest people you might like to meet. If you have a collection of Venetian glass paperweights, you'll probably choose to be a member of one or more world communities of people who share this interest. Some of those people may live in Berlin and have collections they'd be delighted to show you. If you have a ten-year-old daughter you'll be taking with you to Berlin, you might query whether there is anyone in Berlin who has a ten-year-old, shares your language, and is willing to spend time with you during your visit. If you find two or three suitable people, you have created a small—and probably temporary—community of interest.

I recently visited Africa and took a lot of pictures of chimpanzees. If the information highway were available now, I would put out a message saying that if anyone else from the safari wanted to exchange photographs, he or she should put them on the same bulletin board where I had posted my chimpanzee photos. I would be able to set it up so only fellow safari members could have access to that bulletin board.

Already, thousands of newsgroups on the Internet and countless forums on commercial on-line services have been set up as locations for small communities to share information. For example, on the Internet there are lively text-based discussion groups with such names as alt.agri-culture.fruit, alt.animals.raccoons, alt.asian-movies alt.coffee, bionet.-biology.cardiovascular, soc.religion.islam, and talk.philosophy.misc. But these topics aren't nearly so specialized as some of the subjects I expect electronic communities will address in the future. Some communities will be very local, and some will be global. You won't be overwhelmed by the number of choices of communities any more than you are now by the telephone system. You'll look for a group that interests you in general, and then you'll search through it for the small segment you want to join. I can imagine the administration of every municipality, for example, becoming the focus of an electronic community.

Sometimes I get annoyed by a traffic light near my office that always stays red longer than I think it should. I could write a letter to the city, telling the folks who program the lights that the timing isn't optimal, but that would just be one cranky letter. On the other hand, if I could find the "community" of people who drive the route I do, we could send a strong complaint to the city. I could find these others by sending a message to people who live near me or by posting a message on a community affairs bulletin board that showed a map of the intersection accompanied by the message: "During the morning rush hours hardly anyone goes left at this intersection. Does anyone else think the cycle should be shortened?" Anyone who agreed with me could add to my message. It would make it easier to fight City Hall.

As on-line communities grow in importance, they will increasingly be where people will turn to find out what the public is really thinking.

--------------------------➤

People like to know what's popular, which movies friends are watching, and what news others think is interesting. I want to read the same "newspaper front page" as those I'm going to meet with later today, so we can have something in common to talk about. You will be able to see what places on the network are being looked at often. There will be all sorts of "hot lists" of the coolest places.

Electronic communities, with all the information they reveal, will also create problems. Some institutions will have to make big changes as on-line communities gain power. Doctors and medical researchers are already having to contend with patients who explore medical literature electronically and compare notes with other patients who have the same serious disease. Word of unorthodox or unapproved treatments spreads fast in these communities. Some patients in drug trials have been able to figure out, by communicating with other patients in the trial, that they are receiving a placebo rather than the real medication. The discovery has prompted some of them to drop out of the trials or to seek alternate, simultaneous remedies. This undermines the research, but it is hard to fault patients who are trying to save their lives.

It's not just medical researchers who will be affected by so much access to information. One of the biggest concerns is parents having to contend with children who can find out about almost anything they want to, right from a home information appliance. Already, rating systems are being designed to allow parental control over what kids have access to. This could become a major political issue if the information publishers don't handle it properly.

On balance, the advantages will greatly outweigh the problems. The more information there is available, the more choices we will have. Today, devoted fans plan their evenings around the broadcast times of their favorite television shows, but once video-on-demand gives us the opportunity to watch whatever we like whenever we like, family or social activities, rather than a broadcaster's time slots, will control our entertainment schedules. Before the telephone, people thought of their neighbors as their only community. Almost everything was done with others who lived nearby. The telephone and the automobile allowed us to stretch out. We may visit face-to-face less often than we did a century ago because we can pick up the telephone, but this doesn't mean we have become isolated. It has made it easier for us to talk to each other and stay in touch. Sometimes it may seem too easy for people to reach you.

A decade from now, you may shake your head that there was ever a time when any stranger or a wrong number could interrupt you at home with a phone call. Cellular phones, pagers, and fax machines have already made it necessary for businesspeople to make explicit decisions that used to be implicit. A decade ago we didn't have to decide whether we wanted to receive documents at home or take calls on the road. It was easy to withdraw to your house, or certainly to your car. With modern technology you have to decide when and where you want to be available. In the future, when you will be able to work anywhere, reach anyone from anywhere, and be reached anywhere, you will be able to determine easily who and what can intrude. By explicitly indicating allowable interruptions, you will be able to reestablish your home—or anywhere you choose—as your sanctuary.

The information highway will help by prescreening all incoming communications, whether live phone calls, multimedia documents, e-mail, advertisements, or even news flashes. Anyone who has been approved by you will be able to get through to your electronic in-box or ring your phone. You might allow some people to send you mail but not to telephone. You might let others call when you have indicated you're not busy and let still others get through anytime. You won't want to receive thousands of unsolicited advertisements every day, but if you are looking for tickets to a sold-out concert, you'll want to get responses to your solicitations right away. Incoming communications will be tagged by source and type—for instance, ads, greetings, inquiries, publications, work-related documents, or bills. You'll set explicit delivery policies. You'll decide who can make your phone ring during dinner, who can reach you in your car, or when you're on vacation, and which kinds of calls or messages are worth waking you for in the middle of the night. You'll be able to make as many distinctions as you need and to change the criteria whenever you want. Instead of giving out your telephone number, which can be passed around and used indefinitely, you will add a welcome caller's name to a constantly updated list indicating your level of interest in receiving his messages. If someone not on any of your lists wants to get to you, he'll have to have someone who is listed forward the message. You'll always be able to demote someone to a lower level or delete a name altogether from all level lists. If you do that, to get your attention the caller will have to send you a paid message, as discussed in chapter 8.

The changes in technology will start to influence architecture. As the ways in which homes are used change, the buildings will evolve. Computer-controlled displays of various sizes will be built into the design of the house. Wires to connect components will be installed during construction, and thought will be given to the placement of screens in relation to windows to minimize reflection and glare. When information appliances are connected to the highway, there will be less need for many physical things—reference books, stereo receivers, compact discs, fax machines, file drawers, and storage boxes for records and receipts. A lot of space-consuming clutter will collapse into digital information that can be recalled at will. Even old photographs will be able to be stored digitally and called up on a screen instead of having to sit in a frame.

I've been giving these details a lot of thought because I'm building a house now, and in it I'm trying to anticipate the near future. My house is being designed and constructed so that it's a bit ahead of its time, but perhaps it suggests things about the future of homes. When I describe the plans, people sometimes give me a look that says, "You're sure you really want to do this?"

Like almost anyone who contemplates building a house, I want mine to be in harmony with its surroundings and with the needs of the people who will occupy it. I want it to be architecturally appealing. Mostly, though, I want it to be comfortable. It's where my family and I will live. A house is an intimate companion or, in the words of the great twentieth-century architect Le Corbusier, "a machine for living in."

My house is made of wood, glass, concrete, and stone. It's built into a hillside and most of the glass faces west over Lake Washington to Seattle to take advantage of the sunset and Olympic mountain views.

My house is also made of silicon and software. The installation of silicon microprocessors and memory chips, and the software that makes them useful, will let the house approximate some of the features the information highway will, in a few years, bring to millions of houses. The technology I'll use is experimental today, but over time portions of what I'm doing could become widely accepted and will get less expensive. The entertainment system will be a close enough simulation of how media usage will work that I will be able to get a sense of what it will be like to live with various technologies.

It won't, of course, be possible to simulate the highway's applications, which require that a lot of people be connected. A private information highway is a little like only one person having a telephone. The really interesting highway applications will grow out of the participation of tens or hundreds of millions of people, who will not just consume entertainment and other information, but will create it, too. Until millions of people are communicating with one another, exploring subjects of common interest and making all sorts of multimedia contributions, including high-quality video, there won't be an information highway.

The cutting-edge technology in the house I'm building won't just be for previewing entertainment applications. It will also help meet the usual domestic needs: for heat, light, comfort, convenience, pleasure, and security. This technology will be replacing older forms that we take for granted now. It wasn't that long ago that the public would have been amazed at the idea of a house with electric lights, flush toilets, telephones, and air-conditioning. My goal is a house that offers entertainment and stimulates creativity in a relaxed, pleasant, welcoming atmosphere. These desires aren't very different from those of people who could afford adventurous houses in the past. I'm experimenting to find out what works best, but there's a long tradition of that, too.

In 1925, when William Randolph Hearst, the newspaper magnate, moved into his California castle, San Simeon, he wanted the best in modern technology. In those days it was awkward and time-consuming to tune radio receivers to stations, so he had several radios installed in the basement of San Simeon, each tuned to a different station. The speaker wires ran to Hearst's private suite on the third floor, where they were routed into a fifteenth-century oak cabinet. At the push of a button, Hearst could listen to the station of his choice. It was a marvel in its day. Today this is a standard feature on every car radio.

I am certainly in no way comparing my house with San Simeon, one of the West Coast's monuments to excess. The only connection I'm making is that the technological innovations I have in mind for my house are not really different in spirit from those Hearst wanted in his. He wanted news and entertainment, all at a touch. So do I.

I began thinking about building a new house in the late 1980s. I wanted craftsmanship but nothing ostentatious. I wanted a house that would accommodate sophisticated, changing technology, but in an unobtrusive way that made it clear that technology was the servant, not the master. I didn't want the house to be defined by its use of technology. Originally the house was designed as a bachelor pad, but when Melinda and I got married we changed the plan to make it more suitable for a family. For instance, the kitchen was improved so it could better accommodate a family. However, the appliances have no more advanced technology than you'd find in any other well-appointed kitchen. Melinda also pointed out and corrected the fact that I had a great study but there was no place designated for her to work.

I found some property on the shore of Lake Washington within easy commuting distance of Microsoft. In 1990, work on a guest cottage began. Then, in 1992, we began excavating and laying the foundation for the main residence. This was a big job, requiring a lot of concrete, because Seattle is an earthquake zone at least as perilous as California.

Living space will be about average for a large house. The family living room will be about fourteen by twenty-eight feet, including an area for watching television or listening to music. And there will be cozy spaces for one or two people, although there will also be a reception hall to entertain one hundred comfortably for dinner. I enjoy having get-togethers for new Microsoft employees and summer hires. The house will also have a small movie theater, a pool, and a trampoline room. A sport court will sit amid some trees near the water's edge, behind a dock for water-skiing, one of my favorite sports. A small estuary, to be fed with groundwater from the hill behind the house, is planned. We'll seed the estuary with sea-run cutthroat trout, and I'm told to expect river otters.

If you come to visit, you'll drive down a gently winding driveway that approaches the house through an emergent forest of maple and alder, punctuated with Douglas fir. Several years ago, decomposing duff from the forest floor of a logging area was gathered and spread across

Computer rendering of the Gateses' future home,
showing the view from the northwest across Lake Washington

the back of the property. All kinds of interesting things are growing now. After a few decades, as the forest matures, Douglas fir will dominate the site, just as the big trees did before the area was logged for the first time at the turn of the twentieth century.

When you stop your car in the semicircular turnaround, although you will be at the front door you won't see much of the house. That's because you'll be entering onto the top floor. First thing, as you come in, you'll be presented with an electronic pin to clip to your clothes. This pin will connect you to the electronic services of the house. Next, you will descend either by elevator or down a staircase that runs straight toward the water under a sloping glass ceiling supported by posts of Douglas fir. The house has lots of exposed horizontal beams and vertical supports. You'll have a great view of the lake. My hope is that the view and the Douglas fir, rather than the electronic pin, will be what interest you most as you descend toward the ground floor. Most of the wood came from an eighty-year-old Weyerhaeuser lumber mill that was being torn down out on the Columbia River. This wood, harvested nearly a hundred years ago, came from trees that were as much as 350 feet tall, between 8 and 15 feet in diameter. Douglas fir is one of the strongest woods in the world for its weight. Unfortunately, new-growth Douglas fir tends to split if you try to mill it into beams, because the grain is not as tight in a seventy-year-old tree as it is in a five-hundred-year-old one. Almost all of the old-growth Douglas fir has been harvested now, and any that remains should be preserved. I was lucky to find old-growth timbers that could be reused.

The fir beams support the two floors of private living spaces you'll be descending past. Privacy is important. I want a house that will still feel like home even when guests are enjoying other parts of it.

At the bottom of the stairs, the theater will be on the right, and to the left, on the south side, will be the reception hall. As you step into the reception hall, on your right will be a series of sliding glass doors that open onto a terrace leading to the lake. Recessed into the east wall will be twenty-four video monitors, each with a 40-inch picture tube, stacked four high and six across. These monitors will work cooperatively to display large images for artistic, entertainment, or business purposes. I had hoped that when the monitors weren't in use they could literally disappear into the woodwork. I wanted the screens to display wood-grain patterns that matched their surroundings. Unfortunately I could never achieve anything convincing with current technology, because a monitor emits light while real wood reflects it. So I settled for having the monitors disappear behind wood panels when they're not in use.

The electronic pin you wear will tell the house who and where you are, and the house will use this information to try to meet and even anticipate your needs—all as unobtrusively as possible. Someday, instead of needing the pin, it might be possible to have a camera system with visual-recognition capabilities, but that's beyond current technology. When it's dark outside, the pin will cause a moving zone of light to accompany you through the house. Unoccupied rooms will be unlit. As you walk down a hallway, you might not notice the lights ahead of you gradually coming up to full brightness and the lights behind you fading. Music will move with you, too. It will seem to be everywhere, although, in fact, other people in the house will be hearing entirely different music or nothing at all. A movie or the news will be able to follow you around

Computer rendering of the Gateses' future home, showing the staircase and formal dining room

the house, too. If you get a phone call, only the handset nearest you will ring.

You won't be confronted by the technology, but it will be readily and easily available. Handheld remote controls will put you in charge of your immediate environment and of the house's entertainment system. The remote will extend the capabilities of the pin. It will not only let the house identify and locate you, it will also allow you to give instructions. You'll use the controls to tell the monitors in a room to become visible and what to display. You'll be able to choose from among thousands of pictures, recordings, movies, and television programs, and you'll have all sorts of options available for selecting information.

A console, which will be the equivalent of a keyboard that lets you give very specific instructions, will be discreetly visible in each room. I want consoles that are noticeable to those who need them, but that don't invite attention. A characteristic, easy-to-identify feature will alert the user to the identity and whereabouts of the consoles. The telephone has already made this transition. It doesn't attract particular attention to

- ▶

itself; most of us are comfortable putting a nondescript phone on an end table.

Every computerized system should be made so simple and natural to use that people don't give it a second thought. But simple is difficult. Still, computers get easier to use every year, and trial-and-error in my house will help us learn how to create a really simple system. You will be able to be indirect about your instructions and requests. For example, you won't have to ask for a song by name. You will be able to ask the house to play the latest hits, or songs by a particular artist, or songs that were performed at Woodstock, or music composed in eighteenth-century Vienna, or songs with the word "yellow" in their titles. You will be able to ask for songs that you have categorized with a certain adjective, or songs that haven't been played before when a particular person was visiting the house. I might program classical music as background for contemplating and something more modern and energetic to play while I'm exercising. If you want to watch the movie that won the 1957 Academy Award for best picture, you can ask for it that way—and see *The Bridge on the River Kwai.* You could find the same movie by asking for films starring Alec Guinness or William Holden or ones about prison camps.

*Prototype of
a home control console*

If you're planning to visit Hong Kong soon, you might ask the screen in your room to show you pictures of the city. It will seem to you as if the photographs are displayed everywhere, although actually the images will materialize on the walls of rooms just before you walk in and vanish after you leave. If you and I are enjoying different things and one of us walks into a room where the other is sitting, the house will follow predetermined rules about what to do. For example, the house might continue the audio and visual imagery for the person who was in the room first, or it might change programming to something it knows both of us like.

A house that tracks its occupants in order to meet their particular needs combines two traditions. The first is the tradition of unobtrusive service, and the other is that an object we carry entitles us to be treated in a certain way. You're already used to the idea that an object can authenticate you. It can inform people or machinery that you have permission to do something such as open a locked door, get on an airplane, or use a specific line of credit—yours—to make a purchase. Keys, electronic entry cards, driver's licenses, passports, name badges, credit cards, and tickets are all forms of authentication. If I give you the key to my car, the car allows you to get in, start the engine, and drive away. You might say that the car trusts you because you carry its keys. If I give a parking attendant a key that fits my automobile's ignition but not its trunk, the car lets him drive but not open the trunk. It's no different with my house, which will make various amenities available to you based on the electronic key you carry.

None of this is really so radical. Some visionaries are predicting that within the next ten years there will be lots of robots wandering around helping us out with various household chores. I am certainly not preparing for that, because I think it will be many decades before robots are practical. The only ones I expect to see in widespread use soon are intelligent toys. Kids will be able to program them to respond to different situations and even to speak in the voices of favorite characters. These toy robots will be able to be programmed in a limited number of ways. They will have limited vision, know the distance to the wall in each direction, the time, the lighting conditions, and accept limited speech input. I think it would have been cool to have had a toy-size car I could have talked to and programmed to respond to my instructions. Other than toys, the other major uses for robotic devices I see are for military applications. The reason I doubt intelligent robots will provide much help in actual housework in the foreseeable future is that it takes a great deal of visual intelligence and dexterity to prepare food or change diapers. Pool cleaning, lawn mowing, and perhaps even vacuum cleaning can be done with a relatively dumb system, but once we get beyond tasks where you just push something around, it is very hard to design a machine that would be able to recognize and respond to all of the contingencies that come along.

The systems I am building into the house are designed to make it easier to live in, but I won't know for sure if they are worthwhile until I move in. I'm experimenting and learning all the time. The design team used my guest cottage, which was built before the house, as a sort of test laboratory for home instrumentation. Because some people like the temperature warmer than others do, the cottage's software sets its temperature in reaction to who is inside, and the time of day. The cottage knows to make the temperature toasty on a cold morning before a guest is out of bed. In the evening, when it's dark outside, the cottage's lights dim if a television is on. If someone is in the cottage during the day, the cottage matches its inside brightness to that of the outdoors. Of course the occupant can always give explicit directions to overrule the settings.

This sort of instrumentation can provide significant energy savings. A number of electric utilities are testing a network to monitor the use of energy in individual homes. This would end the expensive practice of having meter readers come to each home every month or two, but more important, computers in the home and at the utility company will be able to manage the minute-by-minute demand for power at various times of the day. Energy-demand management can save a lot of money and help the environment by reducing peak loads.

Not all our experiments in the guest cottage have been successful. For example, I had installed speakers that descended from the ceiling when needed. The speaker enclosures were to be suspended away from walls, in an optimal acoustical position. But after trying this out in the cottage, it reminded me too much of James Bond gadgets, so in the main house we've settled for concealed speakers.

A house that tries to guess what you want has to be right often enough that you don't get annoyed by miscalculations. I went to a party at a house that had a computerized home-control system. The lights were set to go out at ten-thirty, which is when the owner usually went to bed. At ten-thirty the party was still going on, but sure enough, the lights went out. The host was away for what seemed like a long time trying to get them back on. Some office buildings use motion detectors to control the lighting in each room. If there hasn't been any major activity for a few minutes, the lights go off. People who sit nearly motionless at their desks learn to wave their arms periodically.

It isn't that hard to turn lights on and off yourself. Light switches are extremely reliable and very easy to use, so you run a risk whenever you start replacing them with computer-controlled devices. You have to install systems that work an incredibly high percentage of the time, because your payoff in convenience can be eliminated by any lack of reliability or sensitivity. I'm hoping the house systems will be able to set the lights automatically at the right levels. But, just in case, every room also has wall switches that can be used to override the computer's lighting decisions.

If you regularly ask for light to be unusually bright or dim, the house will assume that's how you want it most of the time. In fact, the house will remember everything it learns about your preferences. If in the past you've asked to see paintings by Henri Matisse or photographs by Chris Johns of *National Geographic*, you may find other works of theirs displayed on the walls of rooms you enter. If you listened to Mozart horn concertos the last time you visited, you might find them on again when you come back. If you don't take telephone calls during dinner, the phone won't ring if the call is for you. We'll also be able to "tell" the house what a guest likes. Paul Allen is a Jimi Hendrix fan and a head-banging guitar lick will greet him whenever he visits.

The house will be instrumented so it records statistics on the operations of all systems, and we'll be able to analyze that information to tune the systems.

When we are all on the information highway, the same sort of instrumentation will be used to count and keep track of all sorts of things, and the tallies will be published for anyone who cares to pay attention.

We see precursors of this tabulation today. The Internet already carries information about local traffic patterns, which is great for deciding on alternate commuting routes. Television news programs often show traffic as seen by cameras in helicopters and use the same helicopters to estimate freeway speeds during rush hours.

A trivial but amusing example is taking place today thanks to student programmers on several college campuses. They have instrumented a soft-drink vending machine by connecting the hardware to the machine's empty-indicator light, and the machine publishes information constantly on the Internet. It's a bit of frivolous engineering, but each week hundreds of people from all over the world check whether there's any 7UP or Diet Coke left in a vending machine at Carnegie Mellon University.

The information highway may still report on vending machines, as well as showing us live video from many public places, up-to-the-second lottery numbers and sports betting odds, current mortgage rates, or inventory numbers for certain kinds of products. I expect that we will be able to call up live pictures from various places around the city and ask for overlays to show spaces for rent with a list of the prices and the dates they are available. Counts of crime reports, campaign contributions by area, and almost any other kind of public or potentially public information will be ours for the asking.

I will be the first home user for one of the most unusual electronic features in my house. The product is a database of more than a million still images, including photographs and reproductions of paintings. If you're a guest, you'll be able to call up portraits of presidents, pictures of sunsets, airplanes, skiing in the Andes, a rare French stamp, the Beatles in 1965, or reproductions of High Renaissance paintings, on screens throughout the house.

A few years ago I started a small company, now called Corbis, in order to build a unique and comprehensive digital archive of images of all types. Corbis is a digital stock agency for a large variety of visual material—ranging from history, science, and technology to natural history, world cultures, and fine arts. It converts these images into digital form using high-quality scanners. The images are stored at high resolution in a database that has been indexed in inventive ways that will make it easy for someone to find exactly the right image. These digital images will be available to commercial users such as magazine and book publishers as well as to individual browsers. Royalties are paid to the image owners. Corbis is working with museums and libraries, as well as a large number of individual photographers, agencies, and other archives.

I believe quality images will be in great demand on the highway. This vision that the public will find image-browsing worthwhile is obviously totally unproven. I think the right interface will make it appealing to a lot of people.

If you can't decide what you feel like seeing, you will be able to scan randomly and the database will show you various images until something interests you. Then you'll be able to explore related pictures in depth. I'm looking forward to being able to scan and to asking for "sailboats" or "volcanoes" or "famous scientists."

Although some of the images will be of artworks, that doesn't mean I believe that reproductions are as good as the originals. There's nothing like seeing the real work. I believe that easy-to-browse image databases will get more people interested in both graphic and photographic art.

In the course of my business travels, I've been able to spend some time in museums seeing the originals of some great art. The most interesting piece of "art" I own is a scientific notebook, kept by Leonardo da Vinci in the early 1500s. I've admired Leonardo since I was young because he was a genius in so many fields and so far ahead of his time. Even though what I own is a notebook of writings and drawings, rather than a painting, no reproduction could do it full justice.

Art, like most things, is more enjoyable when you know something about it. You can walk for hours through the Louvre, admiring paintings that are at best vaguely familiar, but the experience becomes much more interesting when there is someone knowledgeable walking with you. The multimedia document can play the role of guide, at home or in a museum. It can let you hear part of a lecture on a work given by the preeminent scholar on the subject. It can refer you to other works by the same artist or from the same period. You can even zoom in for a closer look. If multimedia reproductions make art more approachable, those

who see the reproduction will want to see originals. Exposure to the reproductions is likely to increase rather than diminish reverence for real
art and encourage more people to get out to museums and galleries.

A decade from now, access to the millions of images and all the
other entertainment opportunities I've described will be available in
many homes and will certainly be more impressive than those I'll have
when I move into my house in late 1996. My house will just be getting
some of the services a little sooner.

I enjoy experimenting, and I know some of my concepts for the
house will work out better than others. Maybe I'll decide to conceal the
monitors behind conventional wall art or throw the electronic pins into
the trash. Or maybe I'll grow accustomed to the systems in the house, or
even fond of them, and wonder how I got along without them. That's
my hope.

11

RACE FOR
THE GOLD

It seems as though every week some company or consortium an-
nounces it has won the race to build the information highway. Inces-
sant hoopla about megamergers and bold investments has created a gold
rush atmosphere—people and companies pressing headlong toward an
opportunity, hoping to cross a finish line or stake a claim they believe
will assure them of success. Investors seem enchanted with highway-
related stock offerings. Media coverage of the race is unprecedented,
especially considering that both the technology and the demand are unproven. This is quite different from the early, unchronicled days of the
personal-computer industry. Today's frenzy can be intoxicating, especially for those who hope to be contenders, but the truth is that in this
race everyone is barely at the starting line.

When it finally is run, there will be many winners, some unexpected.
One result of the California gold rush was the rapid economic development of the West. In 1848, only 400 settlers were drawn to California.
Most were engaged in agriculture. Within one year the gold rush had attracted 25,000 settlers. A decade later, manufacturing was a much bigger

part of California's economy than gold production, and the state's per capita wealth was the nation's highest.

Over time, big money will be made with the right investment strategies. There are large numbers of very different sorts of companies jockeying for what they perceive will be the post position. And much of their jockeying is being covered as important news. In this chapter I'd like to try to put into perspective what's going on.

In the rush to build the information highway, no one has seen any gold yet, and there's a lot of investing to be done before anyone does. The investments will be driven by faith that the market will be large. Neither the full highway nor the market will exist until a broadband network has been brought to most homes and businesses. Before that can happen, the software platforms, applications, networks, servers, and information appliances that will make up the highway all have to be built and deployed. Many pieces of the highway won't be profitable until there are tens of millions of users. Achieving that goal will require hard work, technical ingenuity, and money. Today's frenzy is helpful in this regard, because it encourages investment and experimentation.

No one yet knows for sure what the public wants from the information highway. The public itself can't know, because it hasn't had experience with video-capable interactive networks and applications. Some early technology has been tried, but there have been only a few such trials. They have offered movies, some shopping, and a lot of novelty, which soon wears off. As a result, all that has really been learned so far is that limited interactive systems generate limited results. It will be impossible to get much of a sense of the highway's real potential until dozens of new applications have been built. However, it's tough to justify building applications without confidence in the market. Until at least one credible trial proves that the revenue generated can justify the fixed costs of the system, everyone who insists his company will spend billions building the information highway to connect it to homes is posturing. My view is that the highway won't be a sudden, revolutionary creation but that the Internet, along with evolution in the PC and PC software, will guide us step by step to the full system.

Some posturing is unfairly elevating expectations and contributing to the excesses of Information Highway Frenzy. A surprising number of people are speculating about the direction technology will take. Some of these conjectures ignore practicality or preferences the public has already demonstrated or are unrealistic about how soon the pieces will come together. Everyone should be free to theorize, but speculation suggesting that the full information highway's major impact on consumers will come before the turn of the century is flat wrong.

Companies investing now in the information highway are, at best, making informed guesses. Skeptics bring up good reasons why they think it won't be as big or early an opportunity as I think it will be. I believe in this business. Microsoft is investing more than $100 million a year on research and development for the highway. It will almost certainly take five years or more of this kind of investing before the results of the R&D bring in enough revenue to make the money back, so we're making a $500 million bet. It could prove to be a half-billion-dollar losing bet. Our shareholders are allowing us to make it on the basis of our previous successes, but that's no guarantee. Naturally we expect we'll be successful, and like the others running the race, we have a rationale for why. We believe our software-development skills and our commitment to PC evolution will allow us to get a return on our investment.

Comprehensive trials of broadband connections to PCs and television sets should get under way in 1996 in North America, Europe, and Asia, financed by companies willing to take a risk and hoping that the results will give them a head start. Some of the trials will be "me too" efforts aimed at showing that a particular network operator can build and operate a high-bandwidth network. The primary goal of the trials should be to make available a platform for software developers to build and explore new applications on, to test the applications' appeal and financial viability.

When Paul Allen and I saw that picture of the first Altair computer, we could only guess at the wealth of applications it would inspire. We knew applications would be developed but we didn't know what they would be. Some were predictable—for example, programs that would let a PC function as the terminal for a mainframe computer—but the most important applications, such as the VisiCalc spreadsheets, were unexpected.

--------------------------->

These forthcoming trials will give companies the opportunity to look for the equivalents of the spreadsheet—unexpected killer applications and services that will capture the imagination of consumers—and build a financial case for rolling out the highway. It's almost impossible to guess what applications will or won't appeal to the public. Customers' needs and desires are so personal. For instance, I hope to be able to use the highway to stay up-to-date on medical advances. I'd like to find out about health risks for someone in my age group, and ways to avoid them. So I want fitness and medical applications as well as ones that would enable me to continue educating myself in other areas I'm interested in. But that's just me. Will other users want medical advice? New kinds of games? New ways of meeting people? Home shopping? Or just a few more movies?

The trials will determine which are the most popular applications and services. These will probably include simple extensions of existing communication functions, such as video-on-demand and high-speed connections between personal computers. In addition, there will be a few wild new services that catch the fancy of the public and inspire further innovation, investment, and entrepreneurship. Those are what I'm looking forward to seeing. If the early trials don't excite consumers, there will have to be more trials, and the building of the full highway will be delayed. In the meantime, the Internet, connected PCs, and PC software will continue to improve and become an even better foundation to build on. Hardware and software prices will continue to come down.

It's interesting to watch how different large companies respond to these opportunities. No one wants to admit to uncertainty. Phone and cable companies, TV stations and networks, computer hardware and software companies, newspapers, magazines, movie studios, and even individual authors are all formulating strategies. From a distance their plans appear similar, but the details are really quite different. It's like the old story about the blind men and the elephant. Each one has a hold of a different part of the elephant and from his own small amount of information is drawing sweeping and erroneous conclusions about what the whole animal looks like. Here, instead of trying to guess the appearance of a large beast, we're investing billions of dollars based on a vague understanding of the true shape of the market.

Competition is a boon for consumers, but it can be tough on investors, especially those who invest in a product that doesn't exist yet. At the moment there is a nonexistent business being called the "information highway." It has generated zero dollars in revenue. The building of the highway will be a learning process, and some companies will lose their shirts. What seem to be lucrative niches today may wind up as highly competitive markets, with low margins. Or they may prove downright unpopular. Gold rushes tend to encourage impetuous investments. A few will pay off, but when the frenzy is behind us, we will look back incredulously at the wreckage of failed ventures and wonder, "Who funded those companies? What was going on in their minds? Was that just mania at work?"

Entrepreneurship will play a major role in shaping the development of the information highway, the same way it shaped the personal-computer business. Only a handful of companies that made mainframe software managed the transition to personal computers. Most successes came from little start-ups, run by people who were open to new possibilities. This will be true on the information highway, too. For every large existing company that succeeds with a new application or service, ten start-ups will flourish and fifty more will flash into existence and momentary glory before slipping into obscurity.

This is a hallmark of an evolving entrepreneurial market; rapid innovation occurs on many fronts. Most of it will be unsuccessful, regardless of whether it's attempted by a large or a small company. Large companies tend to take fewer risks, but when they crash and burn, the combination of their sheer ego and the scale of their resources means they wind up digging a bigger crater in the ground. By comparison, a start-up usually fails without much notice. The good news is that people learn from both the successes and the failures, and the net result is rapid progress.

By letting the marketplace decide which companies and approaches win and which lose, many paths are explored simultaneously. Nowhere is the benefit of a market-driven decision more apparent than in an unproven market. When hundreds of companies try different risk-taking approaches to discover the level of demand, society gets to the right solution a lot faster than it would with any form of central planning. The range of uncertainties about the information highway is very large, but the marketplace will design an appropriate system.

Governments can help assure a strong competitive framework and should be willing, though not overeager, to intercede if the marketplace fails in some particular area. After the trials have yielded sufficient information, they can determine the "rules of the road"—the basic framework guidelines within which companies can compete. But they should not attempt to design or dictate the nature of the information highway, because governments cannot outsmart or outmanage the competitive marketplace, particularly while there are still questions about customer preference and technological development.

The U.S. government is deeply involved in rule-making for communications companies. Federal regulations currently prevent cable and phone companies from offering a general-purpose network that would put them in competition with each other. The first thing most governments have to do to help the highway start is to deregulate communications.

The old approach in most countries was to create monopolies in the various forms of telecommunication. The theory behind this approach was that companies wouldn't make the huge investments necessary to run telephone wires out to everyone unless they had the incentive of being the exclusive supplier. A set of rules drawn up by the government binds the monopoly holders to act in the public interest with restricted but essentially guaranteed profit. The outcome has been a very reliable network with broad services but limited innovation. Later regulations extended the concept to cable television as well as to local telephone systems. Both federal and local governments granted monopolies and curtailed competition in exchange for regulatory control.

A highway that delivers both telephone and video services is not allowed under current U.S. laws. Economists and historians can argue the pros and cons of whether granting regulated monopolies was a good idea back in 1934, but today there is a general agreement that the rules should be changed. As of mid-1995, however, policy makers haven't been able to agree on exactly when or in what ways. Billions of dollars are at stake and lawmakers have found it easy to get lost in the complicated details of how competition should start. The problem is to figure out how to move from the old system to a new one while keeping most of the participants happy. This dilemma is the reason telecommunications reform has been in limbo for years. Congress was embroiled much of the summer of 1995 in a debate, not about whether the telecommunications industry should be deregulated, but rather about how it should be deregulated. I hope that by the time you read this, the information highway will be legal in the United States!

Outside the United States, matters are complicated by the fact that in many countries the regulated monopolies have been agencies owned by the government itself. They were called PTTs because they managed postal, telephone, and telegraph services. In some countries the PTT is being allowed to go ahead and develop the highway, but when government organizations are involved, things often move slowly. I think the pace of investment and deregulation worldwide will increase in the next ten years because politicians are recognizing that this issue is critical if their countries are to remain competitive in the long term. In many election campaigns candidates' platform planks will include policies that will allow their country to lead in the creation of the highway. The political use of these issues will make them more visible, which will help clear various international roadblocks.

Countries like the United States and Canada, where a high percentage of homes have cable television, are at an advantage because the competition between cable companies and phone companies will accelerate the pace of investment in the highway infrastructure. Great Britain, however, is the farthest along in actually using a single network to provide both television and cable services. The cable companies there were allowed to offer phone service in 1990. Foreign companies, primarily U.S. phone and cable companies, made major investments in fiber infrastructure in the United Kingdom. British consumers now can choose to get telephone service from their cable TV company. This competition has forced British Telecom to improve its rates and services.

If we look back in ten years, I think we'll see a clear correlation between the amount of telecommunications reform in each country and the state of its information economy. Few investors will want to put money into places that don't have great communications infrastructures. There are so many politicians and lobbyists involved in creating new regulations in so many countries, I'm sure the entire spectrum of different regulatory schemes will be tried. The "right" solution will vary somewhat in different countries.

One area it's clear government should stay out of is compatibility. Some have suggested that governments set standards for networks, to guarantee that they interoperate. In 1994, legislation was put before a subcommittee in the U.S. House of Representatives calling for all set-top boxes to be made so they would be compatible. This sounded like a great idea to those who drafted the legislation. It would ensure that if Aunt Bessie invested in a set-top box, she could be confident it would work if she moved to another part of the country.

Compatibility is important. It makes the consumer-electronics and personal-computer businesses thrive. When the PC industry was new, many machines came and went. The Altair 8800 was superseded by the Apple I. Then came the Apple II, the original IBM PC, the Apple Macintosh, IBM PC AT, 386 and 486 PCs, Power Macintoshes, and Pentium PCs. Each of these machines was somewhat compatible with the others. For instance, all were able to share plain-text files. But there was also a lot of incompatibility because each successive computer generation showcased fundamental breakthroughs the older systems didn't support.

Compatibility with prior machines is a great virtue in some cases. Both PC-compatibles and the Apple Macintosh provide some backwards compatibility. However, they are incompatible with each other. And at the time the PC was introduced, it was not compatible with IBM's prior machines. Likewise, the Mac was incompatible with Apple's earlier machines. In the world of computing, technology is so dynamic that any company should be able to come out with whatever new product it wants and let the market decide if it has made the right set of trade-offs. Because the set-top box is in every sense a computer, it stands to reason it will follow the same pattern of rapid innovation that has driven the PC industry. In fact, the set-top box will be sold to a far more uncertain market than the PC was, so the case for letting it be market driven is even stronger. It would be foolish to impose the constraint of government-dictated design on an unfinished invention.

The original set-top box compatibility legislation in the United States ultimately died in Congress in 1994, but related issues arose in 1995, and I expect that similar efforts will be made in other countries. It seems easy to legislate reasonable-sounding constraints, but if we don't watch out, those constraints could strangle the market.

The highway will develop at a different pace in different communities and in different countries. When I travel abroad, the foreign press often asks how many years behind the developments in the United States their country is. It's a difficult question. The advantages that the United States has are the size of the market, the popularity of the personal computer in American homes, and the way the phone and cable companies will compete with each other for current and future revenues. Of the various technologies that will be part of building the highway, U.S.-based companies are leaders in almost every one: microprocessors, software, entertainment, personal computers, set-top boxes, and network-switching equipment. The only significant exceptions are display technology and memory chips.

Other countries have advantages of their own. In Singapore, the population density and political focus on infrastructure makes it certain that this nation will be a leader. A decision by the Singaporean government to make something happen means quite a bit in this unique country. The highway infrastructure is already under construction. Every developer will soon be required to provide every new house or apartment with a broadband cable in the same way he is required by law to provide lines for water, gas, electricity, and telephone. When I visited with Lee Kuan Yew, the seventy-two-year-old senior minister who was the political head of Singapore from 1959 to 1990, I was extremely impressed with his understanding of the opportunity and his belief that it is a top priority to move ahead at full speed. He views it as imperative that his small country continue to be a premier location in Asia for high-value jobs. I was quite blunt in asking Mr. Lee if he understood that the Singaporean government would be giving up the tight control over information it exercises today as a way of ensuring shared values that tend to keep societal problems in check. He said Singapore recognizes that in the future it will have to rely on methods other than censorship to maintain a culture that sacrifices some Western-style freedom in exchange for a strong sense of community.

In China, however, the government seems to believe it can have it both ways. Post and Telecommunications Minster Wu Jichuan told reporters at a news briefing, "By linking with the Internet we don't mean absolute freedom of information. I think there is general understanding about this. If you go through customs, you have to show your passport. It's the same with management of information." Wu said Beijing will adopt unspecified "management measures" to control inflows of data on all telecommunications services as they evolve in China. "There is no contradiction at all between the development of telecoms infrastructure and the exercise of state sovereignty. The International Telecommunications Union states that any country has sovereignty over its own telecoms." He may not understand that to implement full Internet access and maintain censorship, you would almost have to have someone looking over the shoulder of every user.

In France, the pioneering on-line service, Minitel, has fostered a community of information publishers and stimulated broad familiarity with on-line systems generally. Even though both terminals and bandwidth are limited, Minitel's success has fostered innovations and provided lessons. France Telecom is investing in a packet switch data network.

In Germany, Deutsche Telekom lowered the price of ISDN service dramatically in 1995. This has led to a significant increase in the number of users connecting personal computers. Bringing down ISDN prices was clever, because lower prices will foster the development of applications that will help hasten the arrival of a broadband system.

The level of PC penetration in business is even higher in the Nordic countries than in the United States. These countries understand that their highly educated workforces will benefit from having high-speed connections to the rest of the world.

Although the interest in high-tech communications systems is probably greater in Japan than in any other country, it is very difficult to predict the fate of the information highway there. The use of personal computers in businesses, schools, and homes is significantly less wide-spread in Japan than in other developed countries. This is partly because of the difficulty of entering kanji characters on a keyboard, but also because of Japan's large and entrenched market for dedicated word-processing machines.

Japan is second only to the United States in the number of companies investing in developing both highway building blocks and the highway's content. Many large Japanese companies have excellent technology and a record of taking long-term approaches to their investments. Sony owns Sony Music and Sony Pictures, which includes Columbia Records and Columbia Studios. Toshiba has a large investment in Time Warner. NEC's corporate slogan, "Computers & Communication," coined in 1984, anticipating the highway, is an indication of its commitment.

The cable industry in Japan was overregulated until quite recently, but the rate of change is impressive. The Japanese phone company, NTT, has the largest valuation of any public company in the world and will play a leadership role in every aspect of the highway system.

In South Korea, although significantly fewer PCs per capita are being sold there than in the United States, more than 25 percent of the machines are going into homes. This statistic demonstrates how countries with a strong family structure that put great emphasis on getting ahead by educating children will be fertile ground for products that provide educational advantages. One appropriate use of governmental authority will be the creation of incentives to encourage low-cost connections for schools and to ensure that the highway reaches rural areas and low-income areas too.

Australia and New Zealand are also interested in the highway, partly because of the great geographic distance between them and other developed countries. The phone companies in Australia are being privatized and the market opened to competitors, encouraging forward-looking plans. New Zealand has the most open telecommunications market in the world, and its newly privatized phone company has set an example of how effective privatization can be.

I doubt that any of the developed countries, including all of Western Europe, North America, Australia, New Zealand, and Japan, will end up more than a year or two ahead of or behind the others unless poor political decisions are made. Within each country some communities will get service earlier than others because of their economic demographics. Networks will go into richer neighborhoods first because that's where residents are likely to spend more. Local regulators may even find themselves competing to create favorable environments for the early deployment of the highway. No taxpayer money will be needed to build the highway in industrialized countries with pro-competition regulations. The speed with which the highway is brought directly into homes will correlate in large part with the per capita gross domestic product (GDP) of a country. Despite this, even in developing countries the connections into businesses and schools will have a huge impact and reduce the income gap between these countries and developed ones. Areas such as Bangalore in India, or Shanghai and Guangzhou in China, will install highway connections to businesses that they will use to offer the services of their highly educated workers to the global market.

In many countries nowadays, the top political leaders are making plans to encourage highway investment. The competition among nations trying either to take the lead in development or to make sure they don't fall behind is creating a very positive dynamic. As different countries try different approaches, everyone will watch to see what works best. Some national governments may rationalize that if they decide they must have a network right away and private enterprise is not willing to build it, they will have to help build or fund pieces of their information highway. A government bootstrap could, in principle, cause an information highway to be built sooner than might happen otherwise, but the very real possibility of an unattractive outcome has to be considered carefully. Such a country might end up with a boondoggle, white-elephant information highway built by engineers out of touch with the rapid pace of technological development.

Something like this happened in Japan with the Hi-Vision high-definition television project. MITI, the powerful Ministry of International Trade and Industry, and NHK, the government-run TV broadcasting company, coordinated an effort among Japanese consumer-electronics companies to build a new analog HDTV system. NHK committed to broadcasting shows a few hours a day in the new format. Unfortunately, the system was rendered obsolete before it was ever deployed, when it became clear that digital technology was superior. Many Japanese companies found themselves in a difficult position. Privately, they knew the system was not a good investment, but they had to maintain their public commitments to the government-sponsored format. As I write this, the "plan of record" in Japan remains to move to this analog system, although nobody actually expects it to happen. Japan will, however, benefit from the investment in developing high-definition cameras and displays that the Hi-Vision project encouraged.

Building the information highway will not be as simple as saying "Run fiber everywhere." Any government or company getting involved will need to track new developments and be prepared to shift directions. Such flexibility requires technological expertise that, with the attendant risks, is better covered by industry.

Competition in the private sector will be fierce on many fronts. Cable, phone, and other companies will compete to provide the fiber, wireless, and satellite infrastructure. Hardware companies will fight to sell servers, ATM switches, and set-top boxes to network companies, and PCs, digital TVs, telephones, and other information appliances to consumers. At the same time companies in the software business, including Apple, AT&T, IBM, Microsoft, Oracle, and Sun Microsystems, will be offering software components to network providers. Eventually, millions of companies and individuals will be selling software applications and information, including entertainment, across the network that springs up.

I've discussed at some length how critical it is that the physical infrastructure be built out to provide broadband connections to homes. I described the competition in the United States, and the strategies of the telephone and cable industries, the major players. The cable companies are younger and smaller than the big telephone companies and tend to be more entrepreneurial. Cable television networks provide customers with one-way broadband video through a web of coaxial, and sometimes fiber-optic, cable. Although the penetration rate worldwide is quite low—189 million subscribers—cable systems run past nearly 70 percent of all American homes, and into 63 million of them. Already, cable systems are gradually being converted to carry a digital signal, and a number of cable companies are working to provide PC users with connections to the Internet and on-line services. They're gambling that many PC users accustomed to downloading information on a telephone line at 28,800 bits per second will be willing to pay more to download information through their television cable at 3 million bits per second.

As for the phone companies, they are much stronger financially. The American telephone system is the world's largest switched-distributed network providing point-to-point connections. The combined local telephone exchange market, with annual revenues of about $100 billion, is far more profitable than the $20 billion U.S. cable business. The seven regional Bell operating companies (RBOCs) will compete with their former parent, AT&T, to provide long-distance, cellular, and new services. But, like phone companies around the world, the RBOCs are new to the competitive world, just emerging from their heritage as heavily regulated utilities.

The local phone companies will be motivated by increased competition. They are in a defensive position. Other phone companies and cable companies are going to want to offer telephone as well as other communications services in their areas. New regulations will unleash this competition and, as I've already noted, the cost of long-distance voice-telephone service will drop dramatically. If that happens, phone companies will be deprived of much of their current profitable revenue.

The companies providing local service have slowly been introducing advanced digital transmission capabilities into their networks. They haven't felt pressure to hurry, because until now it seemed they were protected from competition by the large financial barriers to market entry. They knew a potential rival would have to make a duplicate investment of, say, $100 million in equipment in order to compete in a given community. But the costs of switching equipment and fiber are coming down every year.

This means the companies are faced with the sort of decision that has confronted almost everyone who has contemplated buying a PC. Do you wait for prices to come down and performance to improve, or do you bite the bullet and start getting use out of the equipment sooner? The dilemma will be acute for some network companies. They will have to move very fast and upgrade constantly. A company will get bargain prices if it waits long enough before making investments in cabling and switches, but it may never recover the market share it will have lost to less cautious competitors.

Phone companies, despite their enviable revenues, could be strapped for the cash required to fund the expensive upgrade of the new network, because regulatory rate commissions may not permit them to raise telephone rates or even to use profits from current service to cross-subsidize this new kind of business. Shareholders, accustomed to attractive dividends from the RBOCs, might balk at a diversion of profits to build the information highway. For more than a hundred years telephony has been quietly making its profits as a regulated monopoly. Suddenly the RBOCs must become growth companies, which is about as radical as turning a tractor into a sports car. It can be done (just ask the folks at the Lamborghini Company, which makes both), but it's hard to do.

The opportunity to provide ISDN to PC users will provide new revenues to phone companies that want to bring the price levels down to establish a mass market. I expect ISDN adoption to get off to a faster start than PC cable modes. Phone companies are doing some clever work to find out how to use their twisted-pair connections for at least the last few hundred feet to the home and still deliver broadband data rates. Phone and cable companies can both succeed as demand for new services increases their revenue opportunities.

The ambitions of cable and phone companies go well beyond simply providing a pipe for bits. Imagine you are running a bit-delivery company. Once you own a network in a given area and have hooked up most of the homes, how can you make more money? By getting customers to consume more bits, but there are only twenty-four hours in a day for people to watch TV or sit at their PCs. If you can't ship more bits, an alternative is to have a financial interest in the bits being shipped. Many see the highway as a sort of economic food chain, with the delivery and distribution of bits at the bottom, and various types of applications, services, and content layered on top. Companies in the bit-distribution business are attracted to the idea of moving themselves up the food chain—profiting from owning the bits rather than from just delivering them. This is why cable companies, regional telephone companies, and consumer-electronics manufacturers are rushing to work with Hollywood studios, television and cable broadcasters, and other content businesses.

Some companies are investing because they are afraid not to. For a long time distribution has been pretty lucrative, largely because of the monopolies granted by the government. As these monopolies disappear and competition begins, bit distribution might become less profitable. Companies that hope to participate in the creation of the applications and services and enter the content business through investment and/or influence want to move now, while the opportunities are open. Some of these companies may choose to give away or subsidize the set-top box that connects up the television set. Part of their strategy could be to offer, for a single monthly fee, the connectivity to the highway, the set-top box, and a package of programming, applications, and services to go with it. Cable TV systems work this way, and telephone companies in the United States used to, before deregulation.

Network operators that include the set-top box as part of the standard service fee will attract customers who might hesitate to spend several hundred dollars to buy one. As I explained, in the early years there is a real danger that the box will quickly become obsolete, so why buy one? Although supplying the boxes will increase the up-front capital required by the network operator, the outlay will be worth it if it helps create a critical mass of users. But government regulators worry that allowing the network operators to have control of the boxes will put them in a position to capitalize on their privileged position. A network operator that owns the boxes could also seek to exert control over what software, applications, and services run on those boxes. There could be limited choices for studios that wanted to sell their movies. Whether or not to allow various services equal access to the wires and boxes is one of the tough issues deregulation is going to have to address. One argument for equal access is that if multiple services can use the same wire, the government can avoid setting standards for those services and their interoperability.

Retailers would like the opportunity to sell you the set-top boxes. After all, they already sell the TV sets and PCs, so why not the set-top box too? Consumer-electronics companies want to compete to manufacture the boxes. They want to be able to offer many models—fancy, expensive ones for gadget buffs and simple ones for other folks. If the network company supplies the boxes, there is no profit for the retailers. The cellular telephone industry solved this competition with a partial subsidy: You acquire your cellular phone from any retailer, but the price is partially underwritten by the cellular company that you commit to buy service from.

Cable and phone industries will be the primary, but not the only, competitors to provide the network. Railroad companies in Japan, for example, recognize that the rights-of-way they have for their tracks would be ideal for long fiber-optic cable runs. Electric, gas, and water utilities in many countries point out that they, too, run lines into homes and businesses. Some of them have argued that the energy savings from computerized management of home heating alone might defray much of the cost of stringing fiber-optic cables because energy demand would be lowered, which reduces the need for expensive new generating plants. In France most of the cable TV connections are owned by two big water companies. But outside France, at least, conventional utility companies seem less obvious candidates for building highway connections.

You may wonder why I haven't mentioned direct-broadcast satellites and other technologies as mainstream competitors of the telephone and cable companies. As I said earlier, current satellite technology is a good interim step. It delivers a great broadcast video signal, but there would have to be a major technological breakthrough before it could provide a unique video bandwidth feed to every television set and PC. For the United States market it would have to go from today's 300-channel-per-satellite system to a 300,000-channel system, even assuming fewer than 1 percent of the displays needed a unique feed simultaneously.

Because these satellites also have a problem delivering data from the home back into the network (the back channel) to provide true interactivity, applications such as videoconferencing aren't possible. A partial solution is to use the phone for the back channel. Direct-broadcast satellites such as the Hughes Electronics' DIRECTV system use your regular home telephone line to submit back to their billing center a record of any pay-per-view programs you have chosen. With a special add-in circuit, direct-broadcast satellites can send data to PCs as well as to television sets. Data broadcasting is a valuable interim conduit for some applications.

Teledesic, a company that my friend, cellular telephone pioneer Craig McCaw, and I have invested in, is working on overcoming the limits of satellite technology by using a large number of low-orbit satellites. The scope of the proposed system is quite ambitious. It involves nearly 1,000 satellites orbiting fifty times closer to Earth than traditional geostationary satellites. Being closer to Earth means these satellites require 2,500 times less power and have increased two-way channel resources. This solves the back-channel problem. Also, the significant transmission delay associated with satellites is also overcome. Over long distances these low-orbit satellites can provide transmission speeds comparable to those available on fiber. Teledesic has regulatory, technical, and financial challenges and it will be several years before we'll know whether the company can overcome them. If it can, Teledesic or other systems like it may be the first, the cheapest, or indeed the only way to bring the highway to many parts of Earth. Most of the population of Asia and Africa, for example, is unlikely to have local access to fiber connections within the next twenty years.

Another rapidly advancing technology is ground-based wireless communication. Television signals, which have been broadcast over the air using wireless VHF and UHF, will be carried primarily on fiber. The purpose of this change is to enable everyone to have a personal video feed and interact. Meanwhile, voice and other low-data-rate connections are moving from the wired infrastructure to wireless transmission in order to support increased mobility. The ideal system would allow for the sort of personalized high-quality video and mobility I talked about having with a wallet PC. So far, that combination cannot be supported by any of today's technologies, because wireless systems can't provide the bandwidth for individual video feeds that a fiber network can.

Early on, competitors will race to supply the first interactive services to communities, but once all of the attractive territories are served by one company or another, rivals will begin head-to-head competition by entering markets already served by others. Interestingly, in the cable TV business, the few places a second system was constructed, the "overbuilder" never made money. Having two or more general-purpose connections running into every home would aid competition, but the extra cost is immense.

Servers for the information highway will have to be large computers with gigantic storage capacity that run twenty-four hours a day, seven days a week. Competition to supply them will be intense. Various companies have different ideas about the right design for the servers, and strategies for developing them. Not surprisingly, the positions held by the various potential competitors are influenced by their areas of expertise. If your only tool is a hammer, pretty soon every new problem starts to look like a nail that needs pounding. Minicomputer companies such as Hewlett Packard envision using clusters of minicomputers as servers. A variety of companies that primarily make personal computers believe that inexpensive PCs, connected together in large numbers, will prove to be the most cost-effective and reliable approach. Mainframe specialists such as IBM are adapting their big machines to be servers. They cherish a fond hope that the information highway will be the last bastion of Big Iron.

Software companies naturally see their product as the answer. Software is so inexpensive to duplicate that substituting it for costly hardware reduces system costs. Another competition *is* shaping up to supply the software platforms that will run these servers. Oracle, a database-management company that makes software for mainframes and mini-computers, envisions the server as a supercomputer or minicomputer running Oracle software. AT&T, with its experience in the network business, will probably try to embed most of the system's intelligence in the servers and switches of the network and put relatively little processing power in information appliances such as PCs and set-top boxes.

At Microsoft, our only "hammer" is software. We expect that the highway's intelligence will be evenly divided between servers and information appliances. This arrangement is sometimes called "client/server" computing, which means that the information appliances (the clients) and the servers will run cooperating software applications. We don't believe that giant supercomputers, mainframes, or even clusters of mini-computers will be necessary. Instead, Microsoft, like many of the PC manufacturers, sees the server as a network of dozens to hundreds of what are essentially personal computers. They won't have the familiar cases, monitors, and keyboards, and may be housed together in large racks at the headquarters of a cable system or the central office of a telephone system. It will take special software technology to harness the computing horsepower of thousands of such machines. Our approach is to make the coordination of the highway a software problem and then use the highest-volume (and therefore cheapest) computers to do the work—the same ones used in the PC industry.

Our approach focuses on taking full advantage of all the advances going on in the PC industry, including the software. The PC will be one of the primary devices used on the highway. We think the set-top box should share as many technical features as possible with the PC to make it easy for developers to create applications and services that will work with both. This will allow the Internet to evolve upward into the highway in a compatible fashion. We believe tools and applications available on the PC today can be used to build new applications. For instance, we think set-top boxes should be able to run most of the CD-ROM titles for PCs that will appear over the next decade. One could argue that we are thinking too narrowly by trying to imagine the new world in terms of the PC. But there are more than 50 million PCs sold every year worldwide. The population of installed PCs will provide a substantial starter market for a prospective developer of any application or service.

Even if there were suddenly a million of one type of set-top box in use, it still would represent a tiny market compared to the opportunity for multimedia titles for the PC. A developer could afford to spend only a small fraction of its R&D on customers with these specialized boxes. Only the very largest companies are able to invest in new applications without concerning themselves about the near-term audience size. We believe that most of the innovation that will occur will be extending existing markets, and that using the PC/Internet market is the likeliest means of extending to interactive TV and the highway. But similar arguments could be made in favor of other computer platforms or even home game machines.

Other software companies are equally confident about their own strategies for set-top box software. Apple proposes to use Macintosh technology, and Silicon Graphics intends to adapt its workstation operating system, which is a form of UNIX. One small company even wants to repurpose an operating system that is currently used primarily in the antilock-brake systems of commercial trucks!

Hardware manufacturers are making similar decisions about which approach to set-top boxes they want to take. Meanwhile, consumer-electronics companies are determining what sorts of information appliances—from wallet PCs to TVs—they will build and what software they will use.

The battle among software architectures will play out over a long period and may involve potential competitors who have not yet declared their interest. All software components will be compatible to a degree, the way all of today's computer systems share certain degrees of compatibility. You can connect nearly any computer to the Internet, and the same will be true for the highway.

There are open questions such as to what extent these platforms will share a personality or user interface. A single common user interface is great—unless you happen not to like it. Will Mom, Dad, Grandma, the preschooler, and the Generation X-er all have the same taste? Must one size fit all in this, the most flexible medium? Here, too, good arguments can be made in all directions, so interface is another area in which the industry will have to experiment, innovate, and let the market decide.

There are other, similar decisions awaiting the judgment of the marketplace. For instance, will advertising play a large role in underwriting information and entertainment, or will customers pay directly for most services? Will you control all of what you see when you first turn on a TV or other information appliance, or will your network provider get some part of your first screen to show you information it controls?

The market will also influence technical aspects of network design. Most experts believe that the interactive network will use asynchronous transfer mode (ATM), but today ATM costs too much to use. If ATM equipment prices behave like other chip-related technologies, they will come down rapidly. However, if for some reason they stay high or don't drop quickly enough, signals may have to be translated into some other form before they enter a consumer's home.

A wide range of skills, from a wide range of companies, will be necessary to put the information highway together sufficiently for a mass market to begin. It will be tempting for a company strong in one or more of the necessary disciplines to try to find a way to do every piece and ignite the market all by itself, but I think this would be a mistake.

I have always believed businesses that concentrate on a very few core competencies will do the best. One of the lessons of the computer industry—as well as of life—is that it is almost impossible to do everything well. IBM and DEC and other companies in the old computer industry tried offering everything, including chips, software, systems, and consulting. When the pace of technology was accelerated by the microprocessor and PC standards, the diversified strategy proved vulnerable, because, over time, competitors who had focused on specific areas did better. One company did great chips, another did great PC design, yet another did great distribution and integration. Each successful new company picked a narrow slice and focused on it.

Beware! Mergers that are attempts to bring all aspects of highway expertise into one organization should be viewed skeptically. Much of the press coverage about the highway has concerned just such huge business deals. Media companies are merging and trying different configurations. Some phone companies are buying cable companies. McCaw Cellular wireless communications company was bought by wire-based AT&T. Disney has purchased Capital Cities–ABC and Time-Warner proposed buying Turner Broadcasting. It will be a long time before the corporations making these investments can assess how wise they were.

Right or wrong, deals like these fascinate the public. For example, when the proposed $30 billion merger between Bell Atlantic and TCI fell through, the press speculated about whether it was a setback for the information highway. The answer is no. Both companies still have very aggressive investment plans for building the highway's infrastructure.

The highway's arrival will depend on the evolution of the PC, the Internet, and new applications. Companies merging, or failing to merge, is no indication of progress or the lack of it. The deals are like background noise; they keep rumbling along whether or not anyone is listening. Microsoft plans to reach out to hundreds of companies, including movie studios, television networks, and newspaper and magazine publishers. We hope to work with them so that together we can assemble their respective content assets and build applications for CD-ROMs, the Internet, and the highway.

We believe in alliances and are eager to participate in them. Our core mission, however, is to build a number of software components for the information highway. We are providing software tools to a number of hardware companies building new applications. Many media and communications companies from around the world will be working with us and observing the ways customers respond to the applications. It will be critical to listen to customer feedback.

You too will be able to read about the results of the highway trials. Are people gravitating toward new types of multiplayer games? Are they socializing in new ways? Are they working together across the network? Are they shopping in the new marketplace? Are exciting applications you never would have imagined coming along? Are people willing to pay for these new capabilities?

The answers to these questions are the key to how the Information Age develops. Mergers and mania are fun to watch. But if you want to know how the race to build the information highway is really going, keep your eye on PCs connected to the Internet, and on the software applications that are popular in highway trials. At least that's what I'm going to do.

12

CRITICAL ISSUES

This is an exciting time in the Information Age. It is the very beginning. Almost everywhere I go, whether to speak to a group or to have dinner with friends, questions come up about how information technology will change our lives. People want to understand how it will make the future different. Will it make our lives better or worse?

I've already said I'm an optimist, and I'm optimistic about the impact of the new technology. It will enhance leisure time and enrich culture by expanding the distribution of information. It will help relieve pressures on urban areas by enabling individuals to work from home or remote-site offices. It will relieve pressure on natural resources because increasing numbers of products will be able to take the form of bits rather than of manufactured goods. It will give us more control over our lives and allow experiences and products to be custom tailored to our interests. Citizens of the information society will enjoy new opportunities for productivity, learning, and entertainment. Countries that move boldly and in concert with each other will enjoy economic rewards.

Whole new markets will emerge, and a myriad new opportunities for employment will be created.

When measured by decades, the economy is always in upheaval. For the past few hundred years, every generation has found more efficient ways of getting work done, and the cumulative benefits have been enormous. The average person today enjoys a much better life than the nobility did a few centuries ago. It would be great to have a king's land, but what about his lice? Medical advances alone have greatly increased life spans and improved standards of living.

Henry Ford, in the first part of the twentieth century, *was* the automotive industry, but your car is superior to anything he ever drove. It's safer, more reliable, and surely has a better sound system. This pattern of improvement isn't going to change. Advancing productivity propels societies forward, and it is only a matter of time before the average person in a developed country will be "richer" in many ways than anyone is today.

Just because I'm optimistic doesn't mean I don't have concerns about what is going to happen to all of us. As with all major changes, the benefits of the information society will carry costs. There will be dislocations in some business sectors that will create a need for worker retraining. The availability of virtually free communications and computing will alter the relationships of nations, and of socioeconomic groups within nations. The power and versatility of digital technology will raise new concerns about individual privacy, commercial confidentiality, and national security. There are, moreover, equity issues that will have to be addressed. The information society should serve all of its citizens, not only the technically sophisticated and economically privileged. In short, a range of important issues confronts us. I don't necessarily have the solutions, but, as I started off the book saying, now is a good time for a broad discussion. Technological progress will force all of society to confront tough new problems, only some of which we can foresee. The pace of technological change is so fast that sometimes it seems the world will be completely different from one day to the next. It won't. But we should be prepared for change. Societies are going to be asked to make hard choices in such areas as universal availability, investment in education, regulation, and the balance between individual privacy and community security.

While it is important that we start thinking about the future, we should guard against the impulse to take hasty action. We can ask only the most general kinds of questions today, so it doesn't make sense to come up with detailed, specific regulations. We've got a good number of years to observe the course of the coming revolution, and we should use that time to make intelligent rather than reflexive decisions.

Perhaps the most widespread and personal anxiety is, "How will I fit into the evolving economy?" Men and women are worried that their own jobs will become obsolete, that they won't be able to adapt to new ways of working, that their children will get into industries that will cease to exist, or that economic upheaval will create wholesale unemployment, especially among older workers. These are legitimate concerns. Entire professions and industries will fade. But new ones will flourish. This will be happening over the next two or three decades, which is fast by historical standards, but may turn out to be no more disruptive than the pace at which the microprocessor revolution brought about its changes in the workplace, or the upheavals in the airline, trucking, and banking industries over the last decade.

Although the microprocessor and the personal computer that it enabled have altered and even eliminated some jobs and companies, it is hard to find any large sector of the economy that has been negatively affected. Mainframe, minicomputer, and typewriter companies have downsized, but the computer industry as a whole has grown, with a substantial net increase in employment. As big computer companies such as IBM or DEC have laid people off, many of those workers have found employment within the industry—usually at companies doing something related to PCs.

Outside the computer industry it is also hard to find a complete business sector hurt by the PC. There are some typesetters who were displaced by desktop-publishing programs—but for every worker in that situation there are several whose jobs desktop publishing created. All the change hasn't always been good for all the people, but as revolutions go, the one set in motion by the personal computer has been remarkably benign.

Some people worry that there are only a finite number of jobs in the world, and that each time a job goes away someone is left stranded with no further purpose. Fortunately, this is not how the economy works. The economy is a vast interconnected system in which any resource that is freed up becomes available to another area of the economy that finds it most valuable. Each time a job is made unnecessary, the person who was filling that job is freed to do something else. The net result is that more gets done, raising the overall standard of living in the long run. If there is a general downturn across the economy—a recession or a depression—there is a cyclical loss of jobs, but the shifts that have come about as a result of technology have tended, if anything, to create jobs.

Job categories change constantly in an evolving economy. Once all telephone calls were made through an operator. When I was a child, long-distance calls from our home were made by dialing "0" and giving an operator the number, and when I was a teenager, many companies still employed in-house telephone operators who routed calls by plugging cables into receptacles. Today there are comparatively few telephone operators, even though the volume of calls is greater than ever. Automation has taken over.

Before the Industrial Revolution, most people lived or worked on farms. Growing food was mankind's main preoccupation. If someone had predicted back then that within a couple of centuries only a tiny percentage of the population would be needed to produce food, all those farmers would have worried about what everyone would do for a living. The great majority of the 501 job categories recognized in 1990 by the U.S. Census Bureau didn't even exist fifty years earlier. Although we can't predict new job categories, most will relate to unmet needs in education, social services, and leisure opportunities.

We know that when the highway connects buyers and sellers directly, it will put pressure on people who are currently acting as middlemen. This is the same sort of pressure that mass merchants such as Wal-Mart, Price-Costco, and other companies with particularly efficient consumer-merchandising approaches have already put on more traditional stores. When Wal-Mart moves into a rural area, the merchants in the local towns feel the pinch. Some survive, some do not, but the net economic effect on the region is modest. We may regret the cultural ramifications, but warehouse stores and fast-food chains are thriving because consumers, who vote with their dollars, tend to support outlets that pass their productivity savings along in the form of lower prices.

Reducing the number of middlemen is another way of lowering costs. It will also cause economic shifts, but no faster than the changes happened in retailing in the last decade. It will take many years for the highway to be utilized so widely for shopping that there will be significantly fewer middlemen. There is plenty of time to prepare. The jobs those displaced middlemen change to might not even have been thought of yet. We'll have to wait and see what kinds of creative work the new economy devises. But as long as society needs help, there will definitely be plenty for everyone to do.

The broad benefits of advancing productivity are no solace for someone whose job is on the line. When a person has been trained for a job that is no longer needed, you can't just suggest he go out and learn something else. Adjustments aren't that simple or fast, but ultimately they are necessary. It isn't easy to prepare for the next century, because it's almost impossible to guess the secondary effects of even the changes we can foresee, much less those we can't. A hundred years ago, people saw the automobile coming. It was sure to make fortunes, and also to run over some jobs and industries. But specifics would have been hard to predict. You might have warned your friends at the Acme Buggy Whip Company to polish up their résumés, and perhaps learn about engines, but would you have known to invest in real estate for strip malls?

More than ever, an education that emphasizes general problem-solving skills will be important. In a changing world, education is the best preparation for being able to adapt. As the economy shifts, people and societies who are appropriately educated will tend to do best. The premium that society pays for skills is going to climb, so my advice is to get a good formal education and then keep on learning. Acquire new interests and skills throughout your life.

A lot of people will be pushed out of their comfort zones, but that doesn't mean that what they already know won't still be valuable. It does mean that people and companies will have to be open to reinventing themselves—possibly more than once. Companies and governments can help train and retrain workers, but the individual must ultimately bear principal responsibility for his education.

A first step will be to come to terms with computers. Computers make almost everyone nervous before they understand them. Children are the primary exception. First-time users worry that a single misstep will cause them to ruin the computer or lose everything stored in it. People do lose data, of course, but very rarely is the damage irreversible. We have worked to make it harder to lose data and easier to recover from mistakes. Most programs have "Undo" commands that make it simple to try something, then quickly reverse it. Users become more confident as they see that making mistakes won't be catastrophic. And then they begin to experiment. PCs provide all kinds of opportunities for experimentation. The more experience people have with PCs, the better they understand what they can and can't do. Then PCs become tools instead of threats. Like a tractor or a sewing machine, a computer is a machine we can use to help us get certain tasks done more efficiently.

Another fear people express is that computers will be so "smart" they will take over and do away with any need for the human mind. Although I believe that eventually there will be programs that will re-create some elements of human intelligence, it is very unlikely to happen in my lifetime. For decades computer scientists studying artificial intelligence have been trying to develop a computer with human understanding and common sense. Alan Turing in 1950 suggested what has come to be called the Turing Test: If you were able to carry on a conversation with a computer and another human, both hidden from your view, and were uncertain about which was which, you would have a truly intelligent machine.

Every prediction about major advances in artificial intelligence has proved to be overly optimistic. Today even simple learning tasks still go well beyond the world's most capable computer. When computers appear to be intelligent it is because they have been specially programmed to handle some task in a straightforward fashion—like trying out billions of chess moves in order to play master-level chess.

The computer has the potential to be a tool to leverage human intelligence for the foreseeable future. However, information appliances won't become mainstream for publishing information until almost everyone is a user. It would be wonderful if everyone—rich or poor, urban or rural, old or young—could have access to one. However, personal computers are still too expensive for most people. Before the information highway can become fully integrated into society, it must be available to virtually every citizen, not just the elite, but this does not mean that every citizen has to have an information appliance in his house. Once the majority of people have systems installed in their homes, those who do not can be accommodated with a shared appliance at a library, school, post office, or public kiosk. It's important to remember that the question of universal access arises only if the highway is immensely successful—more successful than many commentators expect. Amazingly, some of the same critics who complain the highway will be so popular it will cause problems also complain it won't be popular at all.

The fully developed information highway will be affordable—almost by definition. An expensive system that connected a few big corporations and wealthy people simply would not be the information highway—it would be the information private road. The network will not attract enough great content to thrive if only the most affluent 10 percent of society choose to avail themselves of it. There are fixed costs to authoring material; so to make them affordable, a large audience is required. Advertising revenue won't support the highway if a majority of eligible people don't embrace it. If that is the case, the price for connecting will have to be cut or deployment delayed while the system is redesigned to be more attractive. The information highway is a mass phenomenon, or it is nothing.

Eventually the costs of computing and communications will be so low, and the competitive environment so open, that much of the entertainment and information offered on the highway will cost very little. Advertising income will allow a lot of content to be free. However, most service providers, whether they are rock bands or consulting engineers or book publishers, will still ask that users make a payment. So the information highway will be affordable, if used judiciously, but it won't be free.

A large portion of the money you will spend on highway services you spend today for the same services in other forms. In the past you may have shifted money you spent on records to buying compact discs, or from movie tickets to videotape rentals. Soon your spending for videotape rentals will go to video-on-demand movies. You will redirect part of what you now spend on printed-periodical subscriptions to interactive information services and communities. Most of the money that now goes to local telephone service, long-distance service, and cable television will be available to spend on the highway.

Access to government information, medical advice, bulletin boards, and some educational material will be free. Once people are on the highway, they will enjoy full egalitarian access to vital on-line resources. Within twenty years, as commerce, education, and broad-scale communications services move onto the highway, an individual's ability to be part of mainstream society will depend, at least in part, on his or her using it. Society will then have to decide how to subsidize broad access so that all users will be equal, both geographically and socioeconomically.

Education is not the entire answer to the challenges presented by the Information Age, but it is part of the answer, just as education is part of the answer to a range of society's problems. H. G. Wells, who was as imaginative and forward-looking as any futurist, summed it up back in 1920. "Human history," he said, "becomes more and more a race between education and catastrophe." Education is society's great leveler, and any improvement in education goes a long way toward equalizing opportunity. Part of the beauty of the electronic world is that the extra cost of letting additional people use educational material is basically zero.

Your education in personal computers can be informal. As I've said, my fascination began with game playing, as years later Warren Buffett's did. My dad got hooked when he used a computer to help him prepare his taxes. If computers seem intimidating to you, why not try doing the same sort of thing? Find something a personal computer does that will make your life easier or more fun and latch on to that as a way of getting more involved. Write a screenplay; do your banking from home; help your child with her homework. It is worth making the effort to establish a level of comfort with computers. If you give them a chance, you will most likely be won over. If personal computing still seems too hard or confusing, it doesn't mean you aren't smart enough. It means we still have work to do to make them easier.

The younger you are, the more important this is. If you are fifty or older today, you may be out of the workforce before you'll need to learn to use a computer—although I think if you don't learn, you'll be missing out on the chance for an amazing experience. But if you are twenty-five today and not comfortable with computers, you risk being ineffective in almost any kind of work you pursue. To begin with, finding a job will be easier if you have embraced the computer as a tool.

Ultimately, the information highway is not for my generation or those before me. It is for future generations. The kids who have grown up with PCs in the last decade, and those who will grow up with the highway in the next, will push the technology to its limits.

We have to pay particular attention to correcting the gender imbalance. When I was young, it seemed that only boys were encouraged to mess around with computers. Girls are far more active with computers today than twenty years ago, but there are still many fewer women in technical careers. By making sure that girls as well as boys become comfortable with computers at an early age we can ensure that they play their rightful role in all the work that benefits from computer expertise.

My own experience as a child, and that of my friends raising children today, is that once a kid is exposed to computing, he or she is hooked. But we have to create the opportunity for that exposure. Schools should have low-cost access to computers connected to the information highway, and teachers need to become comfortable with the new tools.

One of the wonderful things about the information highway is that virtual equity is far easier to achieve than real-world equity. It would take a massive amount of money to give every grammar school in every poor area the same library resources as the schools in Beverly Hills. However, when you put schools on-line they all get the same access to information, wherever it might be stored. We are all created equal in the virtual world, and we can use this equality to help address some of the sociological problems that society has yet to solve in the physical world. The network will not eliminate barriers of prejudice or inequality, but it will be a powerful force in that direction.

The question of how to price intellectual property, such as entertainment and educational materials, is fascinating. Economists understand a lot about how the pricing of classical manufactured goods works. They can show how rational pricing should reflect cost structure in a very direct manner. In a market with multiple competing qualified manufacturers, prices tend to drop to the marginal cost of making one more of whatever they are selling. But this model doesn't work when applied to intellectual property.

A basic economics course describes the curves of supply and demand, which intersect at the price appropriate for a product. But supply-and-demand economics gets into trouble when it comes to intellectual property, because ordinary rules regarding manufacturing costs don't apply. Typically there are huge up-front development costs for intellectual property. These fixed costs are the same regardless of whether one copy or a million copies of the work are sold. George Lucas's next movie in the *Star Wars* series will cost millions to make, regardless of how many people pay to see it in theaters.

The pricing of intellectual property is more complicated than most pricing because today it is relatively inexpensive to manufacture copies of most intellectual property. Tomorrow, on the information highway, the cost of delivering a copy of a work—which will amount to the same thing as manufacturing it—will be even lower, and dropping every year because of Moore's Law. When you buy a new medicine, you're paying mostly for what the drug company spent for research, development, and testing. Even if the marginal cost of making each pill is minimal, the pharmaceutical company still may have to charge quite a bit for each, especially if the market is not huge. The revenue from the average patient has to cover a sufficient share of the development expenses and generate enough profit to make investors glad they took the substantial financial risks involved in developing a new drug. When a poor country wants the medicine, the manufacturer faces a moral dilemma. If the pharmaceutical company doesn't waive or drastically reduce its patent-licensing fees, the medicine won't be available to poor countries. However, if a manufacturer is to be able to invest in R&D, some users must pay more than the marginal cost. Prices for drugs vary greatly from country to country and discriminate against poor people in rich countries except where governments cover medical costs.

One possible solution, a scheme whereby a rich person pays more to buy a new medicine, to see a movie or to read a book, may seem inequitable; however, it is identical to a system already in place today—taxation. Through the income tax and other taxes, people with high incomes pay more for roads, schools, the army, and every other government facility than the average person does. It cost me more than $100 million last year to get those services because I paid a significant capital gains tax after selling some Microsoft shares. I have no complaint, but it is an example of the same services being provided at vastly different prices.

The pricing for highway access may be set politically rather than on the basis of costs. It is going to be expensive to enfranchise people in remote locations because the cost of bringing wiring to far-flung homes and even small communities is very high. Companies may not be eager to make the necessary investment, and the geographically disenfranchised may not be in a position to make the investment on their own behalf. We should expect heated debate about whether the government should subsidize connections to rural areas, or impose regulations that cause urban users to subsidize rural ones. The precedent for this is a doctrine known as "universal service," which was created to subsidize rural mail, phone, and electrical services in the United States. It dictates a single price for the delivery of a letter, a phone call, or electrical power regardless of where you live. It applies even though it is more expensive to deliver services in rural areas, where homes and businesses are farther apart than in areas of concentrated population.

There was no equivalent policy for the delivery of newspapers or radio or television reception. Nonetheless, these services are widely available, so clearly under some circumstances government intervention isn't necessary to ensure high availability. The U.S. Postal Service was founded as part of the government on the assumption that that was the only way to provide truly universal service. UPS and Federal Express might disagree on this point, however, because they have managed to provide broad coverage and make money. The debate as to whether, or to what degree, government needs to be involved to guarantee broad access to the information highway is certain to rage on for many years.

The highway will let those who live in remote places consult, collaborate, and be involved with the rest of the world. Because many people will find the combination of rural lifestyle and urban information attractive, network companies will have an incentive to run fiber-optic lines to high-income remote areas. It is likely that some states, or communities, or even private real estate developers will promote their areas by providing great connectivity. This will lead to what one might call the "Aspen-ization" of parts of the country. Interesting rural communities with high marks for quality of life will deliberately set out to attract a new class of sophisticated urban citizen. Taken as a whole, urban areas will tend to get their connections before rural ones.

The highway will spread information and opportunity across borders to developing nations, too. Cheap global communications can bring people anywhere into the mainstream of the world economy. An English-speaking Ph.D. in China will be able to bid against colleagues in London for consulting work. Knowledge workers in industrialized countries will, in a sense, face new competition—just as some manufacturing workers in industrialized countries have experienced competition from developing nations over the past decade. This will make the information highway a powerful force for international trade in intellectual goods and services, just as the availability of relatively inexpensive air cargo and containerized shipping helped propel international trade in physical goods.

The net effect will be a wealthier world, which should be stabilizing. Developed nations, and workers in those nations, are likely to maintain a sizable economic lead. However, the gap between the have and have-not nations will diminish. Starting out behind is sometimes an advantage. It lets those who adopt late skip steps, and avoid the mistakes of the trailblazers. Some countries will never have industrialization. They will move directly into the Information Age. Europe didn't adopt television until several years after the United States. The result was higher picture

-------------------------->

quality, because by the time Europe set its standard a better choice was available. As a result, Europeans have enjoyed better-looking television pictures for decades.

Telephone systems are another example of how starting late can provide an advantage. In Africa, China, and other parts of the developing world, many citizens who have phones use cellular instruments. Cellular telephone service is spreading rapidly in Asia, Latin America, and other developing regions, because it does not require that copper wires be strung. Many people in the cellular industry predict that improvements in technology will mean that these areas may never get a conventional copper wire–based telephone system. These countries will never have to cut down a million trees for telephone poles or string a hundred thousand miles of telephone lines only to rip them all down and bury the entire network. The wireless telephone system will be their first telephone system. They will get increasingly better cellular systems wherever they can't afford a full broadband connection.

The presence of advanced communications systems promises to make nations more alike and reduce the importance of national boundaries. The fax machine, the portable videocamera, and Cable News Network are among the forces that brought about the end of communist regimes and the Cold War, because they allowed news to pass both ways through what was called the Iron Curtain.

Now, commercial satellite broadcasts to nations such as China and Iran offer citizens glimpses of the outside world that are not necessarily sanctioned by their governments. This new access to information can draw people together by increasing their understanding of other cultures. Some believe it will cause discontent and worse, a "Revolution of Expectations," when disenfranchised people get enough data about another lifestyle to contrast it with their own. Within individual societies, the balance of traditional versus modern experiences will shift as people use the information highway to expose themselves to a greater range of possibilities. Some cultures may feel under assault, as people pay greater attention to global issues or cultures, and less to traditional local ones.

"The fact that the same ad can appeal to someone in a New York apartment and an Iowa farm and an African village does not prove these situations are alike," commented Bill McKibben, a critic of what he sees as television's tendency to override local diversity with homogenized common experiences. "It is merely evidence that the people living in them have a few feelings in common, and it is these barest, most minimal commonalties that are the content of the global village."

Yet if people choose to watch the ad, or the program the ad supports, should they be denied that privilege? This is a political question for every country to answer individually. It will not, however, be easy to filter a highway connection so that it selects and takes in only some elements.

American popular culture is so potent that outside the United States some countries now attempt to ration it. They hope to guarantee the viability of domestic-content producers by permitting only a certain number of hours of foreign television to be aired each week. In Europe the availability of satellite and cable-delivered programming reduced the potential for government control. The information highway is going to break down boundaries and may promote a world culture, or at least a sharing of cultural activities and values. The highway will also make it easy for patriots, even expatriates, deeply involved in their own ethnic communities to reach out to others with similar interests no matter where they may be located. This may strengthen cultural diversity and counter the tendency toward a single world culture.

If people do gravitate to their own interests and withdraw from the broader world—if weight lifters communicate only with other weight lifters, and Latvians choose to read only Latvian newspapers—there is a risk that common experiences and values will fall away. Such xenophobia would have the effect of fragmenting societies. I doubt this will happen, because I think people want a sense of belonging to many communities, including a world community. When we Americans share national experiences, it is usually because we're witnessing events all at the same time on television—whether it is the *Challenger* blowing up after liftoff, the Super Bowl, an inauguration, coverage of the Gulf War, or the O. J. Simpson car chase. We are "together" at those moments.

Another worry people have is that multimedia entertainment will be so easy to get and so compelling, some of us will use the system too much for our own good. This could become a serious problem when virtual-reality experiences are commonplace.

One day a virtual-reality game will let you enter into a virtual bar and make eye contact with "someone special," who will note your interest and come over to engage you in conversation. You'll talk, impressing this new friend with your charm and wit. Perhaps the two of you will decide, then and there, to go to Paris. Whoosh! You'll be in Paris, gazing together at the stained glass of Notre Dame. "Have you ever ridden the Star Ferry in Hong Kong?" you might ask your friend, invitingly. Whoosh! VR will certainly be more engrossing than video games have ever been, and more addictive.

If you were to find yourself escaping into these attractive worlds too often, or for too long, and began to be worried about it, you could try to deny yourself entertainment by telling the system, "No matter what password I give, don't let me play any more than half an hour of games a day." This would be a little speed bump, a warning to slow your involvement with something you found too appealing. It would serve the same purpose as a photo of some very overweight people you might post on your refrigerator to discourage snacking.

Speed bumps help a lot with behavior that tends to generate day-after regrets. If someone elects to spend his or her free hours examining the stained glass in a simulation of Notre Dame, or chatting in a make-believe bar with a synthetic friend, that person is exercising his or her freedom. Today a lot of people spend several hours a day with a television on. To the extent we can replace some of that passive entertainment with interactive entertainment, viewers may be better off. Frankly, I'm not too concerned about the world whiling away its hours on the information highway. At worst, I expect, it will be like playing video games or gambling. Support groups will convene to help abusers who want to modify their behavior.

A more serious concern than individual overindulgence is the vulnerability that could result from society's heavy reliance on the highway.

This network, and the computer-based machines connected to it, will form society's new playground, new workplace, and new classroom. It will replace physical tender. It will subsume most existing forms of communication. It will be our photo album, our diary, our boom box.

This versatility will be the strength of the network, but it will also mean we will become reliant on it.

Reliance can be dangerous. During the New York City blackouts in 1965 and 1977, millions of people were in trouble—at least for a few hours—because of their dependence on electricity. They counted on electric power for light, heat, transport, and security. When electricity failed, people were trapped in elevators, traffic lights stopped working, and electric water pumps quit. Anything really useful is missed when you lose it.

A complete failure of the information highway is worth worrying about. Because the system will be thoroughly decentralized, any single outage is unlikely to have a widespread effect. If an individual server fails, it will be replaced and its data restored. But the system could be susceptible to assault. As the system becomes more important, we will have to design in more redundancy. One area of vulnerability is the system's reliance on cryptography—the mathematical locks that keep information safe.

None of the protection systems that exist today, whether steering-wheel locks or steel vaults, are completely fail-safe. The best we can do is make it as difficult as possible for somebody to break in. Despite popular opinions to the contrary, computer security has a very good record. Computers are capable of protecting information in such a way that even the smartest hackers can't get at it readily unless someone entrusted with information makes a mistake. Sloppiness is the main reason computer security gets breached. On the information highway there will be mistakes, and too much information will get passed along. Someone will issue digital concert tickets that prove to be forgeable, and too many people will show up. Whenever this sort of thing happens, the system will have to be reworked and laws may have to be revised.

Because both the system's privacy and the security of digital money depend on encryption, a breakthrough in mathematics or computer science that defeats the cryptographic system could be a disaster. The obvious mathematical breakthrough would be development of an easy way to factor large prime numbers. Any person or organization possessing this power could counterfeit money, penetrate any personal, corporate, or governmental file, and possibly even undermine the security of nations, which is why we have to be so careful in designing the system. We have to ensure that if any particular encryption technique proves fallible, there is a way to make an immediate transition to an alternate technique. There's a little bit of inventing still to be done before we have that perfected. It is particularly hard to guarantee security for information you want kept private for a decade or more.

Loss of privacy is another major concern about the highway. A great deal of information is already being gathered about each of us, by private companies as well as by government agencies, and we often have no idea how it is used or whether it is accurate. Census Bureau statistics contain great amounts of detail. Medical records, driving records, library records, school records, court records, credit histories, tax records, financial records, employment reviews, and charge-card bills all profile you. The fact that you call a lot of motorcycle shops, and might be susceptible to motorcycle advertising, is commercial information that a telephone company theoretically could sell. Information about us is routinely compiled into direct-marketing mailing lists and credit reports. Errors and abuses have already fostered legislation regulating the use of these databases. In the United States, you are entitled to see certain kinds of information stored about you, and you may have the right to be notified when someone looks at it. The scattered nature of information protects your privacy in an informal way, but when the repositories are all connected together on the highway, it will be possible to use computers to correlate it. Credit data could be linked with employment records and sales transaction records to construct an intrusively accurate picture of your personal activities.

As more business is transacted using the highway and the amount of information stored there accrues, governments will consciously set policies regarding privacy and access to information. The network itself will then administer those policies, ensuring that a doctor does not get access to a patient's tax records, a government auditor is not able to look at a taxpayer's scholastic record, and a teacher is not permitted to browse a student's medical record. The potential problem is abuse, not the mere existence of information.

We now allow a life insurance company to examine our medical records before determining whether it chooses to insure our mortality. These companies may also want to know if we indulge in any dangerous pastimes, such as hang gliding, smoking, or stock car racing. Should an insurer's computer be allowed to examine the information highway for records of our purchases to see if there are any that might indicate risky behavior on our part? Should a prospective employer's computer be allowed to examine our communications or entertainment records to develop a psychological profile? How much information should a federal, state, or city agency be allowed to see? What should a potential landlord be able to learn about you? What information should a potential spouse have access to? We will need to define both the legal and practical limits of privacy.

These privacy fears revolve around the possibility that someone else is keeping track of information about you. But the highway will also make it possible for an individual to keep track of his or her own whereabouts—to lead what we might call "a documented life."

Your wallet PC will be able to keep audio, time, location, and eventually even video records of everything that happens to you. It will be able to record every word you say and every word said to you, as well as body temperature, blood pressure, barometric pressure, and a variety of other data about you and your surroundings. It will be able to track your interactions with the highway—all of the commands you issue, the messages you send, and the people you call or who call you. The resulting record will be the ultimate diary and autobiography, if you want one. If nothing else, you would know exactly when and where you took a photograph when you organize your family's digital photo album.

The technology required is not difficult. It should soon be possible to compress the human voice down to a few thousand bits of digital information per second, which means that an hour of conversation will be converted into about 1 megabyte of digital data. Small tapes used for backing up computer hard disks already store 10 gigabytes or more of data—enough to record about 10,000 hours of compressed audio. Tapes for new generations of digital VCRs will hold more than 100 gigabytes, which means that a single tape costing a few dollars could hold recordings of all the conversations an individual has over the course of a decade or possibly even a lifetime—depending on how talkative he is.

These numbers are based only on today's capacities—in the future storage will be much cheaper. Audio is easy, but within a couple of years a full video recording will be possible as well.

I find the prospect of documented lives a little chilling, but some people will warm to the idea. One reason for documenting a life will be defensive. We can think of the wallet PC as an alibi machine, because encrypted digital signatures will guarantee an unforgeable alibi against false accusations. If someone ever accused you of something, you could retort: "Hey, buddy, I have a documented life. These bits are stored away. I can play back anything I've ever said. So don't play games with me." On the other hand, if you were guilty of something, there would be a record of it. There would also be a record of any tampering. Richard Nixon's taping of conversations in the White House—and then the suspicions that he had attempted to alter those tapes—contributed to his undoing. He chose to have a documented political life and lived to regret it.

The Rodney King case showed the evidentiary power of videotape and its limits. Before long every police car, or individual policeman, may be equipped with a digital video camera, with nonforgeable time and location stamps. The public may insist that the police record themselves in the course of their work. And the police could be all for it, to guard against claims of brutality or abuse on one hand and as an aid in gathering better evidence on the other. Some police forces are already video-recording all arrests. This sort of record won't affect just the police. Medical malpractice insurance might be cheaper, or only available, for doctors who record surgical procedures or even office visits. Bus, taxi, and trucking companies have an obvious interest in the performance of their drivers. Some transportation companies have already installed equipment to record mileage and average speed. I can imagine proposals that every automobile, including yours and mine, be outfitted not only with a recorder but also with a transmitter that identifies the car and its location—a future license plate. After all, airplanes have "black box" recorders today, and once the cost drops, there is no reason they shouldn't also be in our cars. If a car was reported stolen, its location would be known immediately. After a hit-and-run accident or a drive-by shooting, a judge could authorize a query: "What vehicles were in the following two-block area during this thirty-minute period?" The black box could record your speed and location, which would allow for the perfect enforcement of speeding laws. I would vote against that.

In a world that is increasingly instrumented, we could reach the point where cameras record most of what goes on in public. Video cameras in public places are already relatively commonplace. They perch, often concealed, around banks, airports, automatic-teller machines, hospitals, freeways, stores, and hotel and office-building lobbies and elevators.

The prospect of so many cameras, always watching, might have distressed us fifty years ago, as it did George Orwell. But today they are unremarkable. There are neighborhoods in the United States and Europe where citizens are welcoming these cameras above streets and parking lots. In Monaco, street crime has been virtually eliminated because hundreds of video cameras have been placed around the tiny principality. Monaco, however, is small enough in area, 370 acres (150 hectares), that a few hundred cameras can pretty much cover it all. Many parents would welcome cameras around schoolyards to discourage or help apprehend drug dealers, child molesters, and even playground bullies. Every city streetlight represents a substantial investment by a community in public safety. In a few years it will require only a relatively modest additional sum to add and operate cameras with connections to the information highway. Within a decade, computers will be able to scan video records very inexpensively looking for a particular person or activity. I can easily imagine proposals that virtually every pole supporting a streetlight should also have one or more cameras. The images from these cameras might be accessed only in the event of a crime, and even then possibly only under court order. Some people might argue that every image from every camera should be available for viewing by everyone at any time. This raises serious privacy questions in my mind, but advocates might argue that it's appropriate if the cameras are only in public places.

Almost everyone is willing to accept some restrictions in exchange for a sense of security. From a historical perspective, people living in Western democracies already enjoy a degree of privacy and personal freedom unprecedented in all of human history. If ubiquitous cameras tied into the information highway should prove to reduce serious crime dramatically in test communities, a real debate would begin over whether people fear surveillance more or less than they fear crime. It is difficult to imagine a government-sanctioned experiment along these lines in the United States because of the privacy issues it raises and the likelihood of constitutional challenges. However, opinion can change. It might take only a few more incidents like the bombing in Oklahoma City within the borders of the United States for attitudes toward strong privacy protection to shift. What today seems like digital Big Brother might one day become the norm if the alternative is being left to the mercy of terrorists and criminals. I am not advocating either position—technology will enable society to make a political decision.

At the same time technology is making it easier to create video records, it is also making it possible to keep all your personal documents and messages totally private. Encryption-technology software, which anyone can download from the Internet, can transform a PC into a virtually unbreakable code machine. As the highway is deployed, security services will be applied to all forms of digital information—phone calls, files, databases, you name it. As long as you protect the password, the information stored on your computer can be held under the strongest lock and key that has ever existed. This allows for the greatest degree of information privacy any individual has ever had.

Many in government are opposed to this encryption capability, because it reduces their ability to gather information. Unfortunately for them, the technology can't be stopped. The National Security Agency is a part of the U.S. government defense and intelligence community that protects this country's secret communications and decrypts foreign communications to gather intelligence data. The NSA does not want software containing advanced encryption capabilities to be sent outside the United States. However, this software is already available throughout the world, and any computer can run it. No policy decision will be able to restore the tapping capabilities governments had in the past.

Today's legislation that prevents the export of software with good encryption capability could harm U.S. software and hardware companies. The restrictions give foreign companies an advantage over U.S.

competitors. American companies almost unanimously agree that the current encryption export restrictions don't work.

Each media advance has had a substantial effect on how people and governments interact. The printing press and, later, mass-circulation newspapers changed the nature of political debate. Radio and then television allowed government leaders to talk directly and intimately with the populace. Similarly, the information highway will have its own influence on politics. For the first time politicians will be able to see immediate representative surveys of public opinions. Voters will be able to cast their ballots from home or their wallet PCs with less risk of miscounts or fraud. The implications for government may be as great as they are for industry.

Even if the model of political decision making does not change explicitly, the highway will bestow power on groups of citizens who want to organize to promote causes or candidates. This could lead to an increased number of special-interest groups and even political parties. Today, organizing a political movement on an issue requires an immense amount of coordination. How do you find the people who share your view? How do you motivate and communicate with them? Telephones and fax machines are great for connecting people one-on-one—but only if you know whom to call. Television lets one person reach millions, but it is expensive and wasteful if most viewers are not interested.

Political organizations require thousands of hours of volunteer time. Envelopes have to be stuffed for direct-mail appeals, and volunteers must go out and contact people by whatever means possible. Only a few issues, the environment being one, are potent enough to overcome the difficulties involved in recruiting enough volunteers to operate an effective political organization.

The information highway makes all communication easier. Bulletin boards and other on-line forums allow people to be in touch one-to-one, or one-to-many, or many-to-many, in very efficient ways. People of similar interests are able to meet on-line and organize without any physical overhead. It will become so easy to organize a political movement that no cause will be too small or scattered. I expect the Internet will be a significant focus for all the candidates and political-action groups for the first time during the 1996 U.S. national elections. Eventually, the highway will become a primary conduit of political discourse.

Direct voting is already used in the United States for specific issues at the state level. For logistical reasons these ballot propositions can occur only when a major election is already taking place. The information highway would allow such votes to be scheduled far more frequently, because they would cost very little.

Someone will doubtless propose total "direct democracy," having all issues put to a vote. Personally, I don't think direct voting would be a good way to run a government. There is a place in governance for representatives—middlemen—to add value. They are the ones whose job it is to take the time to understand all the nuances of complicated issues. Politics involves compromise, which is nearly impossible without a relatively small number of representatives making decisions on behalf of the people who elected them. The art of management—whether of a society or a company—revolves around making informed choices about the allocation of resources. It's the job of a full-time policymaker to develop expertise. This enables the best of them to come up with and embrace nonobvious solutions direct democracy might not allow, because voters might not understand the trade-offs necessary for long-term success.

Like all middlemen in the new electronic world, political representatives will have to justify themselves. The information highway will put the spotlight on them as never before. Instead of being given photos and sound bites, voters will be able to get a much more direct sense of what their representatives are doing and how they're voting. The day a senator receives a million pieces of e-mail on a topic or is able to have his beeper announce the results of a real-time opinion poll from his constituents is not far away.

Despite the problems posed by the information highway, my enthusiasm for it remains boundless. Information technology is already touching lives deeply, as evidenced by a piece of electronic mail a reader of my newspaper column sent me in June of 1995. "Mr. Gates, I am a poet who has Dyslexia, which basically means I can not spell worth a damn, and I would never have any hope of getting my poetry or my novels published if not for this computer Spellcheck. I may fail as a writer, but thanks to you I will succeed or fail because of my talent, or a lack of talent, and not because of my disability."

We are watching something historic happen, and it will affect the world seismically, rocking us the same way the discovery of the scientific method, the invention of printing, and the arrival of the Industrial Age did. If the information highway is able to increase the understanding citizens of one country have about their neighboring countries, and thereby reduce international tensions, that, in and of itself, could be sufficient to justify the cost of implementation. If it was used only by scientists, permitting them to collaborate more effectively to find cures for the still-incurable diseases, that alone would be invaluable. If the system was only for kids, so that they could pursue their interests in and out of the classroom, that by itself would transform the human condition. The information highway won't solve every problem, but it will be a positive force in many areas.

It won't roll out before us according to a preordained plan. There will be setbacks and unanticipated glitches. Some people will seize upon the setbacks to proclaim that the highway never really was more than hype. But on the highway, the early failures will just be learning experiences. The highway is going to happen.

Big changes used to take generations or centuries. This one won't happen overnight, but it will move much faster. The first manifestations of the information highway will be apparent in the United States by the millennium. Within a decade there will be widespread effects. If I had to guess which applications of the network will be embraced quickly and which will take a long time, I'd certainly get some of them wrong. Within twenty years virtually everything I've talked about in this book will be broadly available in developed countries and in businesses and schools in developing countries. The hardware will be installed. Then it will just be a matter of what people do with it—which is to say, what software applications they use.

You'll know the information highway has become part of your life when you begin to resent it if information is not available via the network. One day you'll be hunting for the repair manual for your bicycle and you'll be annoyed that the manual is a paper document that you could misplace. You'll wish it were an interactive electronic document, with animated illustrations and a video tutorial, always available on the network.

The network will draw us together, if that's what we choose, or let us scatter ourselves into a million mediated communities. Above all, and in countless new ways, the information highway will give us choices that can put us in touch with entertainment, information, and each other.

I think Antoine de Saint-Exupéry, who wrote so eloquently about how people came to think of railroad locomotives and other forms of technology as friendly, would applaud the information highway and dismiss as backward-looking those who resist it. Fifty years ago he wrote: "Transport of the mails, transport of the human voice, transport of flickering pictures—in this century as in others our highest accomplishments still have the single aim of bringing men together. Do our dreamers hold that the invention of writing, of printing, of the sailing ship, degraded the human spirit?"

The information highway will lead to many destinations. I've enjoyed speculating about some of these. Doubtless I've made some foolish predictions, but I hope not too many. In any case, I'm excited to be on the journey.

AFTERWORD

The information highway will have a significant effect on all of our lives in the years to come. As I suggested in chapter 9, the greatest benefits will come from the application of technology to education—formal and informal. To help facilitate this in a small way, my portion of the proceeds from this book will go to support teachers who are incorporating computers into their classrooms. Through the National Foundation for the Improvement of Education in the United States and comparable organizations throughout the world, the funds will help teachers create opportunities for students—just as the Mothers' Club at Lakeside made my first exploration of computers possible.

I've worked long hours on this book. I work hard because I love my work. It's not an addiction, and I like doing a lot of other things, but I find my work very exciting. My focus is to keep Microsoft in the forefront through constant renewal. It's a little scary that as computer technology has moved ahead there's never been a leader from one era who was also a leader in the next. Microsoft has been a leader in the PC era. So from a historical perspective, I guess Microsoft is disqualified from leading in the highway era of the Information Age. But I want to defy historical tradition. Somewhere ahead is the threshold dividing the PC era from the highway era. I want to be among the first to cross over when the moment comes. I think the tendency for successful companies to fail to innovate is just that: a tendency. If you're too focused on your current business, it's hard to change and concentrate on innovating.

For me, a big part of the fun has always been to hire and work with smart people. I enjoy learning from them. Some of the smart people we're hiring now are a lot younger than I am. I envy them for having grown up with better computers. They're extraordinarily talented and will contribute new visions. If Microsoft can combine these visions with listening carefully to customers, we have a chance to continue to lead the way. We can certainly keep providing better and better software to make the PC a universally empowering tool. I often say I have the best job in the world, and I mean it.

I think this is a wonderful time to be alive. There have never been so many opportunities to do things that were impossible before. It's also the best time ever to start new companies, advance sciences such as medicine that improve quality of life, and stay in touch with friends and relatives. It's important that both the good and bad points of the technological advances be discussed broadly so that society as a whole, rather than just technologists, can guide its direction.

Now it's back to you. I explained in the Foreword that I was writing this book to help get a dialogue started and to call attention to a number of the opportunities and issues that individuals, companies, and nations will face. My hope is that after reading this book you will share some of my optimism, and will join the discussion about how we should be shaping the future.

INDEX

Note: Page numbers in **boldface** refer to defined terms.

-----------------------►

------------------------------>